Machine Learning Approaches in Cyber Security Analytics

Tony Thomas · Athira P. Vijayaraghavan ·
Sabu Emmanuel

Machine Learning Approaches in Cyber Security Analytics

Springer

Tony Thomas
Indian Institute of Information Technology
and Management-Kerala
Thiruvananthapuram, Kerala, India

Athira P. Vijayaraghavan
Indian Institute of Information Technology
and Management-Kerala
Thiruvananthapuram, Kerala, India

Sabu Emmanuel
Kuwait University
Kuwait City, Kuwait

ISBN 978-981-15-1705-1 ISBN 978-981-15-1706-8 (eBook)
https://doi.org/10.1007/978-981-15-1706-8

This Springer imprint is published by the registered company Springer Nature Singapore Pte Ltd.
The registered company address is: 152 Beach Road, #21-01/04 Gateway East, Singapore 189721, Singapore

Preface

About the Book

With an overwhelming amount of data being generated and transferred over various networks, cybersecurity experts are having a hard time in monitoring everything that gets exchanged and identifying potential cyberthreats and attacks. As cyberattacks are becoming more frequent and sophisticated, there is a requirement for machines to predict, detect, and identify cyberattacks at a faster rate. Machine learning offers various tools and techniques to automate and quickly predict, detect, and identify cyberattacks. This book introduces various machine learning methods for cybersecurity analytics.

The main emphasis will be on the discussion of machine learning algorithms which have potential applications in cybersecurity analytics. There will be discussions on how cybersecurity analytics complements machine learning research. The potential applications include malware detection, biometrics, anomaly detection, cyberattack prediction, and so on.

The proposed book is a research monograph on cybersecurity analytics using various machine intelligence approaches. Most of the contents of the book are out of the original research by the authors. The cybersecurity and machine learning researchers, graduate students, and developers in cybersecurity will be benefited from this book. The prerequisites needed to understand the book are undergraduate-level knowledge mathematics, statistics, and computer science.

Aim and Scope

Nowadays, machine learning techniques have been applied in many areas such as voice recognition, fraud detection, email spam filtering, text processing, search recommendations, and video analysis. Machine learning techniques offer greater data analytics, reduction in the cost of computation, etc. Progress in the varied applications of machine learning techniques has also led to the advancement of the state of the art of machine learning research. In a broad sense, machine learning refers to a series of techniques where a machine is trained to solve a problem. Once a machine is trained, it can give solutions for several instances of the same problem.

Cybersecurity is a fast-growing field demanding a great deal of attention because of remarkable progresses in IoT networks, cloud and Web technologies, online banking, mobile environment, smart grid, etc. So with all of the recent technologies embracing machine learning approaches, one may ask what exactly is machine learning and how it is applied in cybersecurity analytics.

As cyberattacks are becoming more frequent and sophisticated, there is a requirement for machines to predict, detect, and identify cyberattacks at a faster rate. Machine learning offers various tools and techniques to automate and quickly predict, detect, and identify cyberattacks. Diverse machine learning methods have been successfully deployed to address several wide-ranging problems in cybersecurity. This book discusses and highlights different applications of machine learning in cybersecurity. This research monograph presents the latest research in cybersecurity analytics using machine intelligence methods. A major part of the contents of the book are out of the research work carried out by the authors. This book will be useful for cybersecurity and machine learning researchers, graduate students and security product developers.

Thiruvananthapuram, India
February 2019

Tony Thomas
Athira P. Vijayaraghavan
Sabu Emmanuel

Acknowledgements We thank our family, friends and colleagues for their support in helping to make this monograph possible. We thank the Government of Kerala for supporting this project through the Kerala State Planning Board project CRICTR.

Contents

About the Authors

Tony Thomas is an Associate Professor at the Indian Institute of Information Technology and Management, Kerala, India. He received his master's and Ph.D. degrees from IIT Kanpur. After completing his Ph.D., he pursued postdoctoral research at the Korea Advanced Institute of Science and Technology, Daejeon, South Korea. He later worked as a member of research staff at the General Motors Research Lab, Bangalore, India, and the School of Computer Engineering, Nanyang Technological University, Singapore. His current research interests include malware analysis, biometrics, cryptography, machine learning, cyber threat prediction and visualization, digital watermarking, multimedia security and digital forensics.

Athira P. Vijayaraghavan holds an M.Tech. degree in Information Security and Cyber Forensics from SRM Institute of Science and Technology (formerly known as SRM University), Chennai, India, and a B.Tech. degree in Information Technology from Calicut University, Kerala, India. She currently works at Acalvio Technologies, Bengaluru, Karnataka, as a member of technical staff. She worked as a Research Associate at the Indian Institute of Information Technology and Management, Kerala, India, till August 2019. Her current research interests include autonomous deception for malware detection, threat intelligence analysis, malware analysis, memory forensics and cyber threat prediction.

Sabu Emmanuel received his B.E. degree in Electronics and Communication Engineering from the Regional Engineering College, Durgapur (now NIT Durgapur), India, in 1988, his M.E. degree in Electrical Communication Engineering from the Indian Institute of Science, Bangalore, India, in 1998, and his Ph.D. degree in Computer Science from the National University of Singapore, Singapore, in 2002. He was an Assistant Professor at the School of Computer Engineering, Nanyang Technological University, Singapore; an Associate Professor at the Department of Computer Science, Kuwait University; and a Visiting Professor at IIT Palakkad. His current research interests include malware analysis, multimedia and software security and surveillance video processing.

Chapter 1
Introduction

Suppose that we want to build an automated malware detection mechanism for our smartphones. We want this detection mechanism to run in the background and alert the user whenever we install or run a malicious application. In this situation, a rule-based detection mechanism may not work as malware continuously evolve and a set of rules may not be sufficient to characterize an application as malware or goodware. Instead, we may have a detection mechanism which uses statistical models rather than deterministic rules. This statistical model has been exposed to sufficient different samples of known malware and goodware and is asked to distinguish a malware from a goodware based on its experience gained from the known samples. This approach seems to be more realistic in solving many cybersecurity problems than rule-based approaches. This method of problem-solving is referred to as the machine learning (ML) approach. In this book, we attempt to introduce the machine learning approaches in solving various cybersecurity problems. Machine learning algorithms are mathematical models that have been used for tasks such as classification, clustering, regression, and so on. A machine learning model is build by identifying a machine learning algorithm and fixing its parameters using a process known as training using data instances. The model that is built is subsequently used for various tasks. The performance of such a machine learning model depends on various factors such as the algorithm that is used to build the model, number and type of data samples used in the training, set of features chosen from the data samples, and so on. The effectiveness of a machine learning model is measured with its accuracy in classifying or clustering data points or predicting correct values. One can improve the accuracy of a model by training the model with more data or representing the data in better forms. Very often, the increase in training data or better representations provide lot of improvements in the accuracy of the model.

Machine learning finds applications in a variety of domains such as image or pattern recognition, voice recognition, face recognition, biometric authentication, malware detection, anomaly detection, fraud detection, email spam detection, text analytics, social media services, customer support mechanisms, virtual personal

T. Thomas et al., *Machine Learning Approaches in Cyber Security Analytics*, https://doi.org/10.1007/978-981-15-1706-8_1

assistants, search recommendation systems, video analytics, autonomous cars, health care, financial services, and so on. When we look at the cybersecurity domain, we can see that there is a strong need of application of machine learning techniques in addressing various cybersecurity problems. Typical cybersecurity mechanisms require collection, storage, and analysis of large amounts of data. Although there exist a large number of tools for sorting, slicing, and mining these data, it is difficult for a security analyst to infer meaningful information from these data. Further, there do not exist many qualified and experienced cybersecurity professionals who can successfully defend vital systems and networks from cyberattacks. The defensive game is complex and never ending as complexity and scale of attacks are growing rapidly. A small vulnerability or security loophole is enough to open the door for an incident of security breach. With machine learning approaches, many of these tasks can be automated and can be deployed in real time to detect cyberattacks before it happens or before further damage is done. For example, a machine learning model can identify unusual traffic in a network and shut down the connections as they occur or identify a new instance of a malware and may quarantine the malware before they can even execute.

Many machine learning-based cybersecurity systems act as warning systems with a human in the loop to make the final decision. This is due to the belief that machine learning models are not sufficiently accurate when compared to the humans. However, nowadays, machine learning-based cybersecurity systems have become more accurate than humans due to the improvement in machine learning techniques.

Machine learning algorithms are mainly classified into supervised, unsupervised, semi-supervised, and reinforcement learning algorithms. Supervised algorithms are applied to problems where we have a collection of labeled data. Supervised algorithms can be applied for classification and regression problems. Unsupervised algorithms are applied to problems where we do not have labeled data. Unsupervised algorithms are used for clustering, dimensionality reduction, association rule learning, and so on. These algorithms are useful in representing large dataset easier to analyze. Dimensionality reduction techniques can be used to reduce the number of dimensions or features of data to look at and clustering and association rules can be used to group similar data together.

Machine learning techniques are thriving in the areas of image recognition or natural language processing. However, in the cybersecurity domain the situation is different. There are always attackers trying to find weaknesses in machine learning-based cybersecurity systems to bypass the security mechanisms. Hence, machine learning systems in cybersecurity applications have to be robust against adversarial attacks. This is a challenging task. What is worse is that now attackers are able to use machine learning techniques to launch more sophisticated cyberattacks. In this book, we will discuss only machine learning-based cyber defense systems and not about attack techniques.

1.1 Cybersecurity Problems

Machine learning approaches involve predictions based on a set of training data. In the case of cybersecurity, machine learning algorithms help to make use of data from previous cyberattacks and develop the respective predictions. This approach can be used to build an automated cyber defense system which requires only a minimum human intervention. Some of the typical cybersecurity problems where machine learning approaches fit very well are listed and discussed below:

1. regression for detecting XML external entity (XXE) and server-side request forgery (SSRF) attacks;
2. classification for detecting windows, Android, IoT, and other malware;
3. classification for detecting injection attacks such as SQL injection (SQLi), cross-site scripting (XSS), remote code execution (RCE), etc.;
4. classification for detecting malicious scripts;
5. classification for detecting malicious URLs and phishing pages;
6. classification for spam mail detection;
7. classification for biometric authentication and identification;
8. classification for side-channel attack detection;
9. classification for detection of network attacks such as scanning and spoofing;
10. clustering for anomaly detection;
11. clustering for intrusion detection;
12. clustering for insider threat detection;
13. clustering for detection of distributed denial-of-service (DDoS) attacks and mass exploitations; and
14. clustering for forensic analysis of data.

A malware is a malicious software that disrupts the normal working of computer systems or mobile phones or networks. It gathers sensitive information and data, provides illegal access to cybercriminals, modifies or deletes data, blocks access to legal users, displays unwanted advertisements, consumes resources, and so on. Malware are classified as viruses, worms, trojans, ransomware, spyware, adware, rootkits, backdoors, logic bombs, etc. It can appear as executable codes, scripts, active contents, and so on. Some malware appear as stand-alone programs, whereas others appear as disguised or embedded in non-malicious applications or files. Supervised machine learning algorithms are good for malware identification because of the availability of lot of labeled samples of malware and benign samples. These samples can be used to train machine learning models well.

Phishing is a social engineering attack to acquire sensitive information such as usernames, passwords, and credit card details by masquerading as a trustworthy entity in an electronic communication such as email. This occurs while communicating through emails, social networking sites, e-commerce sites, auction sites, banking sites, and so on. Phishing is usually carried out by sending malicious website links in an email/message to the victim typically from a spoofed email address. When the victim clicks the link in the email/message, a malicious copy (phishing page) of the legitimate website opens. The victim enters his username and password or credit card details into the phishing page. The phishing site is running on the attacker's system, and the entered details of victim are fetched to the attacker's system. The attacker then uses this information to log into the legitimate site and may do financial transactions or other malicious activities. Unfortunately, it is usually very difficult to distinguish between legitimate and phishing sites as they can appear as exactly similar. Machine learning techniques can be used in predicting phishing pages using features such as URL, HTML source code, and so on or in identify phishing emails from their header files, body of the mail, etc. These trained models can be used to detect whether an email is malicious or a web page is phishing or not.

Anomalies are patterns in a data that deviate from a defined notion of normal behavior. Anomalies might get induced in a data due to malicious activities or attacks, intrusions, malware attacks, breakdown of a system, and so on. In anomaly detection, we need to determine a region representing normal behavior and declare any observation in the data which does not fall into this region as an anomaly. Both supervised and unsupervised machine learning algorithms such as k-nearest neighbors, k-means clustering, and SVM have been used for anomaly detection. Density-based anomaly detection makes use of the assumption that normal data points occur around a dense neighborhood and anomalies lie far away. Clustering-based anomaly detection makes use of the assumption that data points that are similar tend to belong to similar groups or clusters. The data points that fall outside of these clusters may be treated as anomalies.

Denial-of-service (DoS) and distributed denial-of-service (DDoS) attacks are launched to make a server or service unavailable for users by flooding the server with packets (false client requests). The ultimate goal of DoS or DDoS attack is to exhaust the processing and networking resources of the targets to prevent legitimate users from accessing the services. This results in partial or total unavailability of the services. Flooding of client requests creates a huge increase in the usage of the resources which makes the servers busy with a large number of pending requests to proceed. This ultimately freezes the servers and makes the services unavailable to all. In a distributed denial-of-service (DDoS) attack, multiple devices launch an attack toward one or more targets in a coordinated manner. DDoS attacks are usually very powerful and devastating than DoS attacks because of the many-to-one nature of the attack. Machine learning techniques such as PCA, SVM, and neural networks have been used for DDoS attack detection.

1.2 Machine Learning

Machine learning involves training a model to perform a classification or clustering or regression task. The model is built by training with a set of data points known as training dataset. The trained model is subsequently used to make predictions. The process consists of the following steps:

1. Data collection: In this step, the dataset is collected. The data is separated into training and evaluation datasets. Data from the training set is used to build the model. The test dataset is used to evaluate the model that was built.
2. Data preparation: In this step, the data is transformed, randomized, error corrected, cleared, and normalized to make it suitable for building the machine learning model.
3. Model selection: There are many machine learning models available. Some models are more suitable for image data, some are suitable for sequential data, some are suitable for numerical data, and so on. The most appropriate model needs to be selected based on the problem and the data.
4. Feature extraction: In this step, relevant features from the data are selected and extracted out.
5. Model training: In this step, the parameters of the selected model are determined using the training dataset.
6. Model testing: The model that was built in the previous steps is tested using the test dataset.
7. Model deployment: In the last step, the model that was build is selected and deployed for real-time application.

Machine learning algorithms make assumptions about the dataset. Each data point may be comprised of a vector of features in different scales such as one may be in seconds and another may be in bits, and so on. In order to improve the performance, the data may be subjected to some transformations given below for rescaling.

1. Normalization: It is the process of rescaling one or more features to the range of 0–1.
2. Standardization: It is the process of bringing features represented in different scales to a common scale.
3. Nonlinear expansions: In some cases, it might be desirable to represent the data in a higher dimensional space.

In any machine learning problem, the attributes or features from the data are extracted, so that it can be fed to the algorithm. If the dimension of the input feature vector is high, then it needs to be transformed to a lower dimensional feature vector by extracting only the relevant attributes. The process of reducing the dimension of the feature vector is referred to as feature selection and extracting the relevant features from the data points is referred to as feature extraction. The selected feature vectors are used instead of the original data points without any loss of information for the further computations. For example, in dynamic malware analysis, the attributes could be the system calls made by the application; in the case of image classification, attributes could be RGB values of pixels, and so on. Such attributes are referred to as features, and the vector of attributes is referred to as a feature vector. Feature extraction aims to obtain a relevant and nonredundant representation of the data elements without which an accurate prediction is not possible. Redundant features can make the algorithm biased and can give inaccurate results. Hence, feature extraction is a very critical task which requires a lot of testing, research, and understanding of the data points. Further, general methods for feature selection and extraction may not work in all cases.

One of the challenges in supervised machine learning approaches for many cybersecurity problems is the lack of good labeled training data. It is a hard problem to generate a good training dataset, without which we cannot train our algorithms. Other problems are related to labeling data, cleaning data, understanding the semantics of a data record, and so on.

Unsupervised machine learning algorithms are good for anomaly detection in cybersecurity. Dimensionality reduction techniques and association rules may not be sufficient to find the anomalies in the dataset. Clustering is a useful way to find anomalies by finding ways to cluster "normal" and "abnormal" data points.

1.3 Implementations of ML Algorithms in the Book

With more physical objects moving to the digital space and more devices getting connected to the Internet, there is a tremendous growth and flow in the amount of electronic data. This has resulted in a demand for advanced research in securing the data repositories in the cyberspace from criminals and hackers. Along with finding ways to reduce such attacks, it is necessary to make the system resilient. This can be achieved only through automated data processing tools due to the tremendous amount of data generated in each second. One of the best methods to tackle this issue is to use machine learning. Machine learning makes use of statistical techniques to learn from large data and make automated decisions in real time. Machine learning appears to be the best approach for handling decision problems in cybersecurity due to their accuracy, efficiency, and robustness in decision-making processes. The book looks into the theoretical as well as implementation details of a few machine learning algorithms such as support vector machines, clustering, nearest neighbors, principal component analysis, decision trees, and deep neural networks. The chapters in the book are organized in such a way that the reader gets to understand how different machine learning algorithms can be applied to solve various cybersecurity problems.

In Chap. 4, support vector machines (SVM) are used to address the problem of malware detection in Android OS. SVM is implemented using Weka as it offers a GUI with a user-friendly look and feel. We shall see how SVM is used to solve both classification and regression problems, how features are extracted from Android APKs, and how kernel methods solve nonlinear problems. SVM can also be implemented using sci-kit. Here, we simulate an Android environment and extract the features such as permissions and API calls once it is exploited. The features in a .CSV format are loaded in the Weka tool, which classifies it based on the type of classifier chosen.

Chapter 5 discusses clustering technique which aims in grouping data points that exhibit similar characteristics. Different types of clustering algorithm such as k-means clustering, DBSCAN, hierarchical clustering, etc. are discussed in this chapter. The CPU–RAM usage statistics of malware and goodware samples are observed over a period of time, and each clustering algorithm is used to assess whether the executing application is benign or malicious. Various modules of sci-kit learn such as numpy, pandas, StandardScaler, and other modules such as matplotlib, seaborn, etc. are used in implementing different clustering techniques.

Chapter 6 deals with another machine learning algorithm called nearest neighbors, whose aim is to find the neighbors of the test data point to be classified and finally assign it to the appropriate class. Here, we use nearest neighbors to find the class to which a test fingerprint might belong to. The classes are determined based on the orientation of the fingerprint patterns. A crime record bureau might have to store hundreds of thousands of fingerprints. Fingerprint matching is a time-consuming task, and hence it is necessary to build a primary selection procedure. Here, we demonstrate how nearest neighbors can be used to identify the class of a fingerprint. The local ridge orientation is determined for each fingerprint, which is later used to identify the class of the fingerprint. Various algorithms such as brute force, KD tree, and ball tree, which are used to find the nearest neighbors, are discussed. We also take a look at various types of nearest neighbor algorithms such as k-nearest neighbor, radius-based nearest neighbor, etc.

Chapter 7 deals with dimensionality reduction techniques. Principal component analysis (PCA), a dimensionality reduction technique, is implemented for reducing human facial features so as to minimize the time taken for facial recognition. The chapter discusses PCA algorithm in detail and explains each step of the algorithm with figures. Feature reduction is very crucial for minimizing the time taken for facial recognition. The chapter demonstrates how PCA converts a set of two-dimensional facial image into a set of eigenfaces such that the number of eigenfaces generated is less in number compared to the number of facial template images. PCA makes sure that these eigenfaces represent the most relevant features of the facial image set.

Chapter 8 deals with the most prominent machine learning algorithm, namely, the deep neural networks. We would see how a neural network learns and why it is unsuitable for some image classification problems. Facial recognition algorithms are continuously explored by researchers to increase the accuracy and thereby make the recognition more precise. For an exact match of a facial image with an image from a huge repository, it is important to primarily identify the features. The images need not necessarily be properly aligned; it can be tilted too. A multilayer neural network called convolutional neural network (CNN) is explained in depth, along with how the network extracts facial features and how a Keras model is implemented for facial feature extraction. We have implemented the feature identification module for extracting 15 different features from a facial image. Python programming language is opted for implementing CNN, as python contains numerous modules that aid deep learning.

Chapter 9 discusses decision tree algorithms and how it could be used to detect windows malware. We approach different types of tree construction algorithms mathematically and try to provide the reader a practical understanding. We talk about tapping the memory space of Windows operating system to extract details about an application such as processes and subprocesses spawned by an executable, CPU–memory usage, etc. Though malware detection is a commonly discussed topics today, a large-scale implementation of early detection and prevention of malware continue to be a challenge for researchers. The chapter also discusses the split and pruning criteria used by each algorithm. Though the decision tree algorithms construct a top-to-down tree-like structure as its final output, each differs in the method it adopts to select the root node. We have implemented three different decision tree algorithms. The chapter includes the python code and a detailed explanation of the same.

Chapter 10 which is on adversarial machine learning will take the reader through different techniques that are adopted to craft adversarial data samples to fool a machine learning model, thereby resulting in misclassifications. Since machine learning has been gaining popularity nowadays due to its efficiency and accuracy in predictions and data analytics, methods to reduce its efficiency by attacking predesigned models are also in progress. It is a need of the hour to understand how an ML model can be susceptible to adversarial attacks and how necessary steps can be taken to design new ML models or feature representations resistant to such attacks. The chapter provides an overview of the various adversarial attacks from a cybersecurity perspective. The reader would get to understand in detail the different algorithms that can be used to generate adversarial samples. Two of the algorithms, generative adversarial network (GAN) and fast gradient sign method (FGSM), are explained in detail and their implementations in malware detection and image misclassification are demonstrated.

1.4 Distance Metrics

Many machine learning algorithms require a notion of distance to know the input data pattern, its distribution, and similarities between data points in order to make any decision. A distance metric $d(a, b)$ can be used to compute the distance between any two elements a and b of a set. A good distance metric can considerably improve the performance of a classifier. If the distance between two elements is zero, then the elements can be considered as equivalent and they can be considered as different otherwise. A multivariate distance such as covariance is used to measure the similarities and dissimilarities among data points. Covariance measures how two random variables change together and can be used to calculate the correlation between variables.

In clustering applications, similarity and dissimilarity measures (distance metrics) play an important role. The type of data to be clustered determines the type of similarity measuring technique to be used. An appropriate distance measure is used to determine the similarity of two data points in the dataset. Hence, learning the datasets is an important step in clustering. In this section, we will discuss different distance metrics and their role in various machine learning algorithms. The important distance metrics are listed in Table 1.1 for an easy reference. Let $a = (a_1, a_2, \ldots, a_n)$ and $b = (b_1, b_2, \ldots, b_n)$ be two points in an n-dimensional space, C be the covariance matrix of a and b, $s = s_1 \ldots s_n$ and $t = t_1 \ldots t_n$ be two bit strings, and A and B be two sets.

Table 1.1 Various distance metrics

S. No.	Name of the metric	Formula	Remarks
1	Euclidean distance	$d(a,b) = \sqrt{\sum_{i=1}^{n} (a_i - b_i)^2}$	Straight-line distance
2	Euclidean squared distance	$d(a,b) = \sum_{i=1}^{n} (a_i - b_i)^2$	Easier and faster to compute
3	Manhattan distance	$d(a,b) = \sum_{i=1}^{n} \lvert a_i - b_i \rvert$	Length of grid-like path
4	Chebyshev distance	$\underset{1 \leq i \leq n}{max} (a_i - b_i)$	Chessboard distance
5	Minkowski distance	$d(a,b) = (\sum_{i=1}^{n} \lvert a_i - b_i \rvert^m)^{\frac{1}{m}}$	Generalized distance
6	Cosine similarity	$sim(a,b) = cos(\theta) = \frac{a.b}{\lvert\lvert a \rvert\rvert \lvert\lvert b \rvert\rvert}$	Measures the angle
7	Mahalanobis distance	$d(a,b) = \sqrt{(a-b)^T \times C^{-1} \times (a-b)}$	Multinomial distance
8	Hamming distance	$d(s,t) = \sum_{i=1}^{n} \lvert s_i - t_i \rvert$	Distance between strings
9	Jaccard index	$\sqrt{(A,B)} = \frac{\lvert A \cap B \rvert}{\lvert A \cup B \rvert}$	Measure of similarity of sets
10	Dice coefficient	$S(A,B) = \frac{2\lvert A \cap B \rvert}{\lvert A \rvert + \lvert B \rvert}$	Spatial overlap index

The Euclidean distance $d(a,b)$ between a and b is given by

$$d(a,b) = \sqrt{\sum_{i=1}^{n} (a_i - b_i)^2}. \tag{1.1}$$

Square of the Euclidean distance gives the Euclidean squared distance. It is useful in some clustering algorithms as it is more easier and faster compared to regular Euclidean distance. The output of some clustering algorithms such as Jarvis-Patrick and k-means clustering are not affected if the Euclidean distance is replaced with Euclidean squared distance, whereas the output of hierarchical clustering is likely to change.

The Manhattan distance is the length of a grid-like path between a and b. It is computed as the sum of the differences of the corresponding components of a and b. The formula for Manhattan distance $d(a,b)$ between the points a and b is given by

$$d(a,b) = \sum_{i=1}^{n} |a_i - b_i|. \tag{1.2}$$

The Chebyshev distance between two points is the maximum distance between the points in any single dimension. It is used if the difference between the points is reflected more in a single component rather than all the components considered together. The Chebyshev distance between the points a and b is computed as

$$\max_{1 \le i \le n} (a_i - b_i). \tag{1.3}$$

Minkowski distance is a generalization of the Euclidean, Manhattan, and Chebyshev distances. The formula for Minkowski distance $d(a, b)$ for any $m > 0$ between a a and b is given by

$$d(a, b) = (\sum_{i=1}^{n} |a_i - b_i|^m)^{\frac{1}{m}}. \tag{1.4}$$

When $m = 1, 2$ and ∞, Minkowski distance gives the Manhattan distance, Euclidean distance, and Chebyshev distance, respectively.

The cosine similarity $sim(a, b)$ between a and b is given by

$$sim(a, b) = cos(\theta) = \frac{a.b}{||a||||b||}. \tag{1.5}$$

The cosine similarity metric finds the normalized dot product of any two data points which in turn gives the angle between them. Two vectors with a cosine similarity of 1 have the same orientation; two vectors with a cosine a similarity of 0 are perpendicular to each other; two vectors with a cosine similarity of -1 are in diametrically opposite orientation. Cosine similarity is very popular as it is efficient to compute for sparse vectors.

Mahalanobis distance is a multivariate distance which measures the distance between each data point and the centroid of the entire set of points. Hence, an increase in the Mahalanobis distance leads to an increase in the distance between the data point and the centroid. The Mahalanobis distance between any two points a and b with covariance matrix C is given by

$$d(a, b) = \sqrt{(a - b)^T \times C^{-1} \times (a - b)}. \tag{1.6}$$

The Hamming distance between two bit strings of equal length is the number of positions for which the corresponding bits are different. In other words, the Hamming distance is the number of bits which are need to be changed to convert one string into another. The Hamming distance can also be considered as the Manhattan distance between bit vectors.

The bit vector distance between a and b is determined by calculating the Euclidean or Manhattan or Hamming distance of the vector $c = (c_1, \ldots, c_n)$ from the origin, where $c_i = 1$ if $a_i > b_i$ and 0 otherwise.

The distance metrics discussed so far find the similarity between objects where the objects are n-dimensional vectors or bit strings. Jaccard index is used to find the similarity and dissimilarity between two sets. Jaccard index $\sqrt{(A, B)}$ between two sets A and B is defined as the ratio of the number of elements in the intersection and the number of elements in the union of the sets. That is,

$$\sqrt{(A, B)} = \frac{|A \cap B|}{|A \cup B|}. \tag{1.7}$$

Dice coefficient is another similarity metric for sets like the Jaccard index. For sets A and B of data points, the dice coefficient is computed as

$$S(A, B) = \frac{2|A \cap B|}{|A| + |B|}. \tag{1.8}$$

1.5 Evaluation Metrics in Machine Learning

In this section, we will quickly take a look at some of the common evaluation metrics used in machine learning models. We assume that classification is binary into a positive class and a negative class.

1. Homogeneity Score
   A clustering result is said to satisfy homogeneity if all of its clusters contain only data points which are members of a single class. Let C be the set of classes and K be the class assignments, then the homogeneity score h is calculated as

   $$h = 1 - \frac{H(C|K)}{H(C)}, \tag{1.9}$$

   where $H(C|K)$ is the entropy of C given K and $H(C)$ is the entropy of C.
2. Completeness Score
   A clustering result is said to satisfy completeness if all the data points that are members of a class belong to the same cluster. Completeness score c is calculated as

   $$c = 1 - \frac{H(K|C)}{H(K)}, \tag{1.10}$$

   where $H(K|C)$ is the entropy of K given C and $H(K)$ is the entropy of K.
3. V-Measure Score
   It is obtained as the harmonic mean of the homogeneity and completeness scores. Thus, V-Measure score v is given by

   $$v = 2 \times \frac{h \times c}{h + c}. \tag{1.11}$$

4. Jaccard Similarity Score
   This is same as the Jaccard index. It can be used to obtain the ratio of correctly classified samples.
5. Cohen's Kappa Score
   In multi-class classification problems, measures such as the accuracy, or precision/recall are not suitable to assess the performance of the classifier. In imbalanced datasets, measures such as accuracy can be misleading, and we use measures such as precision and recall or F-measure. Cohen's Kappa score is an ideal measure that can deal with both multi-class and imbalanced class problems. It is given by

$$k = \frac{p_0 - p_e}{1 - p_e}, \tag{1.12}$$

   where p_o is the probability of observed agreement, and p_e is the probability of expected agreement. It computes how much better the classifier is performing over the performance of a classifier that makes random guesses.
6. Confusion Matrix
   The confusion matrix is a 2×2 matrix used for summarizing the performance of a classification algorithm. In this matrix, each row represents an instance in an actual class and column represents an instance in a predicted class (or vice versa). The table gives the numbers of true positives (TP), true negatives (TN), false positives (FP), and false negatives (FN). A true positive is an outcome where an element of a positive class is correctly predicted by the model as belonging to the positive class. A true negative is an outcome where an element of a negative class is correctly predicted by the model as belonging to the negative class. A false positive is an outcome where an element of negative class is incorrectly predicted as belonging to the positive class. A false negative is an outcome where an element of the positive class is incorrectly predicted as belonging to the negative class. Usually, TP, TN, FP, and FP are used to denote the number of true positives, true negatives, false positives, and false negatives, respectively. To determine the confusion matrix, predictions are made for each test data and from the predicted labels and the actual labels the number of true and false predictions made for positive and negative classes is determined. The confusion matrix is given in Table 1.2.

Table 1.2 Confusion matrix

Total	Predicted NO	Predicted YES	
Actual NO	TN	FP	Sum of Actual NOs
Actual YES	FN	TP	Sum of Actual YESs
	Sum of Predicted NOs	Sum of Predicted YESs	

7. Threshold Curve
   Threshold curve is a graph showing the trade-offs in prediction that are obtained by varying the threshold value between classes.
8. Accuracy
   Accuracy is a measure of how often the classifier makes correct predictions. It is calculated as $\frac{TP+TN}{TP+TN+FP+FN}$.
9. Misclassification Rate
   Misclassification rate is the opposite of accuracy. It is a measure of how often the classifier makes false predictions. It is calculated as $\frac{FP+FN}{TP+TN+FP+FN}$.
10. Sensitivity
    Sensitivity measures the ability of the classifier to correctly predict the positive class. It is a measure of how often a classifier predicts the positive class label for a data when the data actually belongs to the positive class. Sensitivity is also known as recall or true positive rate (TPR). It is calculated as $\frac{TP}{TP+FN}$.
11. Specificity
    Specificity measures the ability of the classifier to correctly predict the negative class. It is a measure of how often a classifier predicts the negative class label for a data when the data actually belongs to the negative class. Specificity is also known as selectivity or true negative rate (TNR). It is calculated as $\frac{TN}{TN+FP}$.
12. Precision
    Precision or positive predictive value (PPV) measures how often a classifier is correct when it predicts a positive class label for a data point. It is calculated as $\frac{TP}{TP+FP}$.
13. Negative Predictive Value
    Negative predictive value (NPV) measures how often a classifier is correct when it predicts a negative class label for a data point. It is calculated as $\frac{TN}{TN+FN}$.
14. Prevalence
    Prevalence measures the proportion of a population in the positive class. It is calculated as $\frac{TP+FN}{TP+TN+FP+FN}$.
15. Null Error Rate
    This is a measure of how often a classifier can be wrong during the prediction of the majority class. At times the best classifier for a particular application will sometimes have a higher error rate than null error rate.
16. Cohen's Kappa
    The Cohen's Kappa measure compares how correct the classifier has performed to the expected accuracy. The Kappa score would be high if there is a big difference between the accuracy and the null error rate. It is calculated as

$$\kappa = \frac{(\text{observed accuracy} - \text{expected accuracy})}{(1 - \text{expected accuracy})}. \quad (1.13)$$

17. F1 Score
    It is the harmonic mean of precision and sensitivity, and is calculated as

$$F_1 = 2 \times \frac{\text{Precision} \times \text{Sensitivity}}{\text{Precision} + \text{Sensitivity}}. \quad (1.14)$$

18. Receiver Operating Characteristic (ROC) Curve
    The ROC curves are two-dimensional graphs where false positive rates (x-axis) are plotted against the true positive rates (y-axis). The graph summarizes the performance of a classifier over all possible thresholds.
19. Matthews Correlation Coefficient (MCC)
    MCC is a measure of quality of binary classification and can be calculated directly from the confusion matrix as

$$MCC = \frac{TP \times TN - FP \times FN}{\sqrt{(TP + FP)(TP + FN)(TN + FP)(TN + FN)}}. \tag{1.15}$$

MCC measures the correlation between the observed and predicted classifications. It gives a value between 1 and +1, where +1 represents a perfect prediction, 0 represents random prediction, and 1 represents a complete disagreement between the prediction and the observation. The Matthews correlation coefficient is generally regarded as being one of the best measures to describe the confusion matrix.

1.6 Mathematical Preliminaries

Machine learning uses a lot of mathematical techniques from various areas such as linear algebra, probability, calculus, and optimization. In this section, we briefly outline some of the essential mathematical concepts and techniques required.

1.6.1 Linear Algebra

Vectors are used for representing features and describing algorithms in machine learning. Vector spaces or linear spaces are the basic setting in which we perform linear algebra. A vector space V is a nonempty set of elements called vectors together with a field **F** whose elements are called the scalars. In this book, we will consider only the field of real numbers **R** as the set of scalars. Two operations called vector addition and scalar multiplication are defined on V. Two vectors can be added together to get a third vector, and a vector can be multiplied with a scalar to get another vector. V forms a vector space over the field **R** if it satisfies the following conditions:

1. Additive closure: $v_1 + v_2 \in V$ for all $v_1, v_2 \in V$.
2. Commutativity: $v_1 + v_2 = v_2 + v_1$ for all $v_1, v_2 \in V$.
3. Associativity: $(v_1 + v_2) + v_3 = v_1 + (v_2 + v_3)$ for all $v_1, v_2, v_3 \in V$.
4. Existence of additive identity: There exists $0 \in V$ such that $v + 0 = v$ for all $v \in V$.
5. Existence of additive inverse: For each $v \in V$, there exists an additive inverse $-v \in V$ such that $v + (-v) = 0$.

6. Multiplicative closure: $c.v \in V$ for all $c \in \mathbf{R}$ and $v \in V$.
7. Existence of multiplicative identity: There exists $1 \in \mathbf{R}$ such that $1.v = v$ for all $v \in V$.
8. Compatibility of scalar multiplication: $c_1.(c_2.v) = (c_1c_2).v$ for all $c_1, c_2 \in \mathbf{R}$ and $v \in V$.
9. Distributivity: $c.(v_1 + v_2) = c.v_1 + c.v_2$ and $(c_1 + c_2).v = c_1.v + c_2.v$ for all $c, c_1, c_2 \in \mathbf{R}$ and $v, v_1, v_2 \in V$.

A set of vectors $v_1, \ldots, v_n \in V$ is said to be linearly independent if $c_1.v_1 + \cdots + c_n.v_n = 0$ implies $c_1 = \cdots = c_n = 0$. The span of $v_1, \ldots, v_n \in V$ is the set of all vectors that can be expressed as a linear combination of them. That is,

$$\text{SPAN}\{v_1, \ldots, v_n\} = \{c_1.v_1 + \cdots + c_n.v_n : \forall c_1, \ldots, c_n \in \mathbf{R}\}.$$

A basis of a vector space is a set of vectors that are linearly independent and whose span is the whole of V. A vector space can have several bases. If a vector space is spanned by a finite number of vectors, it is said to be finite-dimensional and it is infinite-dimensional otherwise. The number of vectors in a basis for a finite-dimensional vector space V, denoted as $dim(V)$, is called the dimension of V and it is independent of the basis chosen.

If V is a vector space, then $S \subset V$ is called a subspace of V if it is a vector space on its own. It can be shown that S is a subspace if and only if the following conditions hold:

1. $0 \in s$.
2. $s_1, s_2 \in S \implies s_1 + s_2 \in S$.
3. $s \in S, c \in \mathbf{R} \implies c.s \in S$.

A linear transformation T from a vector spaces V to a vector space W is a function $T : V \to W$, which satisfies the following:

1. $T(v_1 + v_2) = T(v_1) + T(v_2)$ for all $v_1, v_2 \in V$.
2. $T(c.v) = cT(v)$ for all $v \in V$ and $c \in \mathbf{R}$.

A linear transformation from V to itself is called a linear operator.

1.6.2 Metric Spaces

A metric is a generalization of the notion of the distance in Euclidean spaces. A metric space is a set X together with a distance function $d : X \times X \to \mathbf{R}$ that satisfies the following:

1. Non negativity: $d(x_1, x_2) \geq 0$, with equality if and only if $x_1 = x_2, \forall x_1, x_2 \in X$.
2. Symmetry: $d(x_1, x_2) = d(x_2, x_1), \forall x_1, x_2 \in X$.
3. Triangle Inequality: $d(x_1, x_3) \leq d(x_1, x_2) + d(x_2, x_3), \forall x_1, x_2, x_3 \in X$.

1.6.3 Probability

The set Ω of the possible outcomes of a random experiment is called a sample space. Any subset of Ω is called an event. Let F denote the set of all possible events. Probability $P : F \to [0, 1]$ is defined as a measure which satisfies the following axioms:

1. $P(\Omega) = 1$;
2. For any countable collection of disjoint events $\{A_i\} \subset F$,

$$P(\cup A_i) = \sum P(A_i).$$

The triple (Ω, F, P) is called a probability space. A random variable X is a real-valued function (need not be always) defined on a probability space (Ω, F, P).

1.6.4 Optimization

In machine learning, it is required to minimize a cost function known as objective function that measures how poorly the model fits the training data. Optimization deals with finding minima or maxima of an objective function over an input set $X \subset \mathbf{R}^d$ called the feasible set. If X is the entire domain of the objective function, we say that the problem is unconstrained and the problem is said to be constrained otherwise.

Suppose that $f : \mathbf{R}^n \to \mathbf{R}$ is a real-valued function on an n-dimensional Euclidean space. A point $x \in \mathbf{R}^n$ is said to be a local minimum (or local maximum) of f in $\mathbf{R}^n$ if $f(x) \le f(y)$ ($f(x) \ge f(y)$ for local maximum) for all y in some ϵ neighborhood $N_\epsilon(x) \subset \mathbf{R}^n$ of x. If $f(x) \le f(y)$ for all $y \in \mathbf{R}^n$, then x is said to be a global minimum of $f(.)$ in $\mathbf{R}^n$. Similarly if $f(x) \ge f(y)$ for all $y \in \mathbf{R}^n$, then x is said to be a global maximum of $f(.)$ in $\mathbf{R}^n$.

Chapter 2
Introduction to Machine Learning

2.1 Introduction

Predictive modeling is a general concept where a model is built to make predictions. Machine learning algorithms are also predictive models that learn from a training dataset to make predictions. Predictive models can be built for classification or regression problems. Regression models explore relationships between variables and make predictions about continuous variables. Classification involves predicting discrete class labels for data points. For example, predicting whether an android application is a malware or goodware during a malware detection process is a classification task, whereas estimating the threat level of a system is a regression task.

In machine learning, we train the computers with data and make them to take decisions on their own. Although computers have been good at handling and processing huge data, they lacked the capabilities to take decisions on their own. Hence, machine learning techniques have been developed wherein the computers are made to imitate the human brain and make decisions based on some algorithms. These decisions can be in the form labels which can be numeric or symbols. Depending on the nature of the data used to build the model (training data), the machine learning algorithms are classified into the following four categories:

- supervised machine learning,
- unsupervised machine learning,
- semi-supervised machine learning, and
- reinforcement machine learning.

In supervised machine learning, the model is built by training with labeled data. In unsupervised learning, the model works with data points without any label. The aim of an unsupervised algorithm is to organize data into a group of clusters to describe its structure. This makes complex data to look simple and organized. Semi-supervised learning algorithms lie between supervised and unsupervised learning algorithms. In this case, the algorithm is provided with some labeled data and made to work on unlabeled data. Reinforcement algorithms choose an action, based on each data

T. Thomas et al., *Machine Learning Approaches in Cyber Security Analytics*, https://doi.org/10.1007/978-981-15-1706-8_2

point, and then evaluate how good the decision was. The algorithm then changes its strategy to learn better and achieve better results.

Machine learning algorithms can also be classified as either generative or discriminative. A generative classifier such as naive Bayes classifier tries to learn the model that generates the data by estimating the assumptions and distributions of the model. A discriminative classifier such as logistic regression on the other hand just uses the observed data without making many assumptions on the distribution of data. Let x be a data instance and y be its corresponding label. Generative classifiers try to model the conditional probability density function $p(x|y)$ by some unsupervised learning procedure. Bayes theorem is then used to obtain a predictive probability density function $p(y|x)$. The joint probability distribution $p(x, y) = p(x|y)p(y)$ can be used to generate the labeled data instances (x_i, y_i). Discriminative algorithms do not try to estimate how a data point x has been generated, but instead try to estimate the conditional density $p(y|x)$ directly or even just estimating whether $p(y|x)$ is greater than or less than 0.5 as in the case of SVM. Discriminative models are found to be more efficient and better aligned with the supervised learning approach.

Machine learning involves finding a *target function*, $f : X \rightarrow Y$ from the set of input data X to the set of output variables Y. The process of finding this target function $f(.)$ is called the *learning* or *training*. The target function can only be inferred if there are enough labeled data points, that is, the learning is supervised. Since finding the exact target function is hard, in practice, it is approximated by a hypothesis function. The set of all possible hypothesis is referred to as the *hypothesis set*. The learning process in fact involves finding the best *hypothesis function* $h(.)$ that best approximates the unknown target function $f(.)$. The training of the model is carried out using a *training set* which is a representative dataset that is randomly drawn from the dataset. Usually, at least 70% of the data is used for training. The parameters of the model are then tuned using the set of data points drawn from the dataset known as the *tuning set*. Finally, the actual predictive power of the model is verified using a *test set*.

2.1.1 Supervised Machine Learning

Supervised machine learning utilizes a labeled training data for inferring the target function. A labeled data is a pair (x, y) consisting of an input feature vector x and an output label y. The output label is known as the supervisory signal. The learning algorithm generalizes the relationships between feature vector and the label in the training data to new instances of data to correctly determine the class labels of the data.

Let $\{(x_1, y_1)\ldots, (x_n, y_n)\}$ be a labeled training set, where $x_i = (x_{i,1}, \ldots, x_{i,d}) \in X$ for $1 \leq i \leq n$ are the data points and $y_i \in Y$ are their corresponding labels. In supervised learning, the goal is to learn a target function from the dataset to the set of labels, using a training set. It is assumed that the points (x_i, y_i) are independently and identically distributed from a common distribution on the population. The inferred target function can be evaluated through its predictive performance on test data. When $Y \subset \mathbf{R}$ or $\mathbf{Y} \subset \mathbf{R}^d$, the labels are continuous real values or a vector of them. In this case, the learning is called regression. When the labels are discrete values or symbols, the learning is called classification. Whether the problem is regression or classification, the common goal is to find the relationships between the data and the labels.

Spam email filtering is a typical cybersecurity application in which supervised learning algorithms have been widely used. In this case, the dataset M consists of all possible email messages and the label is binary variable. Let the label 0 indicate a legitimate mail and the label 1 indicate a spam mail. A target function $f(.)$ is required to tell us whether a particular email message m is a spam 1 or a legitimate mail 0. We search for a function $f : M \rightarrow \{0, 1\}$, by training one of the machine learning algorithms on a set of n labeled messages $\{(m_1, l_1), (m_2, l_2), \ldots, (m_n, l_n)\}$, where $m_i \in M$ and $l_i \in \{0, 1\}$ for $1 \leq i \leq n$. Some examples for supervised learning algorithms are as follows:

1. linear, logistic, polynomial, and least square regression for regression problems;
2. k-nearest neighbors (k-NN) for classification;
3. decision trees for classification;
4. naive Bayes for classification;
5. support vector machines (SVM) for classification;
6. random forest for classification and regression;
7. ensemble methods for classification and regression.

2.1.2 Unsupervised Machine Learning

In unsupervised machine learning the learning is performed without a labeled training dataset. That is, in unsupervised learning, only the input data x is available and the corresponding label or output data y is not available for training. Hence, unsupervised learning algorithms try to model the underlying structure or distribution in the data in order to discover and present any interesting patterns and classes present in the data. This process is called unsupervised learning as there is no supervisor with correct answers.

Let $X = \{x_1, \ldots, x_n\}$ be a set of n data points, where $x_i = (x_{i,1}, \ldots, x_{i.d}) \in \Omega$ for $1 \leq i \leq n$. It is assumed that the points are drawn independently and identically distributed from a common distribution on the population Ω. The goals of unsupervised learning include finding interesting structures in the data, estimating the probability density function which is likely to have generated the data, quantile estimation, clustering, association, outlier detection, and dimensionality reduction. In clustering, the goal is to discover the inherent groupings in the data and in association rule learning the goal is to discover the rules that describe large portions of the data. Some examples of unsupervised learning algorithms are as follows:

1. k-means clustering for clustering,
2. hierarchical clustering for clustering,
3. factor analysis for clustering,
4. mixture models for clustering,
5. apriori algorithm for association problem,
6. principal component analysis (PCA),
7. singular value decomposition, and
8. independent component analysis.

Most of the clustering algorithms are designed for numerical data which use a notion of distance. Hence, there are some technical difficulties in applying clustering algorithms to cybersecurity problems with categorical data such as URLs, usernames, IP addresses, port numbers, etc.

2.1.3 Semi-supervised Machine Learning

There are some problems in which the training data consists of only a few labeled points and the remaining are unlabeled points. This situation can occur when it is expensive to produce labeled data. In such situations, we use semi-supervised machine learning. Thus, these problems lie in between the supervised and unsupervised learning problems. Generally, it is expensive and time-consuming to produce labeled data, whereas it is cheap and easy to collect and store unlabeled data. Many real-world machine learning problems fall into the category of semi-supervised learning.

In semi-supervised problems, the dataset $X = \{x_1, \ldots, x_{l+u}\}$ is divided into two sets, X_L and X_U. That is, $X = X_L \cup X_U$, where the points in $X_L = \{x_1, \ldots, x_l\}$ are provided with the labels from $Y_L = \{y_1, \ldots, y_l\}$, and for the points in $X_U = \{x_{l+1}, \ldots, x_{l+u}\}$, the labels are not known. This is the standard semi-supervised learning setup. Semi-supervised learning can also occur as a learning under constraints where they operate by introducing constraints on how a learned classifier will behave on unlabeled instances. Semi-supervised learning can be inductive or transductive. In induction, the unknown function is derived from the given data, whereas in transduction, the values of the unknown function for points of interest are derived from the given data. Some types of semi-supervised learning algorithms/techniques are as follows:

1. semi-supervised support vector machines,
2. graph-based models,
3. self-labeled techniques, and
4. generative models.

In intrusion detection problems, large quantities of unlabeled data are available along with relatively small quantities of labeled data. Hence, semi-supervised algorithms are found to be more suitable in building intrusion detection systems (IDS) as they can work with a small amount of labeled data while taking advantage of the large quantities of unlabeled data available.

2.1.4 Reinforcement Machine Learning

Reinforcement learning (RL) is a powerful machine learning technique which combines dynamic programming with supervised learning. It is a learning process through trial and error for optimizing the behavior of an agent interacting with a stochastic environment. The agent performs an action $A(t)$ at each time step t and then perceives a signal $S(t)$ from the environment and receives a reward $R(t)$. Some categories of RL algorithms and techniques are as follows:

1. Monte Carlo,
2. Q-learning (State-action-reward-state),
3. SARSA (State-action-reward-state-action),
4. Q-Learning-Lambda (State-action-reward-state with eligibility traces),
5. SARSA-Lambda (State-action-reward-state-action with eligibility traces),
6. DQN (Deep Q network),
7. DDPG (Deep deterministic policy gradient),
8. A3C (Asynchronous actor-critic algorithm),
9. NAF (Q-Learning with normalized advantage functions),
10. TRPO (Trust region policy optimization), and
11. PPO (Proximal policy optimization).

Reinforcement learning algorithms find applications in various cybersecurity problems such as network intrusion detection, anomaly detection, and so on.

In the following sections, we briefly discuss various machine learning models.

2.2 Linear Regression

Linear regression is one of the oldest and most widely used regression models in machine learning. The goal of linear regression is to fit a linear function to the data by minimizing the sum of the squared errors between predicted and observed values. A linear model makes a prediction $\hat{y}$ of y by computing a weighted sum of features $x_1, \ldots, x_n$ and a bias term b. Let the $w_1, \ldots, w_n$ and b denote the parameters of the model. Now the general form of the model can be given as

$$\hat{y} = w_1 x_1 + w_2 x_2 + \cdots + w_n x_n + b. \tag{2.1}$$

Linear regression models can be trained by minimizing a cost function in the following two ways:

- Computing the parameters of the model that best fit the training set by minimizing a cost function over the training set.
- Using gradient descent which is a technique of iterative optimization that minimizes a cost function by gradually tweaking the model parameters.

Training of a linear regression model involves finding the values of the parameters of the model $w_1, \ldots, w_n$ and b that minimizes the root mean square error (RMSE) or the mean square error (MSE).

2.3 Polynomial Regression

Polynomial regression is a prediction model for nonlinear data. This can be done by adding powers of features as new features and then training a linear model on this extended set of features. The kth-order polynomial regression model in one variable is given by

$$\hat{y} = w_1 x + w_2 x^2 + \cdots + w_k x^k + b, \tag{2.2}$$

where $\hat{y}$ is the predicted value, x is the feature value, and $w_1, \ldots, w_k$ and b are the model parameters. This can be extended to polynomial models in two or more variables. For example, the second-order polynomial in two variables is given by

$$\hat{y} = b + w_1 x_1 + w_2 x_2 + w_3 x_1^2 + w_4 x_2^2 + w_5 x_1 x_2, \tag{2.3}$$

where $\hat{y}$ is the predicted value, x_1 and x_2 are the feature values, and $w_1, \ldots, w_5, b$ are the model parameters.

2.4 Logistic Regression

Logistic regression or logit regression is usually used to estimate the probability that a data instance belongs to a particular category. In logistic regression, the probability of the association between a categorical-dependent variable Y and a set of independent variables $X_1, \ldots, X_n$ are estimated. If the estimated probability is greater than 0.50, the model predicts that the instance belongs to that category and otherwise it does not.

In logistic regression, a mathematical model of the set of independent variables also known as explanatory variables is used to predict a logit transformation of the dependent variable. Suppose that 0 and 1 denote the outcomes of a binary variable. The mean p of this variable will be the probability of getting 1 as the outcome, and $1 - p$ will be the probability of getting 0 as the outcome. The ratio $\frac{p}{1-p}$ is called the odds l, and the logarithm of the odds is known as the logit. Thus, the logit transformation can be written as

$$l = logit(p) = \ln(\frac{p}{1-p}).$$

The inverse of the logit transformation is called the logistic transformation. It is given by

$$p = logistic(l) = \ln(\frac{e^l}{1+e^l}).$$

Let the dependent variable Y has m distinct values, and there are n independent variables $X_1, \ldots, X_n$. The logistic regression model is given by the m equations

$$\ln(\frac{p_i}{p_1}) = \ln(\frac{P_i}{P_1}) + w_{i,1}X_1 + w_{i,2}X_2 + \cdots + w_{i,n}X_n,$$

where $1 \leq i \leq m$, $p_i = Pr(Y = i|X_1, \ldots, X_n)$, $P_1, \ldots, P_m$ represent the prior probabilities of the outcomes, and $w_{i,j}$ are the regression coefficients to be estimated from the data.

2.5 Naive Bayes Classifier

Naive Bayes classifier is a supervised learning algorithm that is based on the Bayes theorem and a set of conditional independence assumptions on the attributes. It combines prior knowledge and observed data to compute explicit probabilities for hypothesis, and it is robust to noise in the input data. The classifier is called naive Bayes classifier because it works under the assumption that the measurements are mutually independent among the features given the target class. This assumption makes the computation of the posterior probabilities based on the Bayes rule much simpler. Let $x = (x_1, \ldots, x_n)$ be a data point with n attributes x_i for $1 \leq i \leq n$ and Y be its label. The goal of the algorithm is to estimate $P(Y|X)$ from the training set, where X is a data point with label Y. This can be estimated using the Bayes rule. From the conditional independence assumption on the attributes x_i, we get

$$P(x_1, \ldots, x_n|Y) = \prod_{i=1}^{n} P(x_i|Y). \quad (2.4)$$

Our goal is to train a classifier that will output the conditional probability distribution of Y, given X. The posterior probability for each class value y can be computed using the Bayes rule as

$$P(Y = y|x_1, \dots, x_n) = \frac{P(Y = y)P(x_1, \dots, x_n|Y = y)}{\sum_y P(Y = y)P(x_1, \dots, x_n|Y = y)}. \tag{2.5}$$

Now using the conditional independence assumption, we get

$$P(Y = y|x_1, \dots, x_n) = \frac{P(Y = y)\prod_i P(x_i|Y = y)}{\sum_y P(Y = y)\prod_i P(x_i|Y = y)}. \tag{2.6}$$

This is the model equation for the naive Bayes classifier which gives the probability distribution of Y, given the observed attribute values. The probability distributions $P(Y)$ and $P(x_i|Y)$ are estimated from the training dataset.

Naive Bayes classifier is used when we have a moderate or large training dataset with data points having several attributes or features, and given the classification parameter, the attributes are conditionally independent. Some well-known applications of naive Bayes classifier include

1. malware detection,
2. spam detection,
3. intrusion detection,
4. DoS and DDoS attack detection, and
5. sentiment analysis.

Spam filtering is a well-known application of naive Bayes classifier. Spam filter is a binary classifier that assigns one of the labels "Spam" or "Not Spam" to all the emails. Many modern mail clients use spam filters based on naive Bayes classifier. SpamBayes, DSPAM, Bogofilter, SpamAssassin, and ASSP are some server-side spam filters that make use of the Bayesian classifier. In social media, naive Bayes is used for sentiment analysis to analyze status updates expressing positive or negative emotions.

Naive Bayes classifier performs well for categorical input variables. Some advantages of naive Bayes classifier are as follows: it converges faster, requires relatively less training data, easier to predict the class of a test data set, and works well for multi-class classification problems.

2.6 Support Vector Machines (SVM)

SVM or support vector machine is a binary classifier which makes use of a decision boundary in a multidimensional space using a subset of the training data called the support vectors. Geometrically, the support vectors are those training data that are closest to the decision boundary known as the hyperplane. SVM is trained by finding the hyperplane that maximizes the margin between the data points that could be separated into two classes. It is possible to perform linear or nonlinear classification, regression, and outlier detection using SVM. SVM is a very popular machine learning model and is used for classification of both small- and medium-sized datasets.

Let $x = (x_1, \ldots, x_n) \in \mathbf{R}^n$ be a point in an n-dimensional Euclidean space. A hyperplane $H(a, b)$ in $\mathbf{R}^n$ is a set of the form $\{x | a^T x + b = 0\}$, where $a = [a_1, \ldots, a_n]^T$ is $n \times 1$ nonzero column vector. That is,

$$H(a, b) = \{x : x = (x_1, \ldots, x_n) \in \mathbf{R}^n \ \& \ a_1 x_1 + \cdots + a_n x_n + b = 0\}.$$

Here, a and b are the parameters of the hyperplane. Thus, a hyperplane in an n-dimensional Euclidean space is an $n - 1$ dimensional subspace that divides $\mathbf{R}^n$ into two disjoint sets. For example, if we consider a straight line as a 1-dimensional space, then a point on it is a 0-dimensional hyperplane of the line. A half-space is a set of points on one side of the hyperplane. The positive half-space $H^+(a, b)$ and the negative half-space $H^-(a, b)$ are given by

$$H^+(a, b) = \{x : x = (x_1, \ldots, x_n) \in \mathbf{R}^n \ \& \ a_1 x_1 + \cdots + a_n x_n + b > 0\}$$

$$H^-(a, b) = \{x : x = (x_1, \ldots, x_n) \in \mathbf{R}^n \ \& \ a_1 x_1 + \cdots + a_n x_n + b < 0\}.$$

A point is classified into one of the classes according to the half-space it lies. That is, if $y = 1$ and $y = -1$ are the labels of the two classes, then a data point x is assigned the label y according to the following computations:

$$y = \begin{cases} +1, & \text{if } x \in H^+(a, b); \\ -1, & \text{if } x \in H^-(a, b). \end{cases} \tag{2.7}$$

An SVM model attempts to produce the best hyperplane that completely separates the vectors into two disjoint classes. However, perfect separation into two disjoint classes may not be possible and the model may not classify some the points correctly. In this situation, SVM finds a hyperplane that maximizes the margin between the classes and minimizes the number of misclassifications. That is, the SVM classifier tries to fit the widest possible street between the classes. This is referred to as large margin classification. If we require that all the data points be strictly off the street, then the classification is known as a hard margin classification. However, in order to build a more flexible model, one is required to have a trade-off between maximizing the margin and minimizing the margin violations of the data points. This type of SVM modeling is known as the soft margin classification. In all the cases, the target of the SVM is to find the optimal hyperplane by maximizing the margin between classes.

Let $u_1, \ldots, u_m$ be the points in the training set with labels $y_1, \ldots, y_m$, respectively. Now the hyperplane parameters (a, b) can be obtained by solving the following quadratic optimization problem:

$$\text{minimize } a^T a = a_1^2 + \cdots + a_n^2, \text{ subject to} \tag{2.8}$$

$$y_i(a^T u_i + b) - 1 \geq 0, \quad \text{for } i = 1, \ldots, m. \tag{2.9}$$

This quadratic optimization problem is known as the primal problem. The solution to this problem can be obtained by looking at the dual of the primal problem which can be written in terms of the Lagrangian multipliers as follows:

$$L = \sum_{i=1}^{m} \alpha_i - \frac{1}{2} \sum_{i=1}^{m} \sum_{j=1}^{m} y_i y_j \alpha_i \alpha_j u_i u_j^T.$$

The optimal Lagrangian multipliers are obtained by maximizing L over α_1's. a can be determined as $\sum_{i=1}^{m} y_i \alpha_i u_i$ and b can be obtained from Karush–Kuhn–Tucker (KKT) conditions.

The simplest way to separate two groups of data is with a linear hyperplane such as a straight line for two-dimensional data or a plane for three-dimensional data or an $n-1$-dimensional hyperplane for n-dimensional data. If two classes can be separated easily with a hyperplane, then they are said to be linearly separable and the corresponding classification is known as the linear SVM classification. However, in practice, many datasets are not linearly separable and a nonlinear region or surface can separate the groups of data points better than a hyperplane. Since finding a nonlinear separating hypersurface is a hard problem, there are some other approaches for handling nonlinear dataset. Some of them are the following:

- enlarging the feature set by adding polynomial features,
- using kernel functions and kernel trick, and
- adding similarity features computed using a similarity function.

Enlarging the feature set by adding polynomial functions of features is one approach for handling nonlinear dataset. However, with low-degree polynomial features one cannot deal with complex datasets, whereas with high-degree polynomial features, the model can become too slow.

If the data points cannot be separated using a linear hyperplane in some Euclidean space, then it may be possible to separate them by a linear hyperplane if mapped into a higher dimensional space. A kernel function can be used to map the data points into a higher dimensional space. In this way, an algorithm behaving nonlinearly in the original input space can be made to behave linearly in a higher dimensional space. Using kernel trick, the classification algorithm can be carried into a higher dimensional space without explicitly mapping the input points into this space. Kernel trick is a clever way to get the same results as if we have added many polynomial features without actually adding them. In this way, the kernel trick acts as a bridge from linearity to nonlinearity for any algorithm where computations can be expressed in terms of dot products (inner product) of vectors.

Suppose, we want a function $f(.)$ that maps input feature vectors into a higher dimensional output space. $f(.)$ can be realized through a kernel function $k(.)$ as follows. A kernel function $k(,)$ on $\mathbf{R}^n \times \mathbf{R}^n$ is a continuous and symmetric function with preferably a positive (semi) definite gram matrix. That is, the kernel matrix $K = (K_{ij}) = (k(u_i, u_j))$ is positive (semi) definite. Gram matrix is a square matrix consisting of pairwise scalar products of elements of a Hilbert space. Then there exists a function $f(.)$ such that the dot product $(f(u), f(v)) = k(u, v)$ for all u, v. This allows to compute the inner product of the nonlinear mappings without explicitly evaluating them. This reduces the complexity of the optimization problem, without any effect on the Lagrangian formulation. The dual of the optimization problem can be written in terms of the Lagrangian multipliers using the kernel function $k(,)$ as follows:

$$L = \sum_{i=1}^{n} \alpha_i - \frac{1}{2} \sum_{i=1}^{n} \sum_{j=1}^{n} y_i y_j \alpha_i \alpha_j (k(x_i, x_j)).$$

Kernels that satisfy the Mercers theorem are positive semidefinite. That is, their kernel matrices have only nonnegative eigenvalues. When the kernel is positive definite, the optimization problem becomes convex and the solution will be unique. However, many widely used kernel functions such as sigmoid kernel which are not strictly positive definite have also shown to perform very well in practice. It has been shown that the kernels which are only conditionally positive definite can perform better than most classical kernels in some applications. When the training set is very large and the data elements have many features, one should always first try with the linear kernel. If the training set is not too large, one can try with the Gaussian RBF kernel. Other kernels may be used for cross-validation and grid search.

The idea of using kernel functions is based on the fact that many algorithms such as SVM can be formulated so that the only way they interact with their data is through computing dot products of the feature vector of the data points. Similarity functions are proposed to take care of some of the limitations of kernel functions. In this case, the similarity features are computed using a similarity function and added. A similarity function measures how much each instance resembles a particular landmark. Some applications of SVM in cybersecurity are

- intrusion detection systems (IDS),
- classification of cyberattacks, and
- malware detection.

We can have one-class or two-class or multi-class SVM models for IDS. A one-class SVM requires only a training dataset containing normal traffic, whereas a two-class SVM requires a training dataset containing both normal and anomalous traffics. A multi-class SVM can be used to categorize a malicious traffic into one of the classes such as denial-of-service (DoS) attack, distributed denial-of-service (DDoS) attack, probing attack, malware attack, and so on.

SVM can also be used for both linear and nonlinear regression problems. In regression problems, instead of trying to fit the widest possible street between two classes while limiting margin violations, the algorithms try to fit as many instances as possible on the street while limiting the margin violations. Kernelized SVM models are used to address the nonlinear regression problems.

2.7 Decision Tree

Decision trees are very commonly used supervised machine learning algorithms that can be used for both classification and regression problems. Decision tree algorithms make use of training data to formulate a set of decision rules. The labels or classes of the test data are predicted based on this set of decision rules. The decision tree algorithm is represented as a tree structure with each non-leaf node acts as a decision-maker and each leaf node represents a class or label. Thus, a decision tree is a predictor $h : X \rightarrow Y$ from the dataset to the set of labels that is defined by traveling from the root of a tree to a leaf. Each non-leaf node is given a particular decision criterion to determine whether the tree has to parse through the left or the right branch. Decisions are made at each node until the leaf node is reached. The class or label of the data point is determined in the leaf node. In a decision tree, each vertex or node represents a feature, each edge or branch represents a decision made, and each leaf represents a class or label.

Entropy is a measure of uncertainty or randomness in information. Entropy has a value between 0 and 1. The higher the entropy, the more random the data is and more difficult it is to draw conclusions from the information. For example, in the case of tossing an unbiased coin, there is no relationship between a toss and the outcome of the toss. In this case, the entropy of the unknown result of the next toss of the coin has a maximum value of 1. This is a situation of maximum uncertainty, and each toss of the coin gives one full bit of information. On the other hand, if the coin is fully biased toward either tail or head, there is no uncertainty in the outcome of any toss. In this case, the entropy has the minimum value of 0. In the case of decision trees, entropy controls how a decision tree decides to split the data and draws its boundaries. That is, while splitting data, the change in entropy called the information gain is calculated. The higher the entropy change, the better would be the split. The entropy $H(X)$ of any element X with features $(x_1, \ldots, x_n)$ in the dataset is measured as

$$H(X) = -\sum_{i=1}^{n} p_i \log_2 p_i, \tag{2.10}$$

where p_i is the probability of the occurrence of x_i. A data point X which has the lowest value for entropy is chosen as the root node of a decision tree.

Information gain $IG(,)$ can be used to measure how much information a feature gives about a class. Decision trees algorithm works on maximizing the information gain. The computation of information gain is based on the decrease in entropy after a dataset is split on an attribute. The information gain of a feature x_i, in decision tree algorithm, is computed as follows:

$$IG(D_p, x_i) = H(D_p) - \frac{n_{left}}{n_p} H(D_{left}) - \frac{n_{right}}{n_p} H(D_{right}), \tag{2.11}$$

where x_i is the feature to perform the split, n_p is the number of samples in parent node, n_{left} is the number of samples in left child node, n_{right} is the number of samples in right child node, $H()$ is the entropy measure, D_p is the training subset of the parent node, D_{left} is the training subset of the left child node, and D_{right} is the training subset of the right child node. A feature with highest information gain is used to split the dataset first.

The construction of a decision tree is based on finding the attribute or feature that has the highest information gain at each stage of the algorithm. In the first step, the entropy of the target is calculated. The second step involves splitting the dataset based on the different attributes of the data. The entropy for each branch of the tree is then computed and added proportionally to get the total entropy for the split. The resulting total entropy is subtracted from the entropy before the split to get the decrease in the entropy which is the information gain. In the third step, the attribute which has the largest information gain is chosen as the decision node. The dataset is divided by the branches and the same process is repeated on every branch until the entropy of a branch becomes 0 and turns into a leaf node.

For an optimal tree to be constructed, the most appropriate attribute to be placed at the root node is to be determined. Further, the entropy with each level in the tree has to be reduced so as to reduce the overall uncertainty. The maximum tree depth is the maximum number of nodes from the root of the tree. Adding new nodes should be stopped once that maximum tree depth has been reached. The deeper the trees, the more complex the model and the more the chance of over-fitting of the training data. The splitting and adding of new nodes must be stopped once the minimum number of training patterns that a node may have called the minimum node records has been attained. New nodes that are added to an existing node are called its child nodes. A terminal node has no child node. Other nodes can have one or two child nodes. Once a node is created, child nodes can be created by calling a node creation function recursively. This function has the maximum depth, current depth of the node, and minimum node records as its arguments. The tree stops growing once the terminal node has been reached and the final prediction is made then.

Data points can be classified using a decision tree by traversing the tree from the root node to a leaf node. First, the attribute specified by the root node is checked for the data point and then one traverse down the tree branch according to the attribute value. This process is repeated at each sub-tree level. The steps to use a decision tree as a classifier to predict the label of a data point are summarized below.

1. Start the search from the root node.
2. At each interior node, evaluate the decision rule for the data point and determine the branch to the child node as specified by the decision rule.
3. Once a leaf node is reached, assign the class assigned to that node as class of the data point.

The stopping criteria in a decision tree are given below:

1. All the leaf nodes are labeled.
2. Maximal node depth is attained.
3. There is no information gain on splitting of any node.

Algorithm 2.1 Decision Tree algorithm

Input: CSV file for each feature
Output: Classified samples with labels assigned

```
if If leaf nodes do not satisfy the early stopping criteria then
    Select attribute that gives the "best" split; assign it as the root node
    repeat
        Begin from the root node as the parent node
        Split parent node at some feature x_i to maximize the information gain
        Assign training samples to new child nodes
    until for each new child node
end if
```

A few decision tree algorithms are the following:

- ID3 (Iterative Dichotomiser 3),
- C4.5 (successor of ID3),
- CART (Classification and regression tree),
- CHAID (Chi-squared automatic interaction detector),
- MARS: extends decision trees to handle numerical data better, and
- Conditional inference trees.

ID3 algorithm which is based on the concept learning system (CLS) algorithm was developed by Ross Quinlan in 1975. ID3 algorithm usually uses nominal features for classification with no missing values. In 1993, Ross Quinlan again proposed the C4.5 algorithm to overcome some of the limitations of the ID3 algorithm. One limitation of ID3 is that it is very sensitive to features with large values. C4.5 uses information gain to overcome this problem. Conditional inference trees use nonparametric tests for splitting nodes, which is corrected by multiple tests to avoid over-fitting. This algorithm gives an unbiased predictor selection and does not require pruning.

2.8 Nearest Neighbor

Nearest neighbor (NN) learning is also known as instance-based learning because these algorithms are based on similarity or distance calculation between the instances. They are a family of algorithms that can be used for both classification and regression problems. k-nearest neighbors (k-NN) is a simple such algorithm with a parameter $k \in \mathbf{Z}^+$ which has an easy interpretation and a low execution time. The algorithm works as follows. Whenever a new data point has to be classified, its k-nearest neighbors from the training data are found using some distance metric. The new data point is assigned to the class of the majority of the k-nearest neighbors. The parameter k determines the number of neighbors to be considered and has a significant impact on the performance of the algorithm. Figure 2.1 shows the curve for the training error rate with different values of k for the k-NN algorithm. When $k = 1$, the closest point

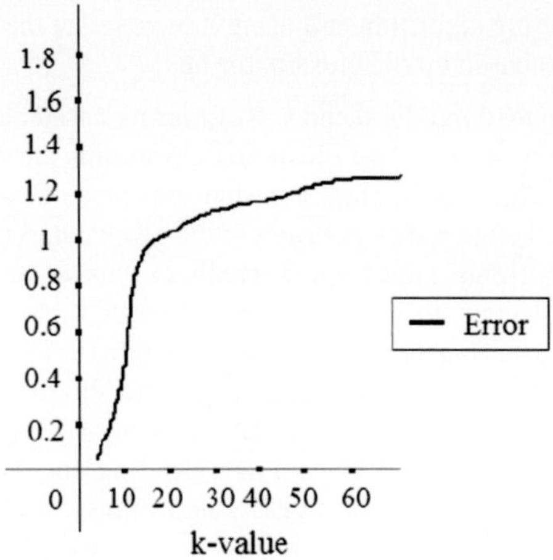

Fig. 2.1 Training error rate

to any training data point is itself. The 1-NN algorithm predicts the same class as the nearest instance in the training set. Hence, in 1-NN the prediction is always accurate with an error rate of 0.

NN algorithms use the entire training dataset for the model representation as it does not require any learning. These classifiers use some or all the patterns available in the training dataset to classify a test pattern. These classifiers look for the similarity between the test pattern and every pattern in the training set.

In k-NN algorithm, predictions are made for a new data point by searching through the entire training set for identifying its k neighbors. Once the k neighbors are identified, regression involves finding the (arithmetic) mean value of these neighbors, whereas classification involves finding the mode of the class values of the neighbors. The k-NN employs some distance metrics such as Euclidean, Manhattan, etc. to find the neighbors.

2.9 Clustering

Clustering is the process of grouping a set of data points or patterns. It partitions the given collection of patterns into a collection of cohesive groups or clusters. The purpose of clustering is to put the patterns that are similar in a way into a cluster so that the patterns that are dissimilar in some other way fall into different clusters. Two patterns are put into the same cluster if and only if the distance (such as Euclidean distance) between them is less than a specified threshold. The important steps in the clustering process can be summarized as follows:

1. representing the patterns as feature vectors,
2. defining a similarity function,

3. selecting a clustering algorithm and using it to generate the clusters, and
4. making decisions based on the clusters formed.

Clustering can be divided into hard and soft clustering based on whether the clusters generated are disjoint or not. Hard clustering algorithms are either hierarchical or partitional. In hierarchical clustering, a nested sequence of partitions is generated, whereas in partitional clustering a partition of the given dataset is generated. Hierarchical clustering algorithms are computationally expensive with nonlinear time and space complexities. Hence, these algorithms are not feasible when the datasets are larger in size. Soft clustering algorithms make use of fuzzy sets, rough sets, artificial neural nets (ANNs), evolutionary algorithms, genetic algorithms (GAs), and so on.

Hierarchical algorithms partition the data as a nested sequence which can be represented using a tree structure known as a dendrogram. The algorithms can be either divisive or agglomerative. In divisive algorithms, all the patterns are put in a single cluster first and the clusters are divided in each successive step. Thus, a top-down strategy is used by divisive algorithms for generating partitions of the data. In divisive algorithms, once two patterns are placed in two different clusters at a level, they remain in different clusters at all subsequent levels. Some divisive algorithms consider only one feature at a time, whereas others consider more than one feature at a time. Accordingly, these algorithms are called monothetic algorithms and polythetic algorithms, respectively. In polythetic clustering, all the possible 2-partitions of the data are found. The partition with the least sum of the sample variances of the two clusters is then chosen as the best 2-partition. From the resulting partition, the cluster with the maximum sample variance is selected and is split into an optimal 2-partition. This process is repeated until we get singleton clusters. Divisive algorithms are not efficient as they require exponential time to analyze the number of patterns or the features. Agglomerative algorithms start with singleton clusters where each input pattern is put in a different cluster. At successive steps, the most similar pair of clusters is merged. In this way, the agglomerative algorithms use a bottom-up strategy. In agglomerative algorithms, once two patterns are placed in the same cluster at a level, they remain in the same cluster at all subsequent levels.

k-means is a popular nondeterministic and iterative clustering algorithm for data points which operates on a given dataset through predefined number of (say k) clusters. k-means algorithm produces k centroids for each of the k clusters generated from the dataset. k-means algorithm is suitable for continuous numeric data with smaller number of dimensions. The steps in k-means algorithm are the following:

1. Select any k patterns from the given set of n patterns as the initial cluster centers (centroid of the clusters).
2. Identify the closest cluster center for each of the remaining $n - k$ patterns and assign the point to that cluster. If there is no change in the assignment of patterns to the clusters then stop.
3. Recompute the new cluster centers based on the current assignment of patterns.
4. Go to Step 2.

There are different ways for selecting the initial cluster centers. These include selecting the first k of the given n patterns, selecting k patterns randomly from the given n patterns, using optimization approach, finding globally optimal solutions, and so on. k-means algorithm has the property that it minimizes the sum of squared deviations of patterns in a cluster from the cluster center. That is, if X_i is the ith cluster and λ_i is its center, then the algorithm minimizes the function,

$$\sum_{i=1}^{k} \sum_{x \in X_i} (x - \lambda_i)^T (x - \lambda_i). \tag{2.12}$$

The k-means clustering algorithm has an interesting application in the profiling of criminals. Criminal profiling is the process of clustering of data on individuals and groups of criminals and their crimes. Criminal profiling can be used to classify the types of criminals who are associated with a cybercrime.

2.10 Dimensionality Reduction

Dimensionality reduction is the process of transforming a dataset with large dimensions into a dataset with smaller dimensions without losing the relevant information in the data. This technique helps in machine learning problems to obtain better features for classification and regression tasks. Some of the benefits of applying dimensionality reduction to the data are as follows:

1. removes redundant features.
2. compresses the data, thereby reducing the memory required.
3. makes the computations faster.
4. allows the usage of algorithms suitable for low-dimensional data.
5. takes care of the multicollinearity problem.
6. allows to plot and visualize the data more precisely which helps in observing the patterns more clearly.

Data can be represented as a matrix with each row representing a data element and each column representing a feature. We call it as the data matrix. Now we will list below some of the common methods for dimensionality reduction.

1. Removing Columns with Missing Values
   In a data matrix, if a column has too many missing values, the corresponding feature is unlikely to carry much useful information. If the number of missing values is greater than a threshold, then that feature can be removed from each data element.
2. Low Variance Filter
   Variance can be used to measure the information in a column of the data matrix. A low variance indicates less information in the column, and the feature corresponding to the column is not good in distinguishing various data points. A threshold can be set, and all the columns with variance less than this threshold can be removed.

3. High Correlation Filter
   Columns in the data matrix with similar trends are likely to carry very similar information. If values in a data column are highly correlated to those of another data column, that data column is not going to provide much new information. Hence, in this case, it is enough to retain only one such column in the data matrix. In this case, we need to measure the correlation between pairs of columns and find the pairs of columns with correlation higher than a given threshold. A column from one such pair needs to be removed.
4. Random Forests/Ensemble Trees
   In random forests or ensembles of decision trees, a large and carefully constructed set of trees against a target attribute is generated. The most informative subset of features is then found out using the statistics of each attribute. That is, many shallow trees which are trained on a small fraction of the total number of attributes are generated. Then the attributes that are often selected as the best splits are retained as an informative feature. The most predictive attributes are determined based on a score calculated on the attribute usage statistics in the random forest.
5. Principal Component Analysis
   Principal component analysis (PCA) is a statistical technique that uses orthogonal transformation to convert a dataset of n dimension into a new dataset of lower dimension, say k where $k < n$ in a different coordinate system called the principal components. The largest possible variance in the data (most of the data information) will be along the first principal component, and the next highest possible variance will be along the succeeding component and so on. By keeping only the first k components, the dimension of the data can be reduced to k from n while retaining most of the data information or the variation in the data.
6. Backward Feature Elimination
   In this case, the feature dimension is reduced by 1 at each stage using an iterative technique until a maximum tolerable error has been reached. In the first iteration, the classification algorithm is trained on n input features. Then one input feature is removed at a time, and the same model is trained on $n - 1$ input features. This is repeated n times corresponding to the n features. We remove the input feature whose removal has produced the smallest increase in the error rate. This reduces the feature dimension to $n - 1$. This process is then repeated using $n - 2$ features and so on. Each iteration m produces a model trained on $n - m$ features and an error rate of ϵ_k. By fixing the maximum tolerable error rate, we determine the smallest number of features necessary to reach the required classification performance with the chosen algorithm.
7. Forward Feature Construction
   This is the inverse process to the backward feature elimination technique. We start with one feature only, progressively adding one feature at a time. That is, we add the feature that produces the highest increase in the performance. Both backward and forward algorithms are quite time and computationally expensive. They are practically applicable only to a dataset with a relatively low number of input columns.

2.11 Linear Discriminant Analysis (LDA)

Linear discriminant analysis (LDA) is a linear classification algorithm that has been proposed to take care of some of the limitations of the logistic regression. Although logistic regression is a simple and powerful linear classification algorithm, it has the following limitations:

1. Restricted to binary classification: Logistic regression is intended for binary or two-class classification problems. Although it can be extended for multi-class classification problems, it has not been much used for this purpose.
2. Unstable when classes are well separated: Logistic regression can become unstable when classes are very separated.
3. Unstable when training data is less: Logistic regression can become unstable when the training data is very less to estimate the parameters.

LDA addresses these problems and is a suitable linear classifier for multi-class as well as binary classification problems. LDA is a type of Bayesian classifier which uses the following classification equation:

$$C(x) = \underset{r \in \{1,2,\ldots,k\}}{argmax}\, Pr(Y = r|X = x), \tag{2.13}$$

where x is a feature vector and $r \in \{1, 2, \ldots, k\}$ is a class label. The classifier computes the conditional probabilities $Pr(Y = r|X = x)$ for each output class $Y = r$ for $r = 1, 2, \ldots, k$. This is the conditional probability for the class r, when x is the feature vector. The class (r) that returns the maximum value for this probability becomes the output of the classifier $C(x)$.

2.12 Boosting

Boosting is a process of converting a weak classifier to a strong classifier or creating a strong classifier from a number of weak classifiers. A strong classifier is very closely correlated to the true classifier, whereas a weak classier is only loosely correlated to the true classifier. The first approach involves building a machine learning model from the training data as discussed in the earlier sections and then converting it into another model that corrects the errors of the first model. In the second approach, a strong learner is obtained from several weak learners by combining the prediction of each weak learner. Weak models are added until the predictions of the combined model on the training set become perfect or a maximum number of models are added. More specifically, the weak learners are executed multiple times on the training data and the final classifier is obtained as a linear combination of different classifiers weighted by their strength. Boosting algorithms are iterative in nature, where the classifiers generated in each round depend on their predecessors and the errors in classifications made in the previous rounds.

Adaptive boosting or AdaBoost is a very successful boosting algorithm developed for both binary classification and regression algorithms. It is an ensemble learning algorithm that is called adaptive because it makes use of multiple iterations to generate a strong learner. AdaBoost algorithm creates a strong learner by iteratively adding a new weak learner to the ensemble during each round of the training. A weight vector is adjusted in each round to correct the classification of the data points that were misclassified in the previous rounds. There are other boosting algorithms such as stochastic gradient boosting that were developed based on AdaBoost.

Chapter 3
Machine Learning and Cybersecurity

3.1 Introduction

Machine learning (ML) may be defined as the ability of machines to learn without being explicitly programmed. Using mathematical techniques across cyberdata, ML algorithms can build models of behaviors and use those models as a basis for making predictions on newly input data. ML techniques can analyze threats and respond to attacks and security incidents quickly in an automated way. ML techniques could be applied to a variety of cybersecurity problems such as

1. spam mail and phishing page detection,
2. malware detection and identification,
3. DoS and DDoS attack detection,
4. anomaly detection,
5. biometric recognition,
6. user identification and authentication,
7. detection of identity theft,
8. social media analytics,
9. detection of information leakage,
10. detection of advanced persistent threats,
11. detection of hidden channels, and
12. detection of software vulnerabilities.

In the following sections, we will briefly discuss some of these cybersecurity problems and solution approaches with ML techniques.

3.2 Spam Detection

Spam is the electronic equivalent of the junk mail that arrives in our mailbox. Spam may be defined as an unsolicited commercial email or an unsolicited bulk email. Spam mails are not only just annoying but can be dangerous. The content of spam

T. Thomas et al., *Machine Learning Approaches in Cyber Security Analytics*, https://doi.org/10.1007/978-981-15-1706-8_3

can be anything such as advertisements of goods and services, pornographic material, financial advertisements, information on illegal copies of software, fraudulent advertisements, fraudulent messages to solicit money, links to malware, phishing websites, etc. The intention of spammers involve making money, running phishing scams, spreading malicious code, etc. Spam can damage computer system and may clog computer networks as well. Spam may also be used for launching denial-of-service (DoS) attacks.

Spam filtering can be performed based on the textual content of email messages. This can be seen as a special case of text categorization, with the categories being spam and non-spam. Text classification techniques such as TF-IDF, naive Bayes, SVM, n-gram, boosting, etc. can be applied for spam filtering based on the textual content. Some of the limitations of these approaches are the requirement of lots of training data, processing power, etc.

Other ML techniques involve, converting emails into feature vectors, where features include token of the email, size, presence of attachment, IP, and number of recipients. We can use ML techniques such as SVM, decision trees, neural network, and so on.

3.3 Phishing Page Detection

Phishing is one of the methods adopted by cybercriminals to obtain user credentials by redirecting users to malicious websites. Malicious web links sent through email, SMS, etc. might contain payloads capable of sniffing sensitive information entered by the user. People are psychologically influenced and the contents of the malicious website are made believable, thereby making users to enter personal details such as username, password, bank account number, credit card details, and so on. Generally, this is achieved by spoofing the websites of reputed organizations, so that the user never doubts an illegitimate activity prior to entering their personal information. These days, phishing sites are not only used for sniffing user credentials but also for spreading malware such as cookie stealers, keyloggers, etc. These malware can steal cookies from the system or capture user keystrokes.

Different kinds of features which are used in existing ML-based detection algorithms can be grouped as

1. URL-based features,
2. domain-based features,
3. page-based features, and
4. content-based features.

Some of URL-based features include number of digits in the URL, total length of URL, number of sub-domains in URL, misspelled domain names, TLD used, and so on. Some of the domain-based features include the presence of domain name or its IP address in well-known blacklisted services, age of the domain, category of the domain, availability of the registrant name, and so on. Some of the page-based features include global and country PageRank, position at the Alexa yop 1 million site, estimated number of visits for the domain on a daily, weekly, or monthly basis, average page views per visit, average visit duration, web traffic share per country, number of references from social networks, the presence of similar websites, and so on. Some content-based features include page titles, meta tags, hidden text, text in the body, images, video, and so on.

Thus, the common features that are used for phishing page detection include its URL, PageRank, SSL certificate, Google indexing, domain, and features based on the web page source code. However, these features have the following limitations. Web pages that are hosted on free web hosting services would never include some of the relevant features possessed by a legitimate web page such as PageRank, age of the domain, SSL certificate, and Google indexing. On the other hand, it is possible for a hacker to promote his phishing page by utilizing black hat SEO techniques such as keyword stuffing to get higher indices for the phishing page in Google search results or link spamming to boost the PageRank of the phishing page. Further, incoming traffic to the website can be increased with the help of third-party tools such as web clicker application which generates thousands of page views within minutes. Thus, a hacker can partially evade the URL and domain-based detection mechanisms by using black hat SEO tools. Hence, we can conclude that URL and domain-based features are not much effective for phishing web page detection.

Phishing page detection is a supervised classification problem. We need labeled data which has samples of phishing pages and legitimate pages in the training phase. The training dataset which we use is a very important component to build a successful detection mechanism. So, we have to use training samples whose classes are precisely known. PhishTank is a well-known public dataset of phishing websites. Site reputation services can be used for collecting legitimate sites. ML techniques such as SVM, decision tree, naive Bayes, etc. have been used for phishing page detection.

3.4 Malware Detection

Malware (malicious software) is any software intentionally designed to cause damage to computer systems and networks. Malware can be divided into the following classes:

- Virus: It is a type of malware that is loaded and launched without the permission of a user and reproduces itself as well as infect other software.
- Worm: This malware type is very similar to the virus but unlike virus it can spread over the network and replicate to other machines on its own.
- Trojan: This malware type appears as a legitimate software but has malicious functionalities hidden in it.
- Adware: This malware type displays advertisements on the computer.
- Spyware: This malware type performs espionage.

- Rootkit: This malware type enables the attacker to access the system and network with root access.
- Backdoor: This malware type provides an additional secret entry point to the system for the attacker.
- Keylogger: This malware type logs all the keys pressed by the user and captures all sensitive data including passwords, credit card numbers, and so on.
- Ransomware: This malware type encrypts all the data in the machine or locks the access and asks the victim to pay a ransom to get the access or decrypted data back.
- Remote administration tool (RAT): This malware type allows an attacker to gain access to the system and makes modifications like a remote administrator.

Existing malware detection mechanisms are classified as static or dynamic or hybrid (combination of static and dynamic) analysis. Static analysis uses features of the source code of the software such as signatures, API calls, function calls, and permissions for detecting its malicious nature without executing the software. On the other hand, dynamic analysis is conducted on the software while it is being executed ideally in a virtual environment. A malware can easily bypass static detection mechanisms using encrypted or obfuscated source code or bypassing the permissions. Dynamic analysis uses runtime features such as system calls, API calls, CPU–memory usage, and so on for malware detection. Most of the existing malware detection mechanisms use machine learning algorithms where permissions, API calls, system calls, system call frequencies, densities, co-occurrence matrix, and Markov chain state transition probability matrix are taken as features. Static analysis can include various techniques such as

1. file format inspection for getting compile time, imported and exported functions, etc.;
2. string extraction for examination of the output;
3. fingerprinting which includes cryptographic hash computation, finding the environmental artifacts such as hard-coded username, filename, and registry strings;
4. scanning with anti-malware scanners; and
5. disassembling where reversing the machine code to assembly language and inferring the software logic and intentions.

In dynamic analysis, the behavior of the software is monitored while it is executed in a virtual environment (sandbox) and the properties and intentions of the software are inferred from that information. This kind of analysis provides information about all behavioral attributes, such as opened files, created mutexes, etc.

ML techniques can be applied in both malware detection and classification of malware into families. Signature-based malware detectors can perform well in detecting malware with known signatures. However, they may not detect polymorphic malware that have the ability to change signatures, as well as new malware with different signatures. In malware classification, unknown malware types are clustered into several groups based on certain features, identified by the ML algorithm. For known malware families, this problem can be narrowed down to classify one of the known malware families. We will now discuss a few Android ML malware detection mechanisms.

A behavior-based malware detection in android systems based on crowdsourcing collects the system calls from the users and sends to a centralized server for analysis. The server will preprocess the data by creating the system call vector per each interaction of the users within their applications. k-means clustering algorithm is used to determine whether the application is malicious or not, where the number of clusters is 2. This approach does not work if the number of users is very less as the k-means clustering algorithm needs large amount of data.

Statistical mining technique is another approach for detecting malware applications in smartphones. In this case, the features such as CPU usage, memory usage, network traffic, battery usage, etc. are collected at every 5 s and then stored in a database. The database is built with the data of several known malware and goodware applications and their variations. Then ML algorithms such as decision trees (DT), logistic regression (LR), naive Bayes classifier (NBC), artificial neural network (ANN), and support vector machine (SVM) are applied to determine whether the application is a malware or not.

Another mechanism for detecting Android malware uses permissions as features. First, a dataset with the permissions in well-known goodware and malware applications are created. Then, feature selection algorithms are used to select relevant features from this dataset. Then, k-means clustering algorithm is used to identify malware from the goodware applications. Finally, it classifies the malware in the cluster using ML algorithms such as J48, random forest, etc. into various types such as trojan, information stealer, etc.

API-level features can also be used for detecting Android malware. In this case, the dangerous APIs, their parameters, and package-level information are extracted, and a classifier such as ID3 DT or C4.5 DT or k-NN or linear SVM is trained based on these features. This detection method can be bypassed by encrypting the byte code which makes the APIs non-available.

Hidden Markov model (HMM) can also be employed for malware detection. This method is based on the observation that every smartphone application involves a series of interaction between the user and the device. Thus, the system calls are correlated with the user operations and can be used to detect malicious activities. It uses process state (set of system calls invoked by the application) transitions and user operational patterns. HMM takes user operations as input, associates process states and transitions with these user operations, and computes a likelihood of the observation sequence. The application is classified as a malware if the likelihood is less than a threshold.

HMM can also be built with system call sequence as observations and the key press sequence as hidden states. The key press and the system call sequence generated by the application are collected, and the hidden key press sequence is obtained using the Viterbi algorithm. The hidden key press sequence is compared with the stored sequence to classify the application as malware or goodware.

MALINE is a tool to detect Android malware applications using system call dependencies. It first collects the system calls generated by the application and stores it in a log file and generates features such as system call dependency graph and system call frequency vector from this log file. A feature dataset is build from several malware and goodware applications. It then uses a machine learning algorithm to determine whether the given application is a malware or not based on these features. One limitation of this approach is that it needs a large training dataset.

3.5 DoS and DDoS Attack Detection

A denial-of-service (DoS) or distributed denial-of-service (DDoS) attack is a malicious attempt to disrupt the normal traffic of a targeted server, service, or network by overwhelming the target or the infrastructure with a flood of the Internet traffic. A DoS attack exploits a victim machine or network by exhausting bandwidth, memory, and its processing capacity. A DoS attack targets the victim by generating numerous malicious packets to prevent legitimate users using different services. DDoS attack is a DoS attack involving more than one computer to target a victim in a coordinated manner.

The detection of a DoS attack is mainly carried out in one of the following two ways of intrusion detection:

1. signature-based intrusion detection and
2. anomaly based intrusion detection.

Signature-based intrusion detection works by comparing the network traffic with known network attack patterns stored in the database. Although this method has fewer false positive alarms, it may not detect zero-day attacks. Anomaly based intrusion detection uses the statistics of network traffic such as packet header information, packet size, and packet rates to detect various intrusions in the network. Although anomaly based intrusion detection mechanisms do not require databases of anomalies to compare (resulting in lesser memory requirement and maintenance), it has difficulty in detecting malicious traffic which is similar to normal traffic, such as low-rate DDoS attacks and has no guarantee on detecting unknown attacks.

Some of the features used by ML models are entropy, number of data bytes transferred from source to destination, number of connections to a host, source and destination IP addresses, byte rate, packet rate, TCP flag ratios, SYN packet statistics and flow statistics, SYN flag presence, classification fields and protocol fields, TCP SYN occurrence, destination port entropy, entropy of source port, UDP protocol occurrence and packet volume, and so on. Machine learning techniques such as SVM, k-nearest neighbor, naive Bayes, k-means, etc. have been used for DoS/DDoS detection.

3.6 Anomaly Detection

Anomaly detection is the process of finding anomalous or abnormal or unexpected patterns in a dataset. Such patterns are termed as anomalies or outliers. The anomalies may not correspond to an cyberattack all the time but can be a new behavior. Anomalies or abnormal or unexpected behavior can be detected and categorized into various attacks and intrusions using ML techniques. Some of the ways to apply clustering techniques for anomaly and intrusion detection are discussed below.

In k-means clustering, the objects are grouped into k disjoint clusters on the basis of the feature vector of the objects to be grouped. A network data mining (NDM) approach along with k-means clustering algorithm can be used to separate time intervals with normal and anomalous traffic in a training dataset. The resulting cluster centroids can be used for fast anomaly detection while monitoring new data.

k-medoids is an algorithm similar to the k-means algorithm that is more robust in the presence of noise and outliers as a medoid is less influenced by outliers or other extreme values than a mean. In k-medoids, each cluster is represented by the most appropriate center object (medoid) in the cluster, rather than by the centroid that may not belong to the cluster. k-medoids can be used to detect network anomalies which contains unknown intrusions and is found to have more accuracy than k-means algorithm.

In EM clustering algorithm, instead of assigning an object to a cluster based on centroid, it assigns the object to a cluster according to a weight representing the probability of membership. New mean of the cluster is computed on the basis of weight measures. EM-based anomaly detection mechanisms are found to outperform both k-mean- and k-medoids-based methods.

Unsupervised and supervised learning algorithms can be combined to form hybrid approaches for anomaly detection. By this, the efficiency and accuracy of anomaly detection can be improved. A combination of k-means and ID3 decision tree is known for classification of anomalous and normal activities in computer address resolution protocol (ARP) traffic.

Machine learning approaches for intrusion detection using artificial neural networks and support vector machine are also known. The experimental results obtained by applying this approach to the KDD CUP99 dataset showed that this approach performs well under U2R- and U2L-type attacks.

A hybrid approach by combining entropy of network features and SVM can overcome the drawbacks of individual approaches, resulting in anomaly detection with high accuracy.

Thus, different ML-based anomaly detection approaches exist. A model is built on the basis of normal and abnormal behavior of the system. There are different ways that can be opted depending on the type of anomaly detection considered. When the model for the system is available, it is tested with the observed traffic. If the deviation is found to be more/less than a predefined threshold, then the traffic is identified as anomalous.

3.7 Biometric Recognition

As today's technology has sneaked into every nooks and corners of modern living, protection of personal data has become more crucial. Furthermore, the increase of security breaches in networks and identity thefts has clearly indicated the need for a stronger authentication mechanism. This corner stoned the advent and flourishing of biometric-based authentication technology which is an effective method for personal authentication. Biometric technology uses our body as a natural identification system through the application of statistical analysis to physiological or behavioral data. Now we are in the age of a technological revolution in the field of biometrics with wide range of research and product developments taking place to utilize the complete benefits of this exciting technology in its entirety.

Biometrics deal with measuring the physiological or behavioral information to verify an individual's identify, and hence it is accurate and reliable. Physiological characteristics pertain to visible parts of the human body. These include fingerprint, finger vein, retina, palm geometry, iris, facial structure, etc. Behavioral characteristics are based on what a person does. These include voiceprints, signatures, typing patterns, keystroke pattern, gait, and so on.

A biometric system is a pattern recognition system that functions by acquiring biometric data from an individual, extracting a feature set, and comparing this feature set against the template set stored in the database. The two different phases involved in any biometric system are enrollment (registration) and verification (authentication). Users' biometric data is collected for future comparison during enrollment phase, and the collected biometric data (biometric template) is stored in the database. In the verification phase, a user provides his/her biometric data template to the system and the system compares this template with the corresponding template of the user in the database. The verification process aims to establish someone's claimed identity. If a positive match is established, the user will be provided with privileges or access to the system or service. In the case of person identification, the entire database needs to be searched against the query biometric template. As the template can belong to anyone in the database, a one-to-many matching is needed to be examined. A good example of a person identification system is automated fingerprint identification service (AFIS), which is used by many law enforcement agencies to identify and track known criminals.

The biological characteristics used for identification or authentication should be quantifiable or measurable, as only quantifiable characteristic can be compared to obtain a boolean result (match or non-match). The different components in a generic biometric system are sensors or data acquisition module, preprocessing and enhancement module, feature extraction module, matching module, and the decision-making module. Capturing user's biometric trait for authentication is performed by the data acquisition module and most of the time the captured data will be in the form of an image. Quality of the acquired biometric data need to be improved for better matching performance in the preprocessing stage. The salient features are then extracted from the enhanced biometric data in the feature extraction stage. The resulting feature template is stored in the database, and it is used for future comparison with query biometric templates in the matching stage. The final decision of the comparison is taken by the decision module based on the match score obtained.

Biometric-based authentication or person identification is currently used in various applications in our life. Biometric systems offer significant advantages over traditional methods of access control such as passwords or tokens in many aspects. Main advantages include the following:

1. Biometric systems are based on who a person is or what a person does, not on what a person knows (password, PIN) or what a person has (token, smart card).
2. Biometrics use a physiological or behavioral characteristic for authentication; it is unique, accurate, and the duplication of a person's biological characteristic which is comparatively difficult.
3. Stealing of the biometric data and its re-usage is difficult. Users are relieved from the need to remember passwords and forgery can be minimized as biometric features cannot be shared.

There are some important characteristics of biometric traits which need to be analyzed before fixing the appropriate biometric trait to be used in a given application. The different characteristics of a biometric trait which need to be taken under consideration are as follows:

1. Uniqueness: The selected trait should be sufficiently unique across individuals.
2. Universality: The selected trait should be possessed by almost all the individuals.
3. Permanence: The selected trait should be invariant for sufficiently long duration.
4. Circumvention: It should be computationally hard for an adversary to spoof the selected trait.
5. Inter/intra-class performance: There should be sufficiently enough distinctive features between the inter-class templates (templates of two different individuals). Intra-class templates (templates of same individual) should only possess a minimum amount of distinctiveness.
6. Collectability: It should be easy to collect the biometric template of the selected trait from users.
7. Acceptability: The target population should be willing to reveal the selected biometric template to the biometric system and the user interface of the system should be as simple as possible.
8. Cost: The infrastructure cost and the maintenance cost of the system which can process the selected trait should be minimal.

Fingerprint and iris are the commonly used biometric traits in most of the biometric systems. This is mainly because of its user convenience (high for fingerprint-based systems) and accuracy (high for iris-based systems). Aadhaar (Aam Aadmi Ka Adhikar), recognized as the worlds largest universal civil ID program and biometric database, is currently used by Government of India to provide social services to the citizens. Both fingerprint and iris biometric traits are taken during Aadhaar enrollment.

Table 3.1 Features and ML techniques

Modality	Features	ML techniques
Face	Distance between eyes, DCT, Fourier transform, Ratio of distance between eyes and nose, Principal components,	PCA, LDA, Kernel PCA, Kernel LDA, SVM, Deep neural network
Iris	DCT, Fourier transform, Wavelet transform, Principal components, Texture features,	PCA, LDA,
Fingerprint	Delta, Core points, Ridge ending, Island, Bifurcation, Minutiae, FFT	Artificial neural networks, Support vector machine, Genetic algorithms, Bayesian training, Probabilistic models
Finger vein	LBP, Minutiae, Bifurcation and end points, Pixel information	SVM, Deep learning
Palm print	Shape, Texture, Palm lines, PCA, LDA coefficients, DCT	Naive Bayes, k-nearest neighbor, HMM
Palm vein	LBP, Minutiae, Bifurcation and end points, Pixel information	SVM, Deep learning
Voice	Linear prediction coefficient (LPC), Cepstral coefficient (CC), MFCC features	Gaussian mixture models, HMM, ANN, SVM deep learning

ML has played a major role in improving the performance of biometric systems. One-to-one or one-to-many matching tasks can be done automatically and seamlessly in biometric systems with ML-based algorithms. The features used and the ML techniques used in various biometric modalities are listed in Table 3.1.

3.8 Software Vulnerabilities

A software vulnerability is a security flaw, glitch, or weakness found in a software system. Vulnerability refers to a flaw in a system that can leave it open to attacks. Software vulnerability is a flaw in software system that can cause a computer software or system to crash or produce invalid output or to behave in an unintended way. Some of the common software vulnerabilities are the following:

1. buffer overflows;
2. numeric over- and underflows;
3. errors in type conversion;
4. operator misuse;
5. bugs in pointer arithmetic;
6. evaluation order logic errors;
7. structure padding errors;

8. precedence errors;
9. errors in macros and preprocessors;
10. string and meta-character vulnerabilities;
11. privilege problems;
12. file permission issues;
13. race conditions;
14. errors in processes, IPC, and threads;
15. environments and signaling issues;
16. SQL injection vulnerability;
17. cross-site scripting (XSS) vulnerability;
18. vulnerability for cross-site request forgery (CSRF);
19. vulnerabilities in file inclusion and access;
20. vulnerabilities in shell invocation, configuration; and
21. access control and authorization flaws.

Software vulnerability detection is the process of confirming whether a software system contains flaws that could be leveraged by an attacker to compromise the security of the software system or that of the platform on which the software system runs. By carefully crafting an exploit for these vulnerabilities, attackers can launch a code injection attack. Code injection attacks are one of the most powerful and common attacks against software applications. A code injection attack allows an attacker to execute a (malicious) code within the privileges of the vulnerable program. Identifying the vulnerabilities and fixing them are very important measures to evaluate and improve the security of the software systems and the platforms on which they are running.

Machine learning can be used to model the syntax and semantics of the code, infer code patterns to analyze large code bases, and assist in code auditing and code understanding. The ML approaches for vulnerability detection methods may be classified as

1. anomaly detection methods and
2. pattern recognition methods.

Anomaly detection methods use features such as API usage patterns, missing checks, lack of input validation, lack of access controls, and so on. ML techniques such as k-nearest neighbors have been used for classification.

Pattern recognition methods identifies vulnerable lines of code along with keywords (specific to programming languages) using ML algorithms. The features used involve system calls and API calls invoked by an application, syntax trees, etc. ML techniques such as logistic regression, multilayer perceptron (MLP), random forests, neural networks, BLSTM, etc. have been used for classification of software vulnerabilities.

Chapter 4
Support Vector Machines and Malware Detection

4.1 Introduction

In this chapter, we shall take a look at what support vector machine (SVM) is, how it works, and then get into the details of applying SVM in malware detection. SVM learning algorithm is a supervised machine learning technique used for both regression and classification problems. Regression models are used in predicting continuous values, and classification models are used in predicting which class a data point is part of. SVMs are mostly used for solving classification problems. At the end of this chapter, we also demonstrate the classification of malware from benign ones.

Malware detection is inevitable nowadays due to the huge increase in the types of malware and their evolving attack strategies. The further sections in this chapter explain how the SVM differentiates a malicious sample from a benign sample by finding an optimal hyperplane in the feature space. Feature space refers to a collection or a set of features that are used to categorize data. Hyperplane is a straight line or a plane or any other nonlinear frontier that is drawn in a feature space in such a way that the entire set of malware remains well separated from goodware. Hyperplanes are easy to construct when the datasets are sparse. In those cases, where the datasets are dense it might be difficult to separate the differently behaving samples from each other. In such cases, a nonlinear hyperplane has to be constructed. Kernel functions in SVM are used to solve nonlinear problems by converting them to a linear problem, which is done by mapping a low-dimensional input space to a higher dimensional space.

For malware detection, an efficient feature extraction is the first step. The training dataset is prepared by downloading samples from any data repository such as Drebin dataset, and then relevant features are extracted from the samples. SVM being a supervised machine learning technique requires data to be labeled as either malware or goodware to classify them in the training stage. These features along with the labels are used to plot the data samples in the feature space to find the optimal hyperplane that effectively separates malware from goodware.

T. Thomas et al., *Machine Learning Approaches in Cyber Security Analytics*, https://doi.org/10.1007/978-981-15-1706-8_4

In the following sections, we shall first take a look into the different malware features and how these features are extracted. Then, we shall look into how training datasets are made use to train the classifier and how the classifier learns to differentiate a malware from a goodware in a testing phase. We shall also learn about the optimal condition of linear separability feature of the hyperplane in an SVM. Learning the hyperplane is the most important phase of SVM. Optimization technique is used to reduce the number of weights that are nonzero to just a few that correspond to important features that would decide how the hyperplane should be constructed. Linear algebraic techniques are used to learn the hyperplane. Kernels are functions that determine the similarity between two inputs. In those cases where the feature vectors are highly dense and it is difficult to find a linear hyperplane, then a kernel method is used in an SVM to map the feature vectors to a higher dimensional space.

4.2 Malware Detection

Malware detection techniques can be broadly classified into the following two:

1. Static analysis, where the malware's behavior is inspected without executing it. Extraction of API calls in the malware and opcode analysis using reverse engineering are a few examples. Each variant of a particular malware has a distinct signature. The signature-based approach uses a cryptographic hash function to generate a hash of each file. The hashes are checked against a database of hashes of already known malware.
2. Dynamic analysis, also known as behavioral analysis, where malware are executed in a controlled environment such as a sandbox to evaluate its behavior and the properties exhibited by it during execution. System calls made by the malware are an example.

Feature selection is an important step when it comes to malware detection using machine learning. A few of its objectives are to reduce the noise, to improve the accuracy and speed for training the classifier, and to minimize the dataset for choosing the best training set. The methods are based on minimizing generalization bounds via gradient descent and are feasible to compute. SVMs can perform badly in the situation of many irrelevant features. Characteristic raw data of a sample includes information regarding headers, possible packers and compressors, size of different sections, strings, entropy, hash of the file, size of the file in bytes, etc. The target is to process raw characteristics into numerical features. To extract numerical features from the acquired data, feature extraction is an important part of the machine learning process. Some other features are size of code in the file, the number of resource languages detected in the file, the number of PE resource types detected in the file, the number of PE sections in the file, decimal value of entry point, i.e., the location in code where control is transferred from the host OS to the file, size of the initialized data, length of the original file name, size of the part of the file that contain all global, uninitialized variables or variables initialized to zero, and so on. Some of the features that can be extracted from Android malware are API calls, permissions, opcodes, system calls, CPU–RAM usage, memory utilization, network utilization, etc. To be able to perform feature selection and/or classification on the data, we must create subsets of the full dataset.

The SVM classifier learns by determining the optimal hyperplane to best separate the data. With a kernel function, the data is projected to a higher dimensional feature space. The primary goal is to find a hyperplane that classifies the training dataset into two classes: benign and malicious based on the labels that we specify. SVM being a supervised machine learning technique takes in data that are labeled beforehand during the training phase. Feature selection methods aim to reduce the dimensionality and enhance the compactness of the feature vector representing the files.

In the experiments carried out in the chapter, we have made use of the SVM classifier trained with a collection of malware–goodware samples to detect Android malware. Relevant permissions and API calls corresponding to each APK sample are stored in a *.csv* file which is further used to train the classifier. Here, we deal with binary classification of data, and SVM is very much capable in handling binary data (True/False or Yes/No or 1/0). There are linear hyperplanes as well as nonlinear hyperplanes to classify data; a variety of kernels like linear, radial-based function, sigmoid, polynomial, and Gaussian may also be used to construct a classifier. The type of hyperplane to be used solely depends on the data distribution in a dataset.

4.3 Maximizing the Margin and Hyperplane Optimization

A hyperplane is a decision boundary and support vector machines are based on optimizing a decision boundary in the data space. A hyperplane is always chosen in such a way that the closest support vectors from both the classes, malware and goodware, are at maximum distance from the frontier. Doubling this distance gives a quantity which is called the margin. In Fig. 4.1, the closest support vectors from the positive as well as negative classes are marked with dotted circles. There should not be a data point within the margin. The $+$ and $-$ symbols in the figure denote goodware and malware samples, respectively, divided by a hyperplane.

The margin would be small if the hyperplane is very close to at least one data point (from both the classes) and further is the hyperplane from the data points, the larger will be its margin. The objective of SVM is to find the optimal separating hyperplane which maximizes the margin of the training data. The classifier is said to have 100% accuracy if no sample point lies in between the margin after finding the hyperplane in the training phase. We need to find that specific decision rule which decides the decision boundary.

Let W be an orthogonal vector to the hyperplane in an inner product space as shown in Fig. 4.2. Length of the vector is unknown. Let $W^T X + b = 0$ be the decision rule that would make use of a decision boundary (the separating hyperplane) to classify the data points. Let X be any data point that is to be classified. We intend to find the

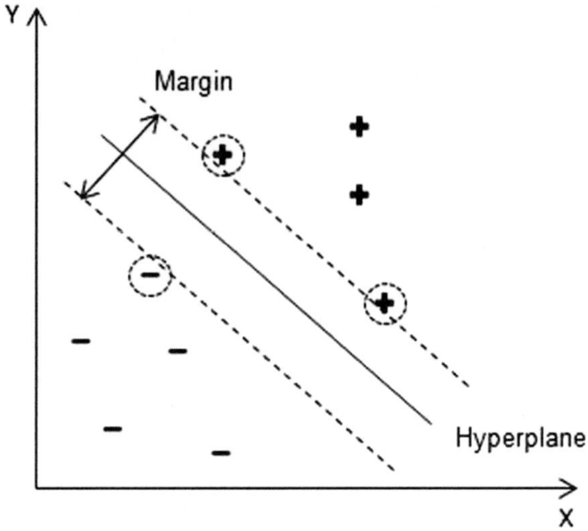

Fig. 4.1 Optimal hyperplane and margin

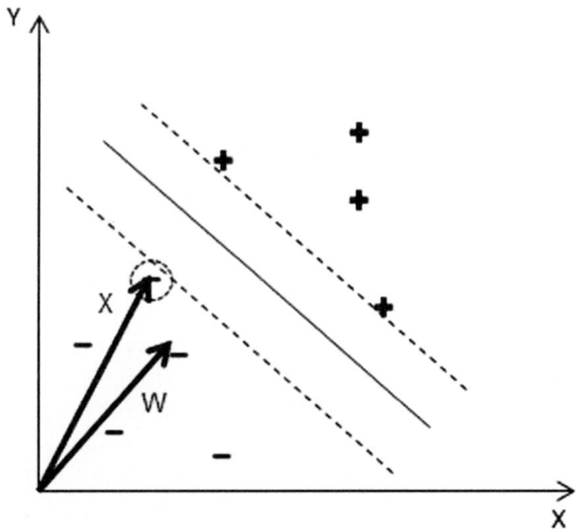

Fig. 4.2 Determining the hyperplane

class to which X might belong to. We project the vector X to the orthogonal W. This projection will give us the distance in the direction of W.

The dot product of the orthogonal W and vector X gives the projection of X onto W. If the projection of X onto W crosses the optimal hyperplane, we say that the sample X belongs to the positive class. Without loss of generality, we represent this as

$$W \cdot X + b \geq 0. \tag{4.1}$$

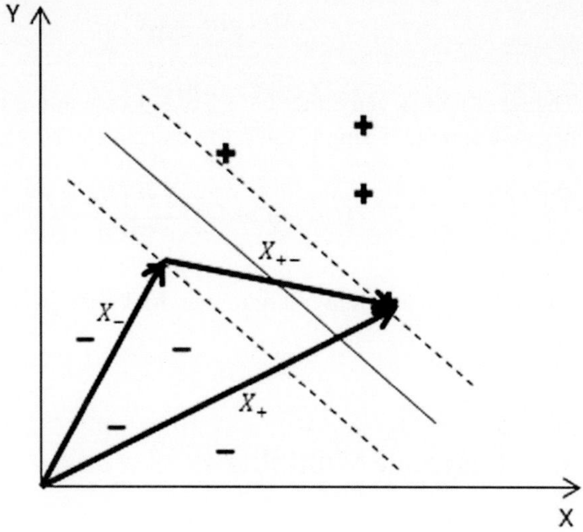

Fig. 4.3 Determining the margin

If Eq. 4.1 holds true, then the data point X is classified as a goodware (class indicated by +). This is called the decision rule of the SVM. Except for the fact that W is orthogonal to the separating hyperplane and can be of any length, no other information is known about W as well as the constant b. Let X_+ and X_- represent any sample from the positive and negative class, then we can say

$$\begin{aligned} W \cdot X_+ + b &\geq 1 \\ W \cdot X_- + b &\leq -1. \end{aligned} \tag{4.2}$$

We require some constraints to determine the values for W and b. Let y_i be the constraint: $y = +1$ for all positive samples and $y = -1$ for all samples belonging to the negative class. Multiplying Eq. 4.2 by y on the left, we get

$$\begin{aligned} y(W \cdot X_+ + b) &\geq 1 \\ y(W \cdot X_- + b) &\geq 1. \end{aligned} \tag{4.3}$$

Thus, the above equations can be written as $y(W \cdot X + b) - 1 \geq 0$ for points on positive or negative class and $y(W \cdot X + b) - 1 = 0$ for points on the margin. These equations give a constraint on the data points lying on the margin. Reiterating our previous point, our aim is to find the maximum margin that separates positive samples from the negative ones. In Fig. 4.3, X_+ and X_- are vectors in the positive and negative samples in the margin respectively. X_{+-} is the difference of the two vectors X_+ and X_-. If a unit normal vector is drawn orthogonal to the optimal hyperplane, then the width of the margin is given by the dot product of the unit normal and the difference $X_{+-} = X_+ - X_-$. That is,

$$Margin = (X_+ - X_-) \cdot \frac{W}{||W||} \tag{4.4}$$

The label y of X can either be $+1$ or -1 depending on whether X is a positive or a negative sample. Using Eq. 4.3, the margin can be written as

$$Margin = \frac{1 - b - (-1 - b)}{||W||} = \frac{2}{||W||}. \tag{4.5}$$

To find the maximum margin, we find max $\frac{2}{||W||}$ or max $\frac{1}{||W||}$ or min $||W||$ or min $\frac{1}{2}||W||^2$.

4.4 Lagrange Multiplier

We make use of Lagrange multipliers to find the extremum of a function with constraints. Lagrange multipliers will result in a new expression that can be minimized or maximized independent of the constraints. All the local minimums and maximums of a function (or local extrema) occur at critical points of the function, where the derivative is zero or undefined. Extremum is any point at which a function's value is at maximum or minimum. To maximize the width of the margin, consider

$$L = \frac{1}{2}||W||^2 - \sum \alpha_i[y_i(W \cdot X_i + b) - 1], \tag{4.6}$$

where W is the vector orthogonal to the separating hyperplane and α_i are multipliers for the constraints. Now we need to find the extremum of this function, for which we find the derivatives and then set it to zero. Taking the partial derivative of L with respect to W, we get

$$\begin{aligned} \frac{\partial L}{\partial W} &= W - \sum \alpha_i y_i X_i = 0 \\ \implies W &= \sum_i \alpha_i y_i X_i. \end{aligned} \tag{4.7}$$

W known as the decision vector indicates that it is a linear sum of the samples. Differentiating L with respect to b, we get

$$\begin{aligned} \frac{\partial L}{\partial b} &= -\sum \alpha_i y_i = 0 \\ \implies &\sum \alpha_i y_i = 0. \end{aligned} \tag{4.8}$$

Our next task is to find the minimum for the expression $\frac{1}{2}||W||^2$ which is a quadratic optimization problem. Now substituting W in Eq. 4.6, we get

$$L = \frac{1}{2}(\sum \alpha_i y_i X_i) \cdot (\sum \alpha_j y_j X_j) - (\sum \alpha_i y_i X_i) \cdot (\sum \alpha_j y_j X_j) - \sum \alpha_i y_i b + \sum \alpha_i. \tag{4.9}$$

Now simplifying this equation and using the constraint given in Eq. 4.8, we get

$$L = \sum \alpha_i - \frac{1}{2} \sum_i \sum_j \alpha_i \alpha_j y_i y_j X_i \cdot X_j, \text{ such that } \alpha_i \geq 0 \ \forall i \text{ and } \sum_i \alpha_i y_i = 0. \tag{4.10}$$

The optimization depends only on the dot product of the pair of samples X_i and X_j. Now, from Eq. 4.1 we get the decision rule in the following form:

$$\sum \alpha_i y_i X_i \cdot u + b \geq 0, \tag{4.11}$$

where u is an unknown sample vector. Hence, we conclude that the total dependence is only on the dot product. The decision rule also depends on the dot product of the unknown sample vector. But this decision rule does not separate samples that are nonlinearly separable. In such cases, we might have to transform the data points to some other space using a function $\phi()$ where they are more easily separable. As said earlier the optimization only depends on the dot product of the vectors. Hence, $\phi()$ can be realized using a kernel function $k()$. If $k()$ is an kernel function, then

$$k(x_i, x_j) = \phi(x_i) \cdot \phi(x_j). \tag{4.12}$$

It is not necessary to know the transformation $\phi()$; it is only enough that we know the dot product of the sample vectors in the other space where samples are more separable. We shall learn more about kernels in the next section.

4.5 Kernel Methods

Here, we try to transform the input data in a lower dimensional space to a higher dimensional linear space. If it is difficult to separate the positive samples from the negative ones lying in a lower dimensional space using a linear hyperplane, we can try to transform it into a higher dimensional space. Let X be a feature matrix with each row corresponding to the feature set of each data point in the dataset. Let $\phi()$ be a function that maps the feature set from lower dimensional space to a higher dimensional space. Then, we calculate the inner product in the higher dimensional space. If $\phi()$ is any function that maps x in the original space to a higher dimensional inner product space, then we apply SVM to $\phi(x)$ instead of x. Let $k()$ be a kernel function and $K = (k_{ij})$ be the corresponding kernel matrix, where $k_{ij} = k(x_i, x_j)$. An inner product $\langle , \rangle$ on a vector space V can be a dot product which satisfies the following conditions:

1. Symmetry: $\langle u, v \rangle = \langle v, u \rangle, \forall\, u, v \in V$;
2. Bilinearity: $\langle \alpha u + \beta v, w \rangle = \alpha \langle u, w \rangle + \beta \langle v, w \rangle, \forall u, v, w \in V, \forall \alpha, \beta \in \mathbf{R}$;

3. Strict positive definiteness:
   $\langle u, u \rangle \geq 0, \forall u \in V$;
   $\langle u, u \rangle = 0 \Leftrightarrow u = 0$.

Thus, an inner product space is a vector space with an inner product defined on it. The major features of kernel methods are as follows:

1. Data is always mapped into a Euclidean feature space. Euclidean space satisfies the classic laws of geometry such as the line joining any two points in the space is straight.
2. The inner product of vectors in the feature space is only considered while implementing algorithms.
3. Kernel functions can be used to compute the vector dot product. This is called the *kernel trick*.

Let $k()$ be a kernel function such that $k(x_i, x_j) = \langle \phi(x_i), \phi(x_j) \rangle$, where x_i and x_j are elements of a vector space V, and $\phi()$ is a mapping from the vector space V to a Hilbert space F. A Hilbert space is an inner product space such that the norm defined by the inner product turns it into a complete metric space. That is,

$$\phi : x_i \in V \mapsto \phi(x_i) \in F. \tag{4.13}$$

An important property of the kernel matrix is its positive semi-definiteness. A matrix M is positive semidefinite iff

1. M is symmetric;
2. $X^T M X \geq 0 \; \forall \; X \in V$.

Let X be the feature set such that $X = \{x_1, x_2, \ldots, x_n\}$ and $k_{ij} = \langle \phi(x_i), \phi(x_j) \rangle$, where k_{ij} represents the (ij)th element of the kernel matrix K. Then

$$\begin{aligned} X^T K X &= \sum_{i=1}^{n} \sum_{j=1}^{n} x_i x_j k_{ij} = \sum_{i=1}^{n} \sum_{j=1}^{n} x_i x_j \langle \phi(x_i), \phi(x_j) \rangle \\ &= \langle \sum_{i=1}^{n} x_i \phi(x_i), \sum_{j=1}^{n} x_j \phi(x_j) \rangle = || \sum_{i=1}^{n} x_j \phi(x_j) ||^2 \geq 0. \end{aligned} \tag{4.14}$$

Further, the matrix K is symmetric. Hence, the matrix K is positive semidefinite. By Mercer's theorem, the kernel function $k()$ can be written as $k(x_i, x_j) = \langle \phi(x_i), \phi(x_j) \rangle$, for some $\phi()$ iff the kernel matrix K is positive semidefinite.

Kernels play an important role in creating linear patterns from nonlinear patterns in a feature space. Different types of kernels are discussed below.

1. Linear kernel: $k(x_i, x_j) = \langle x_i, x_j \rangle$
   Let $\phi(x_i) = x_i$, then $k(x_i, x_j)$ can be written as $k(x_i, x_j) = (x_i \cdot x_j) = (\phi(x_i) \cdot \phi(x_j))$.

2. Inhomogeneous polynomial kernel: $k(x_i, x_j) = (\langle x_i, x_j \rangle + r)^d$, where d is a positive integer and $r \in \mathbf{R}$ is a parameter.
3. Gaussian radial basis function kernel (RBF kernel): $k(x_i, x_j) = exp(-\frac{||x_i - x_j||^2}{2\sigma^2})$, where σ is any parameter.
Here, the generated decision boundaries resemble contour circles around positive and negative samples.
4. Sigmoid kernel (Hyperbolic tangent): $k(x_i, x_j) = tanh(\alpha x_i^T x_j + c)$.
An SVM sigmoid kernel is similar to a two-layer perceptron neural network. Here, α is the slope and c is the intercept. Like RBF kernels, it may exhibit over-fitting problem when used improperly (or configured improperly). A few properties of tanh are as follows: it is similar to the sigmoid function $S(x) = \frac{1}{1+e^{-x}}$; it is differentiable indicating that the slope of the sigmoid curve can be found at any two points; and its value exist between 0 and 1. Commonly used value for α is $\frac{1}{n}$ where n is the dimension of the data.
5. Graph kernel: $k(G, G') = \langle \phi(G), \phi(G') \rangle = \sum_{i=0}^{\infty} \lambda^i \phi^i(G) \phi^i(G')$.
It is a kernel function that computes an inner product on graphs. Here $G = (V, E)$ and $G' = (V', E')$ are any two simple graphs, $0 < \lambda < 1$ is a weight factor, and $\phi^i(G)$ denotes the number of paths of length i in G.
6. String kernel:
String kernel is a function that operates on finite sequences of symbols that are not necessarily of the same length.
7. Tree kernel: $k(T_1, T_2) = \sum_{n_1 \in N_{T_1}} \sum_{n_2 \in N_{T_2}} \Delta(n_1, n_2)$, where N_{T_1} and N_{T_2} are two sets whose elements are the nodes of trees T_1 and T_2, respectively.
Tree kernels compute the number of sub-trees that are common among any two trees T_1 and T_2. $\Delta(n_1, n_2)$ is computed as

$$\Delta(n_1, n_2) = \sum_{i=1}^{|F|} I_i(n_1) I_i(n_2). \tag{4.15}$$

$F = \{f_1, f_2, \ldots\}$ is the set of fragments over which we define an indicator function $I_i(n) = 1$ if the target f_i is rooted at any node n_i and $I_i = 0$ otherwise.
8. Fourier kernel:
Fourier transformation is one of the most commonly adopted methods to analyze time series data. This data which in general is spread over some frequency of events at each time point. A regularized kernel function can be used to calculate the Fourier expansion of two times series as

$$k_F(x_i, x_j) = \frac{1 - q^2}{2(1 - 2q\cos(x_i - x_j)) + q^2}, \tag{4.16}$$

where $0 < q < 1$ and $X \subset [0, 2\pi]^n$. For instance, the Fourier transformation for the convolution of any two functions is equal to the product of the Fourier transforms of these two functions.

9. B-spline kernel: $k(x_i, x_j) = B_{2n+1}(x_i - x_j)$, where B_n is a B-spline and $n \in \mathbf{N}$ Spline is a function that is defined by multiple subfunctions which are polynomials. The kernel is defined on the interval $[-1, 1]$. A B-spline is a linear combination of control points c_i. B-splines are said to be highly efficient for interpolation. Spline kernels are found to perform well in regression problems as well. It is also useful in dealing with large number of sparse data vectors. The degree of any B-spline polynomial can be set independently of the number of control points. B-splines allow control over the shape of a spline surface or curve locally.
10. Cosine kernel: $k(x_i, x_j) = \frac{\langle x_i, x_j \rangle}{||x_i||||x_j||}$
    Cosine similarity calculates the normalized dot product of any two vectors. In the above case, x_i and x_j are any two vectors. This kernel is mainly used for finding the similarity of text documents represented as tf-idf vectors.
11. Wave kernel: $k(x_i, x_j) = \frac{\theta}{x_i - x_j} \sin(\frac{||x_i - x_j||}{\theta})$.

4.6 Permission-Based Static Android Malware Detection Using SVM

In this section, we describe how an android malware can be detected using SVM by utilizing permissions as the static features. Here, we limit our research to android malware, though the procedure discussed below may be implemented in detecting malware found on other platforms such as Windows or for viruses, Trojans, and ransomware. The features of each Android APK are extracted one at an instance using a set of codes written in python programming language. The next step is to create separate CSV files for each feature, which are then used to train the SVM classifier. Our aim is to train an SVM classifier to identify malware and goodware from a set of Android APKs. Here, we have applied cross-validation as the test option in the samples used, meaning that a percentage of samples (as specified) is used as training data and the rest as test data.

To extract the permissions, both the malicious and benign APKs are converted to smali files. During its execution, the entire set of permissions of each APK in a single directory is copied into a text file one after the other. The code used to convert each APK to output files is as follows.

```
from smalisca.core.smalisca_main import SmaliscaApp
from smalisca.modules.module_smali_parser import SmaliParser
import re
import os, sys
import subprocess

#Open a file
path = "F:\\Apps"
dirs = os.listdir(path)
root = "F:\\Apps"
```

```
#This would print all the files and directories
for file in dirs:
    print (file)
    os.chdir("F:\\Apps")
    os.system("java -jar " + "C:\\apktool.jar" + " d " +
        root+"/"+file)
    #This would copy all the permissions of files (both benign
        and malicious) in the directory #into a text file
    p = os.system("C:\\aapt.exe d permissions
        "+path+"/"+file+">> permissions.txt")
print(p)
```

Smali files are obtained by decompiling *.DEX* files using programs included in the smali package called as *backsmali*. In short, *backsmali* is a disassembler and *DEX* files are the executables included in Android APKs. The reverse engineering tool used here is *apktool.jar*. While using *AndroidStudio*, we get to view and edit all of the resources along with the manifest file. The list below shows all the permissions that were taken for training the SVM classifier. The permissions and its corresponding descriptions are given below.

1. ENHANCED_NOTIFICATION: Allows applications to receive information about new notifications.
2. READ_SETTINGS: Allows an application to read the system settings.
3. READ_EXTENSION_DATA: Allows an application requesting DashClock extension data.
4. READ_PROFILE: Allows an application to read the user's personal profile data.
5. WRITE_BADGES: Allows an application to add a badge to its icon.
6. SYSTEM_ALERT_WINDOW: Allows an application to create windows using the type TYPE_APPLICATION_OVERLAY. The windows are intended for system-level interaction with the user.
7. PROCESS_OUTGOING_CALLS: Allows an application to see the number being dialed during an outgoing call with the option to redirect the call to a different number or to abort the call.
8. RESTART_PACKAGES: It allows them to break other applications by removing their alarms, stopping their services, etc.
9. MAPS_RECEIVE: Allows an application to integrate maps from Google Maps.
10. ACCESS_WIFI_STATE: Allows applications to access information about Wi-Fi networks.
11. CALL_PRIVILEGED: Allows an application to call any phone number, including emergency numbers, without going through the Dialer user interface for the user to confirm the call being placed.
12. MODIFY_AUDIO_SETTINGS: Allows an application to modify global audio settings.
13. ACCESS_LOCATION_EXTRA_COMMANDS: Allows an application to access extra location provider commands.

14. BILLING: Allows an application to directly bill you for services through Google Play.
15. BROADCAST_BADGE: Allows an application to display a badge.
16. WRITE_HISTORY_BOOKMARKS: Allows an application to write the user's browsing history and bookmarks.
17. ALLOW_ANY_CODEC_FOR_PLAYBACK: Allows an application to use any installed media decoder to decode for playback.
18. INSTALL_PACKAGES: Allows an application to install packages.
19. PAYMENT: Allows an application to incorporate in-app payment mechanism for any service user avails or any purchase the user do using your application.
20. BIND_NOTIFICATION_LISTENER_SERVICE: Required by a Notification-ListenerService, to ensure that only the system binds to it. NotificationListenerService is a service that receives calls from the system when new notifications are posted or removed, or their ranking is changed.
21. ACCESS_NOTIFICATION_POLICY: Marker permission for applications that wish to access notification policy.
22. MIPUSH_RECEIVE: Allows an application to use push services.
23. SUBSCRIBED_FEEDS_WRITE: Allows an application to access the subscribed feeds ContentProvider.
24. CLEAR_APP_CACHE: Allows an application to clear the caches of all installed applications on the device.
25. RECORD_AUDIO: Allows an application to record audio.
26. GOOGLE_AUTH.WISE: Allows applications to sign in to Google Spreadsheets using the account stored on the device.
27. PERSISTENT_ACTIVITY: Allows an application to make its activities persistent.
28. ADD_VOICEMAIL: Allows an application to add voicemails into the system.
29. READ_LOGS: Allows an application to read the low-level system log files.
30. READ_HISTORY_BOOKMARKS: Allows an application to read the user's browsing history and bookmarks.
31. ACCESS_LOCATION: Applications are given access to the location services supported by the device.
32. READ_VOICEMAIL: Allows an application to read voicemails in the system.
33. READ_DATA: Allows an application to read the data of the file.
34. BROADCAST_STICKY: Allows an application to broadcast sticky intents. A sticky broadcast is a tool Android developer's use for communicating between apps. These broadcasts happen without the user being notified.
35. READ_PHONE_STATE: Allows read-only access to phone state, including the phone number of the device, current cellular network information, the status of any ongoing calls, and a list of any PhoneAccounts registered on the device.
36. LOCATION_HARDWARE: Allows an application to use location features in hardware, such as the geofencing API. Geofencing is a feature in a software program that uses the global positioning system (GPS) or radio-frequency identification (RFID) to define geographical boundaries.

37. WRITE_CALENDAR: Allows an application to write the user's calendar data.
38. WRITE_EXTERNAL_STORAGE: Allows an application to write to external storage.
39. GET_TASKS: Allows an application to get information about the currently or recently running tasks.
40. SYNC_STATUS: Allows an application to check the status of SYNC.
41. SEND_DOWNLOAD_COMPLET ED_INTENTS: Allows the application to send notifications about completed download.
42. PER_ACCOUNT_TYPE: A signature-level permission granted only to the Firefox versions sharing an Android Account type.
43. MANAGE_DOCUMENTS: Allows an application to manage access to documents, usually as part of a document picker.
44. DOWNLOAD_WITHOUT_NOTIFIC ATION: Allows to queue downloads without a notification shown while the download runs.
45. BROADCAST: Allows an application to broadcast something.
46. MOUNT_UNMOUNT_FILESYSTEMS: Allows mounting and unmounting file systems for removable storage.
47. WRITE_VOICEMAIL: Allows an application to modify and remove existing voicemails in the system.
48. ACCESS: Provides access to an application to whatever is specified.
49. READ_GSERVICES: Allows an application to read the Google services map.
50. INTERACT_ACROSS_USERS_FULL: It removes restrictions, where broadcasts can be sent and other types of interactions are allowed.
51. WRITE_INTERNAL_STORAGE: Allows an application to access the directory and store files.
52. WRITE_CALL_LOG: Allows an application to write (but not read) the user's call log data.
53. READ_CALENDAR: Allows an application to read the user's calendar data.
54. RECEIVE_BROADCAST: Allows an application to register itself so that registered events are notified by Android Runtime once the event occurs.
55. GET_ACCOUNTS: Allows access to the list of accounts in the Accounts Service.
56. WRITE_SETTINGS: Allows an application to read or write the system settings.
57. AUTHENTICATE_ACCOUNTS: Allows an application to act as an AccountAuthenticator for the AccountManager to authenticate the user for its service.
58. ACCESS_DOWNLOAD_MANAGER: Allows an application to act as an AccountAuthenticator for the AccountManager.
59. UA_DATA: An application-specific permission that is used to for delivering different APIs.
60. DELETE_PACKAGES: Allows an application to delete packages.
61. ACTIVITY_RECOGNITION: Allows an application to receive periodic updates of your activity level from Google.
62. RECEIVE_SMS: Allows an application to receive SMS messages.

63. REORDER_TASKS: Allows an application to change the particular order of tasks.
64. CAMERA: Required to access the camera device.
65. STOP_APP_SWITCHES: Prevent users from switching to another application.
66. FLASHLIGHT: Allows access to the flashlight.
67. RECEIVE: Allows an application to receive whatever is specified in the manifest file.
68. GET_ACCOUNTS_PRIVILEGED: Allows access to the list of accounts in the Accounts Service.
69. UPDATE_COUNT: This enables an application to provide counter information to the launcher.
70. AUTH_APP: This allows another application to successfully request this permission, which already has been granted to an application that has a signature match.
71. CHANGE_NETWORK_STATE: Allows applications to change network connectivity state.
72. GOOGLE_AUTH.WRITELY: Allows an application to sign in to Google Docs using the account stored on this Android device.
73. RECEIVE_ADM_MESSAGE: This permission ensures that no other application can intercept your ADM messages.
74. SET_ALARM: Allows an application to broadcast an Intent to set an alarm for the user.
75. CHANGE_CONFIGURATION: Allows an application to modify the current configuration such as locale.
76. WAKE_CLOCK: Allows an application to keep the screen turned ON.
77. DISABLE_KEYGUARD: Allows applications to disable the keyguard if it is not secure.
78. TRANSMIT_IR: Allows using the device's IR transmitter, if available.
79. SEND_SMS: Allows an application to send SMS messages.
80. CHANGE_WIFI_MULTICAST_STATE: Allows applications to enter Wi-Fi Multicast mode.
81. READ_SMS: Allows an application to read SMS messages.
82. WRITE_SECURE_SETTINGS: Allows an application to read or write the secure system settings.
83. USE_CREDENTIALS: Allows an application to request authtokens from the AccountManager.
84. UNINSTALL_SHORTCUT: Allows an application to remove any shortcut.
85. READ_CONTACTS: Allows an application to read the user's contacts data.
86. VIBRATE: Allows access to the vibrator.
87. READ_CALL_LOG: Allows an application to read the user's call log.
88. WRITE_MEDIA_STORAGE: Allows an application to modify the contents of the internal media storage.

89. BODY_SENSORS: Allows an application to access data from sensors that the user uses to measure what is happening inside his/her body, such as count of the footsteps taken, heart rate, etc.
90. MANAGE_ACCOUNTS: Allows an application to manage the list of accounts in the AccountManager.
91. INTERNAL_SYSTEM_WINDOW: Allows an application to open windows that are for use by parts of the system user interface.
92. CHECK_LICENSE: Needed to verify the validity of the app's license against Google services.
93. MMS_SEND_OUTBOX_MSG: Sends out all MMSs from the outbox to the network.
94. ACCESS_NETWORK_STATE: Allows applications to access information about networks.
95. ACCESS_COARSE_LOCATION: Allows an application to access approximate location.
96. SUBSCRIBED_FEEDS_READ: Allows an application to access the subscribed feeds ContentProvider.
97. CALL_PHONE: Allows an application to initiate a phone call without going through the Dialer user interface for the user to confirm the call.
98. READ_SYNC_STATS: Allows applications to read the sync stats.
99. BLUETOOTH_ADMIN: Allows applications to discover and pair Bluetooth devices.
100. WRITE_USER_DICTIONARY: Allows write access to user dictionaries.
101. READ: Allows the application to read whatever is specified.
102. READ_USER_DICTIONARY: Allows an application to read the user dictionary.
103. CUSTOM_BROADCAST: Allows the application to either send or receive the intended broadcast.
104. NFC: Allows applications to perform I/O operations over NFC.
105. USE_FINGERPRINT: Allows an app to use fingerprint hardware.
106. READ_OWNER_DATA: Allows read access to owner data saved on the device.
107. INSTALL_SHORTCUT: Allows an application to install a shortcut in Launcher.
108. RECEIVE_WAP_PUSH: Allows an application to receive WAP push messages.
109. SET_ALARM: Allows an application to broadcast an Intent to set an alarm for the user.
110. BLUETOOTH_PRIVILEGED: Allows applications to pair Bluetooth devices without user interaction and to allow or disallow phonebook access or message access.
111. ACCESS_GPS: Allows an application to access the GPS.
112. INTERNET: Allows applications to open network sockets.
113. MODIFY_PHONE_STATE: Allows modification of the telephony state—power on, MMI, etc.

114. BROADCAST_SMS: Allows an application to broadcast an SMS receipt notification.
115. EXPAND_STATUS_BAR: Allows an application to expand or collapse the status bar.
116. WAKE_LOCK: Allows using PowerManager WakeLocks to keep processor from sleeping or screen from dimming.
117. CHANGE_WIFI_STATE: Allows applications to change Wi-Fi connectivity state.
118. WRITE_CONTACTS: Allows an application to write the user's contacts data.
119. RECEIVE_BOOT_COMPLETED: Allows an application to receive the ACTION_BOOT_COMPLETED that is broadcast after the system finishes booting. ACTION_BOOT_COMPLETED can be used to perform application-specific initialization.
120. WRITE_SMS: Allows an Application to write SMS messages.
121. RECEIVE_MMS: Allows an application to monitor incoming MMS messages.
122. WRITE_SYNC_SETTINGS: Allows applications to write the sync settings.
123. INTERACT_ACROSS_USERS: Allows an application to call APIs that allow it to do interactions across the users on the device, using singleton services and user-targeted broadcasts.
124. SET_WALLPAPER_HINTS: Allows applications to set the wallpaper hints.
125. GET_PACKAGE_SIZE: Allows an application to find out the space used by any package.
126. SET_WALLPAPER: Allows applications to set the wallpaper.
127. BIND_APPWIDGET: Allows an application to tell the AppWidget service which application can access AppWidget's data.
128. RECEIVE_USER_PRESENT: The permission is issued once the user begins interacting with the device, for instance, when unlocking the screen.
129. READ_EXTERNAL_STORAGE: Allows an application to read from external storage.
130. REQUEST_IGNORE_BATTERY_OPTIMIZAT IONS: Permission an application must hold in order to use ACTION_REQUEST_IGNORE _BATTERY_ OPTIMIZATIONS. The ACTION_ REQUEST_IGNORE_BATTERY_ OPTIMIZATIONS permission is needed to ask the user to allow an app to ignore battery optimizations.
131. GOOGLE_AUTH: Allows applications to see the usernames of the Google account configured in the device.
132. ACCESS_FINE_LOCATION: Allows an app to access precise location.
133. BATTERY_STATS: Allows an application to collect battery statistics.
134. READ_SYNC_SETTINGS: Allows applications to read the sync settings.
135. BLUETOOTH: Allows applications to connect to paired Bluetooth devices.
136. PACKAGE_USAGE_STATS: Allows an application to collect component usage statistics.
137. INSERT_BADGE: Allows an application to assign badges to notifications.

4.6.1 *Experimental Results and Discussion*

CSV files are created with permissions as features, where 1 is used to indicate if a feature is present and 0 otherwise. These files are given as input to Weka and LibSVM classifier is used to create the classifier.

Now let us take a look at the images of outputs that were obtained after classifying a conglomerate of malicious and benign samples using an SVM classifier. Both malicious and benign samples were downloaded from repositories such as Android Malware Dataset, Kaggle, Drebin, Android Malshare, and APKPure. The details of the data and performance results are given in Tables 4.1 and 4.2.

Figure 4.4 shows the classification errors of malware and goodware. Malware and goodware samples correctly classified are represented using $\times$, and those incorrectly classified are represented in the figure using □. The red-colored □ in the image represents goodware that were misclassified as malware.

The performance of a classification algorithm can be seen in the ROC curve. The number of points in the ROC curve depends on the number of unique values in the input data. As ours is binary classification problem and the input data has 1's and 0's as features (1—if a feature is present and 0—if a feature is absent), we get an ROC curve resembling a triangle. The ROC curve is shown in Fig. 4.5.

Table 4.1 Test data and results

Number of attributes (Features)	137
Number of instances taken	172
Number of malware samples in the dataset	72
Number of goodware samples in the dataset	100
Correctly classified instances	169
Incorrectly classified instances	3
Kappa statistic	0.9642
Mean absolute error	0.0174
Root mean squared error	0.1321

Table 4.2 Performance results

TP Rate	FP rate	Precision	Recall	F-measure	Accuracy
0.986	0.020	0.973	0.986	0.979	0.982

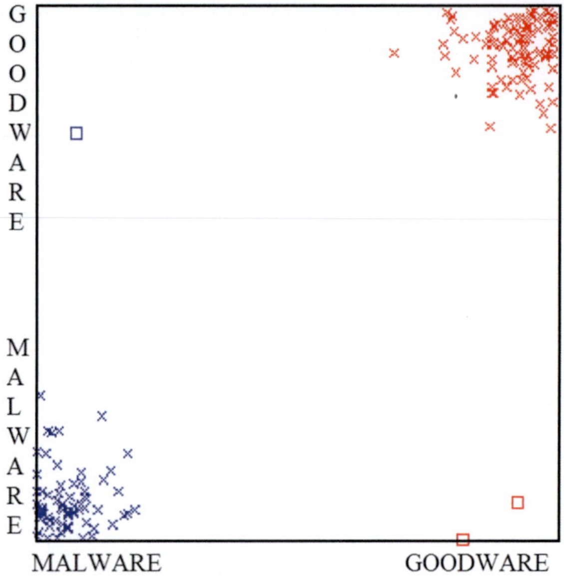

Fig. 4.4 Misclassified versus correctly classified malware and goodware for permissions

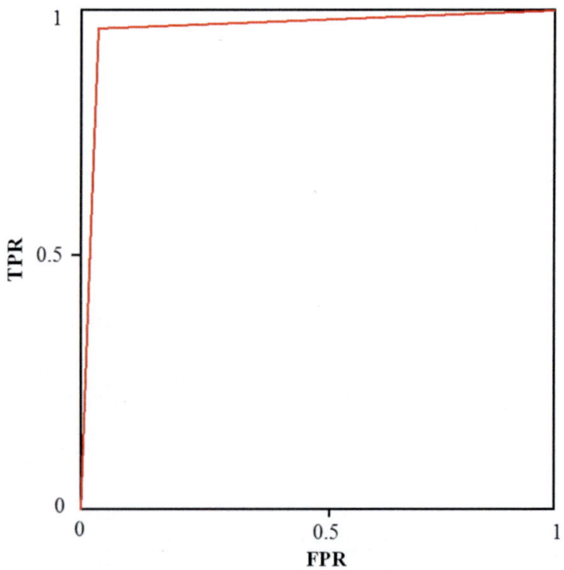

Fig. 4.5 ROC curve for permissions

4.7 API Call-Based Static Android Malware Detection Using SVM

In this section, we describe how an android malware can be detected using SVM by utilizing API calls as the static features. API calls can be extracted both statically and dynamically. Static API calls are those specified in the code when an APK is built, while dynamic API calls are those made use of by an APK during its execution. The code used for extracting the static API calls is given below.

```
from smalisca.core.smalisca_main import SmaliscaApp
from smalisca.modules.module_smali_parser import SmaliParser
import re
import os, sys
import subprocess

app = SmaliscaApp()
app.setup(
#Set log level
app.log.set_level('info')
path = "F:\\ Malware"
dirs = os.listdir( path )
root="F:\\ Malware"
i=0
location = 'F:/apps/Twitter_v5.105.0_apkpure'
#Specify file name suffix
suffix = 'smali'
#Create a new parser
parser = SmaliParser(location, suffix)
parser.run()
results = parser.get_results()
results1=re.findall(r'to_ method \ ':\'(.*?)\'\}',str(results))
results2=re.sub('\ '',"",str(results1)
c=['startService','getDeviceId','createFromPdu','getClassLoader',
'getClass','getMethod','getDisplayOriginatingAddress',
'getInputStream','getOutputStream','killProcess',
'getLine1Number','getSimSerialNumber','getSubscriberId',
'getLastKnownLocation','isProviderEnabled']
b=[0,0,0,0,0,0,0,0,0,0,0,0,0,0,0,0]
print results
for C in c:
    if re.search(r ' ' +C, str(results1)):
        b[i]=1
        print "Found"
    i=i+1
print b
```

The API calls used and their explanation are given below.

1. startService: Requests a given application service to get started.
2. getDeviceId: Gets the id for the device from which an event came from.
3. createFromPdu: To create SMS message from PDU. Protocol Data Unit is a method of sending information over cellular networks.
4. getClassLoader: Returns a class loader to retrieve classes in a package. A class loader is an object that is responsible for loading classes. The class ClassLoader is an abstract class. Given the binary name of a class, a class loader should attempt to locate or generate data that constitutes a definition for the class.
5. getClass: Returns the runtime class of this object.
6. getMethod: Returns a Method object that reflects the specified public member method of the class or interface represented by this class object.
7. getDisplayOriginatingAddress: Returns the originating address, or email from address if this message was from an email gateway.
8. getInputStream: Returns an input stream that reads from this open connection.
9. getOutputStream: Returns an output stream that writes to this connection.
10. killProcess: Kill the process with the given PID.
11. getLine1Number: Returns the phone number string for line 1, for example, the MSISDN for a GSM phone. Mobile Subscriber Integrated Services Digital Network is a unique number to identify a subscription in a GSM mobile network.
12. getSimSerialNumber: Returns the serial number of the SIM.
13. getSubscriberId: Returns the unique subscriber ID, for example, the international mobile subscriber identity (IMSI) for a GSM phone. IMSI is used to identify the user of a cellular network and is a unique identification associated with all cellular networks.
14. getLastKnownLocation: Returns a location indicating the data from the last known location fix obtained from the given provider.
15. isProviderEnabled: Returns the current enabled/disabled status of the given provider.

4.7.1 Experimental Results and Discussion

A binary *.csv* file is created with the extracted API call features for 260 different Android samples, out of which there were 201 malware samples and 59 goodware applications. The details of the data and performance results are given in Tables 4.3 and 4.4.

Figure 4.6 shows the classification errors of malware and goodware. Malware and goodware samples correctly classified are represented using $\times$, and those incorrectly classified are represented in the figure using $\square$. The red-colored $\square$ in the image represents goodware that were misclassified as malware. The ROC curve is shown in Fig. 4.7.

Table 4.3 Test data and results

Number of attributes (Features)	15
Number of instances taken	260
Number of malware samples in the dataset	201
Number of goodware samples in the dataset	59
Correctly classified instances	241
Incorrectly classified instances	19
Kappa statistic	0.7879
Mean absolute error	0.0731
Root mean squared error	0.2703

Table 4.4 Performance results

TP Rate	FP rate	Precision	Recall	F-measure	Accuracy
0.960	0.186	0.946	0.960	0.953	0.927

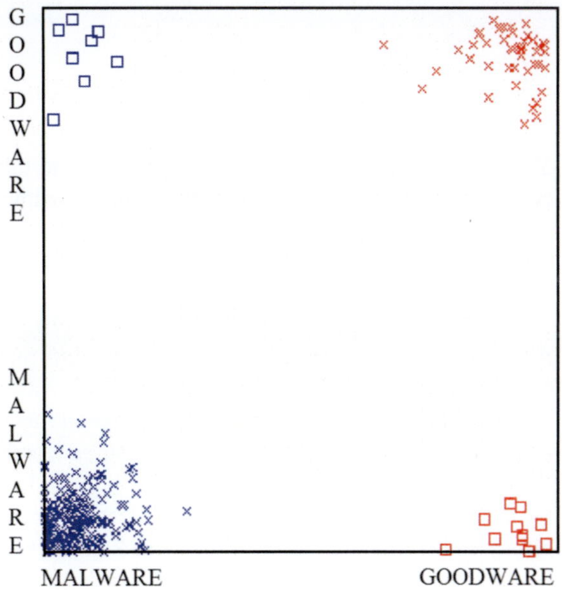

Fig. 4.6 Misclassified versus correctly classified malware and goodware API calls

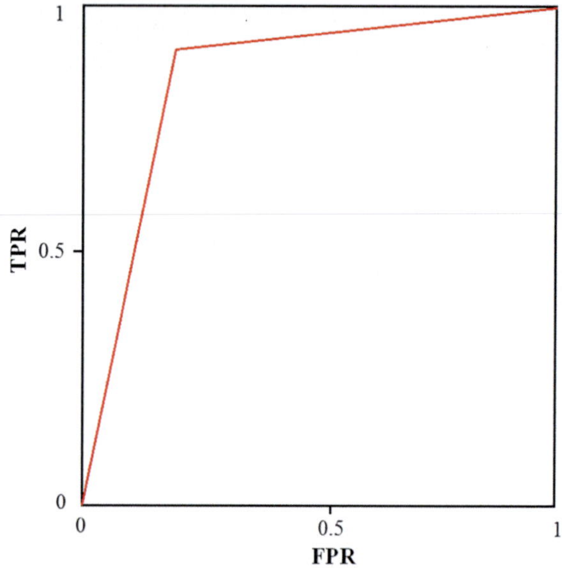

Fig. 4.7 ROC curve for API calls

4.8 Conclusions and Directions for Research

The experiments conducted in this chapter aim to throw light on how a basic SVM classifier can be trained using static Android malware features in the Weka tool. A classifier that appears to have high accuracy measure can deceive us as in the case discussed here. The possibilities for a classifier to have an impressive accuracy measure are more, especially when the feature vector is of high dimension. Though these experiments prove the SVM classifier to be accurate, permissions and static API calls are not the optimal features for detecting malware. This is so because malicious application developers are continuously involved in crafting metamorphic and polymorphic malware that constantly change in functionality, as well as obfuscated applications. It is easy to manipulate the static features such as signatures, permissions, etc. to easily fool a machine learning classifier. Hence, it is very important to tap the dynamic features of malware applications for effective detection. The concept discussed here can be extended for dynamic analysis.

4.8.1 State of the Art

During DDoS attack, computer systems' resources are made unavailable by generating humongous traffic on the network. Even after detecting these attacks on the server side, it becomes impossible to nullify the network congestion. SVM an efficient technique for binary classification can be used to early detect DDoS attacks at the client side. Network packets can be captured and relevant features like flag, protocol, port, IP address, etc. can be extracted to train the model so that it classifies network packets either as normal or abnormal.

Attacks targeting IoT devices have increased due to the rise in number of IoT devices. The most infectious attack among all are those which utilize software vulnerabilities to infect IoT devices. Based on the type of vulnerability that a malware targets, IoT malwares can be classified as HTTP GET, Telnet, and HTTP POST. Sensors installed at different points can collect the incoming traffic, extract feature vectors, and can be used to train the classifier. Traffic is captured at the gateway level rather than the device-level as we intend to detect the network anomaly before the device gets compromised. The most important features to be considered here are the destination IP addresses, and the minimum, maximum, and average packets for each destination IP addresses. As much traffic sessions each of duration 15–20 min are captured. Necessary features are extracted and a binary SVM model is trained. Suitable kernel methods in SVM may be used for the classification task.

The SVM model can be used to provide an extra layer of security to reduce the false positives generated in intrusion detection systems. SVM can, hence, successfully predict the incoming traffic to be malicious or not. A semi-supervised technique, one-class SVM model can be used to construct a classification model trained with non-malicious data (one type of sample alone) so that we can find a hyperplane which will maximize the distance between the origin and the data. Making use of a one-class SVM model with non-labeled benign training set has shown improved accuracy as well. Features are only extracted from the physical layer and MAC layer as they do not encrypt the network frames header. The most important features that can be extracted for classification using SVM are sequence number (SEQ), received signal strength indication (RSSI), network allocation vector (NAV), value injection rate, and inter-arrival or delta time between two consecutive frames.

Chapter 5
Clustering and Malware Classification

5.1 Introduction

In the present time, where people maintain a close relationship with smartphones, it is easier for cybercriminals to gain user's personal data by installing malware without the user's knowledge or authorization. In such a situation where the user's data and privacy are always at threat, it is necessary to build a resilient system so as to curb such attacks. The system should undergo a learning–decision-making process to early detect and defend malware attacks. Different types of machine learning mechanisms are adopted to train the system to predict such kind of malware attacks. One of them is clustering and is discussed in detail in this chapter. The sections in this chapter are organized as follows. At first, we take a look at what clustering is and then the details of the different types of existing clustering algorithms. Understanding how each algorithm works also helps us to get an idea about how the clustering algorithms differ from one another, and how they can be used in clustering similarly behaving malwares and goodwares. We also give the mathematical details of each algorithm. We shall be providing the results of experiments conducted using only some of the algorithms, as to include the entire list of algorithms is out of scope of this book.

Clustering is the process of grouping a set of patterns. It generates a partition of the dataset into cohesive groups of similar patterns. Patterns in the same cluster are similar in some sense, and patterns in different clusters are dissimilar in that sense. The distance between two points belonging to the same cluster is small compared to that between any two points belonging to different clusters. That is, intra-cluster distance is small, whereas intercluster distance is large. Clustering can be applied to unlabeled patterns resulting in unsupervised classification or to labeled patterns resulting in supervised clustering. Unsupervised clustering is a machine learning technique which finds a structure or a meaningful pattern in a set of unlabeled data.

As the number of malware applications is increasing exponentially, it is essential to explore the applicability of clustering in identifying malware applications from benign applications. Thus, the applications should be analyzed to group them either as malware or goodware applications. Clustering methods involve the basic

T. Thomas et al., *Machine Learning Approaches in Cyber Security Analytics*, https://doi.org/10.1007/978-981-15-1706-8_5

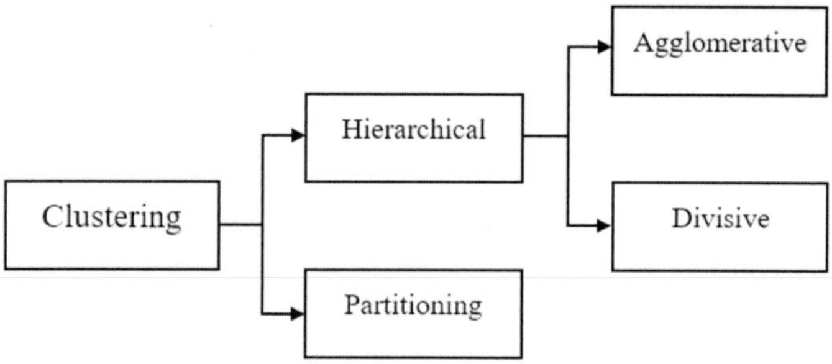

Fig. 5.1 Basic types of clustering

modeling approaches such as centroid based and hierarchical. The basic types of clustering are shown in Fig. 5.1.

As far as clustering is concerned, we concentrate on machine learning to look for similarity while solving a problem, rather than looking for patterns in the malware–goodware dataset. Instead of training a machine learning model for malware detection by using hundreds of samples labeled as goodware or malware, we will teach a model about features such as permissions, API calls, CPU–RAM usage, system calls, etc.

5.2 Algorithms Used for Clustering

Clustering is a main tool used in image processing, information retrieval, data mining, and so on. In this chapter, we make use of clustering for malware–goodware categorization. The aim of cluster analysis is to separate data points depending on their features into nonoverlapping groups. It requires a definite pattern to be determined from the defined datasets. We shall see how clustering acts on an input dataset which is a collection of malicious and benign applications. We shall also measure the clustering accuracy of each technique briefed below. Each of the algorithms will be dealt in detail in the forthcoming sections. The four main types of clustering algorithms are as follows:

1. Exclusive clustering,
2. Overlapping clustering,
3. Hierarchical clustering, and
4. Probabilistic clustering.

The most commonly used algorithms are k-means, fuzzy c-means, hierarchical clustering, and mixture of Gaussians. We shall see each type of algorithms in detail in later sections.

Exclusive clustering as the name suggests allows each data object to exist in only one cluster, whereas *overlapping clustering* allows each data object to exist in two or more clusters.

Partition clustering is a kind of clustering that divides the entire dataset into k nonoverlapping partitions such that each data item only belongs to a single cluster. Partition clustering ensures that an item of a cluster is more nearer to the centroid of the cluster to which it belongs to than to the centroid of its nearby cluster. An objective function is used for clustering in this case. k-means, partition around mediods, and CLARA are a few partition clustering algorithms.

Hierarchical clustering produces nested clusters in the form of a tree structure called dendrograms. The root node is the entire collection of the dataset, and the leaf nodes are the individual data points. The clusters can be obtained by snipping the tree structure at different points. Hierarchical clustering can be of two types: agglomerative and divisive. Agglomerative clustering is a type of clustering in which the elements of a dataset are clustered one after the other by taking into consideration the shortest distance between a data point and every other point in the dataset. The pair separated by the minimum distance forms the new cluster, and then distance between the newly formed cluster and every other data point is evaluated. The process continues until the distance matrix reduces to a singleton matrix. In divisive clustering, clustering is done in a macro-cluster and is continued until every data point becomes a singleton cluster. Balance iterative reducing and clustering using hierarchies (BIRCH) and cluster using representatives (CURE) are a few hierarchical clustering algorithms. It does not demand the value of "k" to be predetermined and instead makes use of a proximity matrix.

In *k-means clustering*, k is a number chosen randomly in the beginning when clustering is about to start. Distance between nearby data points are calculated, and those which are separated by the shortest distance are put into a single cluster. In the further steps, distances between each data point and cluster point are calculated, thereby altering the clusters formed. Further, k-means clustering aims in minimizing the distortion within the clusters.

Unlike k-means clustering which makes use of the concept of a centroid to create clusters, *density-based clustering* clusters the densely packed data points together, while the outliers are assigned to a different cluster. In k-means clustering, the anomalous points show a tendency to pull back the cluster centroid toward them. This creates problem during anomaly detection as the outliers will be assigned to the same cluster to which the other data points belong to. Density-based clustering defines a distance variable which determines the boundary limit for the data points to be clubbed into a single cluster. If P is a point, then data points in the neighborhood of P that are at a distance of ε from P are combined into a single cluster.

Consider a large multidimensional space which has data points densely present at some areas and sparsely separated at some other areas. In such conditions, density-based and *grid-based clustering* are found to produce better outputs. Grid-based clustering is concerned about the value space that surrounds the data points and not data points themselves. The size of the dataset is at least linearly proportional to the computational complexity of most of the clustering algorithms. One of the greatest advantages of grid-based clustering is its low computational complexity, especially for clustering very large datasets.

Constraint-based clustering is a semi-supervised machine learning technique, meaning the training set uses a small set of labeled data and comparatively larger set of unlabeled data. Some of the constrained clustering algorithms are COP k-means, PC k-means, and CMW k-means.

Fuzzy c-means (FCM) is a method of clustering which allows one piece of data to belong to two or more clusters. This method is frequently used in pattern recognition. It is based on minimization of an objective function.

Similarity and dissimilarity measures play an important role in data clustering. As data can be numerical or binary or any other, it is the type of data to be clustered which determines the type of similarity measuring technique to be used. An important step in any clustering is to select a distance measure, which will determine the similarity of two data points in the dataset. Distance calculating algorithms play a major role in clustering. The exact choice for distance calculation can only be made depending on the type of data that is to be clustered. Hence, learning the datasets is the primary step in clustering. We have to study the type of data (which is a combination of malware and goodware in our case) in the dataset before choosing the distance measuring paradigm. Thus, the primary step in clustering machine learning is to get to know the dataset in detail. In this section, we shall learn how to understand the input data and the different methods to calculate the distance between the data points. Choosing the right distance measure for each algorithm is the biggest challenge.

There are many types of distance functions used by clustering algorithms. These distance functions determine the clustering efficiency of each algorithm. Data points belonging to different clusters are far apart compared to data points within the same cluster which are always separated by a very small distance.

Let us consider the following scenario to understand the need of distance metrics in calculating the distance in clustering. The most commonly used distance metric in a two-dimensional plane is the Euclidean distance measure. But as the dimension increases we might have to change the method used for distance calculation. In the case of malware–goodware clustering, the datasets that we have made use of in the experiments have more than two features. Hence, they are points in higher dimensional spaces.

5.3 Feature Extraction

The taxonomy of clustering is shown in Fig. 5.2. For demonstration and easy understanding of malware detection using different clustering techniques, the features CPU usage and RAM usage are extracted from malware and goodware samples. For this, a few Android APKs were installed in an Android emulator, and the CPU–RAM usage were captured using an APK called 'usemon". The "usemon" APK records the CPU usage of the Android emulator. The memory usage was monitored during the following two different situations:

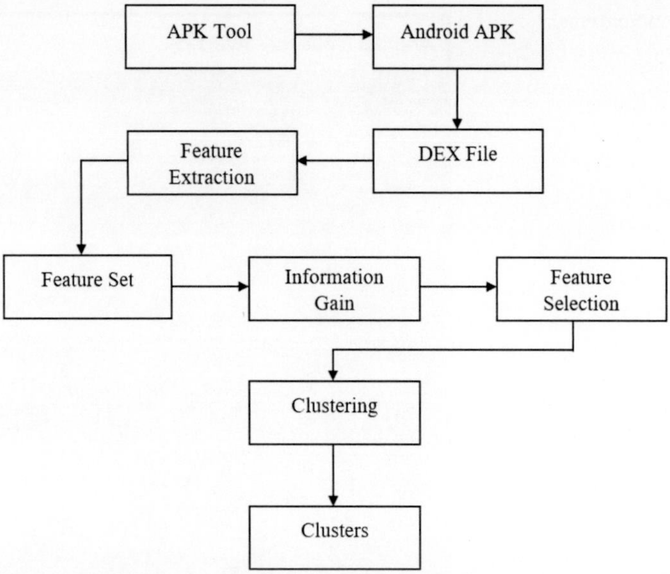

Fig. 5.2 Clustering taxonomy

1. Installation of malware samples and
2. Uninstallation of previously installed malware samples and installation a new set of goodware APKs.

The following steps were used to start the emulator, install the APKs and extract the memory usage statistics of the Android emulator at different instances.

1. Android emulator with the following specifications was selected:
   Virtual device name: AVD
   Selection of device: 2.7" QVGA
   Category: Phone
   x86 images: Lollipop
   OS: Android 5.1
   Graphics: Software-GLES 1.1
   Multi-Core CPU 2
2. Emulator was started using the following command:
   C:\Users\C14\AppData\Local\Android\Sdk\tools>emulator.exe -avd AVD -partition-size 300
3. APK was installed through terminal using:
   C:\Users\C14\AppData\Local\Android \Sdk\platform-tools>adb install $<< PathToTheAndroidAPK >>$
4. usemon APK installed in the emulator was started. usemon has an interesting interface displaying the CPU–RAM statistics. Figure 5.3 shows usemon running in an Android emulator.

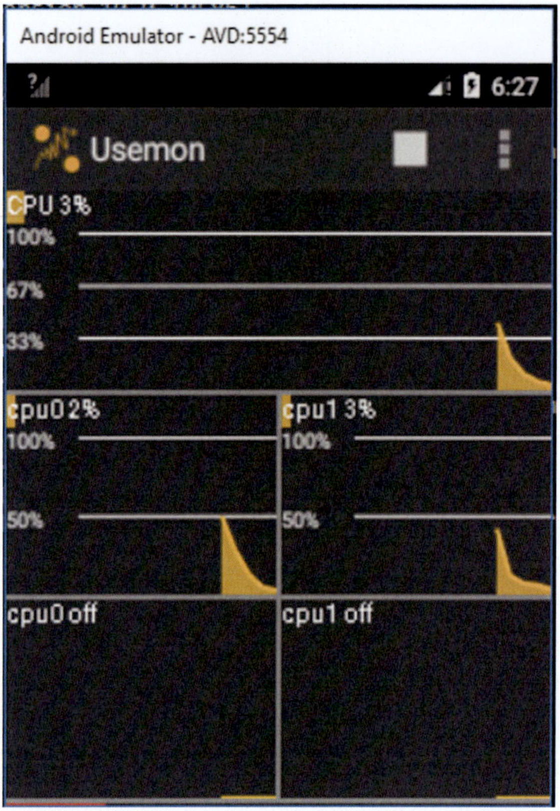

Fig. 5.3 Android emulator

5. To obtain the measure of the memory usage, we made use of SQLite. The commands used to obtain the usemon log were
   C:\Users\C14\AppData\Local\Android \Sdk\platform-tools>adb shell
   root@generic_x86_64 : /# cd data
   root@generic_x86_64:/data # cd data
   root@generic_x86_64:/data/data # cd com.iattilagy.usemon
   root@generic_x86_64:/data/data/com.iattilagy.usemon # cd databases
   root@generic_x86_64:/data/data/com.iattilagy.usemon/databases # exit.
6. Next, the usemon log was extracted to a file name usemon_log using
   C:\Users\C14\AppData\Local\Android \Sdk\platform-tools>adb pull /data /data/com.iattilagy.usemon/databases/usemon_log.db usemon.db.

We created a .CSV file with necessary features “cpu_sum” and “ram_used”, and used it in demonstrating different clustering algorithms.

5.4 Implementation

The experimental results along with the implementation are presented in subsequent sections. The number of samples collected from benign and malicious repository is limited to five each as the experimental results are only meant for demonstration and understanding. A summary of the performance results of three clustering algorithms is given in Table 5.1. The details are given in the subsequent sections.

Mobile devices are vulnerable to different types of threats, and these threats are continuing to grow every year. SMS attacks are a significant type of threat to all mobile users. SMS attack mainly involves the creation and distribution of malware that are designed to make unauthorized calls or send unauthorized text messages without the user's knowledge or consent. These calls and texts are subsequently charged to the user.

The CPU and RAM usage of the five malware and five goodware samples are observed over a period of time. The CPU and RAM usage of these applications at various instances are plotted in Fig. 5.4. In this figure, the data points are color coded based on their corresponding labels. The red dots indicate malicious samples, and green dots indicate benign samples.

Table 5.1 Performance results

Algorithm	Malware type	Number of malware	Accuracy (%)	Feature extracted
k-means	SMS	5	63.88	CPU–RAM usage
DBSCAN	SMS	5	63.88	CPU–RAM usage
Hierarchical	SMS	5	63.88	CPU–RAM usage

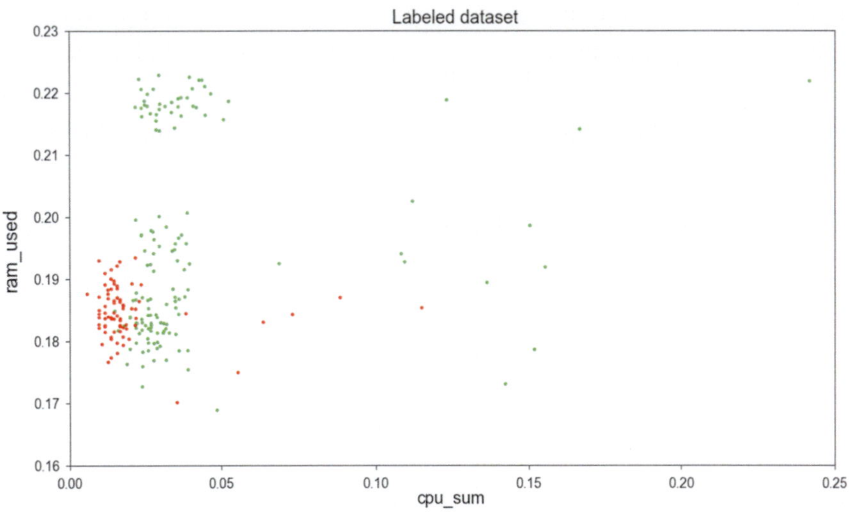

Fig. 5.4 Collection of malware–goodware dataset

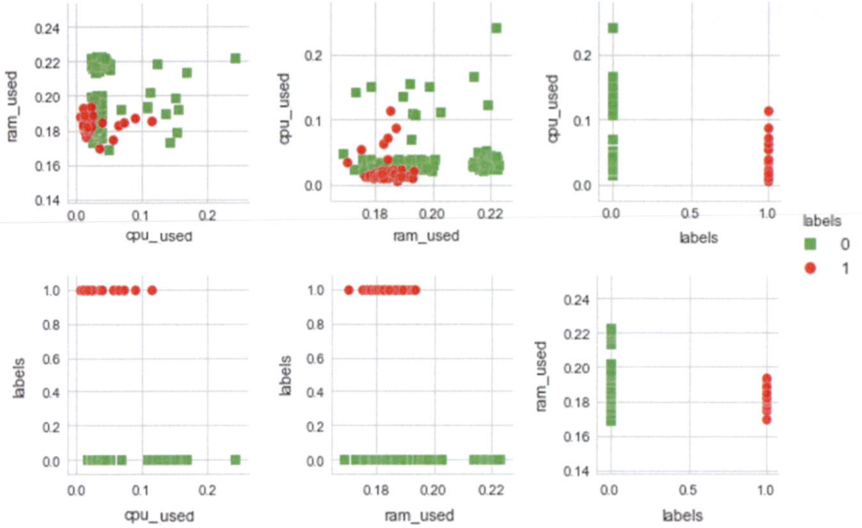

Fig. 5.5 Pair plots of features and labels

Figure 5.5 shows a collective plot of the dataset represented in Fig. 5.4, where green-colored squares represent goodware samples and red-colored circles represent malware samples. CPU usage, RAM usage, and labels of the samples in Fig. 5.4 are plotted against each other for a clear understanding of the data distribution. We can clearly see that some of the samples are well separated based on their CPU and RAM usage, whereas others seem to overlap.

5.5 K-Means Clustering

The k-means clustering algorithm is a very simple algorithm which clusters data into k number of clusters. The value of k is randomly chosen in the beginning, based on which closer data points are grouped into a single cluster. The centroid is now calculated for the newly formed cluster, after which the distance between data points is calculated and nearer ones are re-grouped. The process continues until the centroid already obtained equals the centroid of the newly formed cluster. The k-means clustering uses the objective function

$$J = \sum_{j=1}^{k} \sum_{i=1}^{n} ||x_i^j - c_j||^2, \tag{5.1}$$

where x_i^j is the ith data point in the jth cluster and c_j is the centroid of the jth cluster. The objective function also known as the squared error function is an indicator of the distance of the n data points from their respective cluster centers.

Suppose that we have n sample feature vectors $x_1, x_2, \ldots, x_n$, and we know that they fall into k compact clusters, where $k < n$. Let c_i be the mean of the vectors in the ith cluster. If the clusters are well separated, we can use a minimum-distance classifier to separate them. That is, we can say that x is in the ith cluster if $||x - c_i||$ is the minimum among all the clusters. This suggests the Algorithm 5.1 for finding the k-means clustering.

Algorithm 5.1 k-Means Clustering Algorithm

Input: CSV file for each feature
Output: Clustered samples

Initialisation: Initial values for the centroids (means) $c_1, c_2, \ldots, c_k$

1: **repeat**
2: Use the estimated means $(c_1, c_2, \ldots, c_k)$ to classify the samples into clusters
3: **for** $i \leftarrow 1$ to k **do**
4: Replace c_i with the mean of all of the samples for cluster i
5: **end for**
6: **until** there are no changes in any values of the centroids

We shall now see how similarly behaving samples can be clustered using k-means clustering technique by utilizing the CPU usage and RAM usage as the dynamic features. The code is given below.

```
import numpy as np
import pandas as pd
from matplotlib import pyplot
from sklearn.cluster import KMeans
from sklearn import metrics
import sklearn
from sklearn.model_selection import train_test_split
from sklearn.preprocessing import StandardScaler
import seaborn
from sklearn.metrics import roc_curve, auc, roc_auc_score
pyplot.style.use('ggplot')
seaborn.set(style='ticks')
# Import the dataset
data = pd.read_csv('GM-cpu_ram-labeled.csv')
print(data.shape)
data.head()
# Define the features considered
f1 = data['cpu_sum'].values
f2 = data['ram_used'].values
f3 = data['labels'].values
X = np.array(list(zip(f1, f2)))
print("\nThe centroids are :")
scaler = StandardScaler()
class_names = [1,0]
scaled_X = scaler.fit_transform(X)
cluster_range = range(1,25)
cluster_error = []
for cr in cluster_range:
```

```
    clusters = KMeans(cr)
    clusters.fit(scaled_X)
    cluster_error.append(clusters.inertia_)
clusters_df=pd.DataFrame({"number_of_clusters":cluster_range,"cluster_error":cluster
    _error})
print(clusters_df[0:25])
fig = pyplot.gcf()
fig.set_size_inches(18.5, 10.5)
pyplot.xlabel('number_of_clusters', fontsize=22)
pyplot.ylabel('cluster_error', fontsize=22)
pyplot.plot(clusters_df.number_of_clusters,clusters_df.cluster_error,marker="X")
pyplot.show()
X_train,X_test,y_train,y_test=train_test_split(X,f3,test_size=0.33,random_state=42)
kmeans = KMeans(n_clusters=2, n_init=20)
kmeans.fit(X_train, y_train)
pred_labels = kmeans.predict(X_test)
print("Actual labels are ")
print(y_test)
print("Predicted set of labels are")
print(pred_labels)
centroid = kmeans.cluster_centers_
print("The centroids are")
print(centroid)
fpr, recall, thresholds = roc_curve(y_test,pred_labels)
roc_auc = auc(fpr, recall)
pyplot.figure(figsize=(15,6))
pyplot.plot(fpr,recall,'b',label='AUC=%0.2f'%roc_auc,color='darkorange')
pyplot.title('Receiver Operating Characteristic curve', fontsize=21)
pyplot.legend(loc='lower right')
pyplot.plot([0, 1], [0, 1], color='navy', linestyle='--')
pyplot.xlim([0.0, 1.0])
pyplot.ylim([0.0, 1.0])
pyplot.ylabel('True Positive Rate', fontsize=20)
pyplot.xlabel('False Positive Rate', fontsize=20)
pyplot.show()
print("Area under the ROC curve is ")
print(roc_auc_score(y_test, pred_labels))
seaborn.set_style('whitegrid')
seaborn.pairplot(data, hue='labels', markers=["s", "o"],palette='prism')
pyplot.show()
cnf_matrix = metrics.confusion_matrix(y_test, pred_labels)
print(cnf_matrix)
seaborn.heatmap(cnf_matrix.T,square=True,annot=True,fmt='d',cbar=False,
           xticklabels=class_names,yticklabels=class_names,cmap='summer_r',
           annot_kws={"size":20})
fig.set_size_inches(2,2)
pyplot.xlabel('true_label', fontsize=18)
pyplot.ylabel('predicted_label', fontsize=18)
tn,fp,fn,tp = metrics.confusion_matrix(y_test, pred_labels).ravel()
print(tn)
print(fp)
print(fn)
print(tp)
print("Accuracy Score:%0.06f"%metrics.accuracy_score(y_test,pred_labels))
print("Precision Score : %0.06f" %sklearn.metrics.precision_score(y_test,
                          pred_labels, average='weighted',
                               sample_weight=None))print("Mean Absolute Error :
                               %0.06f"%sklearn.metrics.mean_absolute_error
        (y_test,pred_labels,sample_weight=None,multioutput='raw_values'))
print("F-Score : %0.06f" %sklearn.metrics.f1_score(y_test, pred_labels,
              pos_label=1,average='weighted',sample_weight=None))
print("Homogeneity: %0.6f" % metrics.homogeneity_score(y_test, pred_labels))
print("Completeness: %0.3f" % metrics.completeness_score(y_test, pred_labels))
```

```
print("V-measure: %0.3f" % metrics.v_measure_score(y_test, pred_labels))
print("Jaccard Similarity score : %0.6f" %metrics.jaccard_similarity_score
                    (y_test, pred_labels,normalize=True, sample_weight=None))
print("Cohen's Kappa : %0.6f" % metrics.cohen_kappa_score(y_test, pred_labels,
                                          labels=None, weights=None))
print("Hamming matrix : %0.06f" %metrics.hamming_loss(y_test, pred_labels,
                        labels=None, sample_weight=None, classes=None))
print(metrics.classification_report(y_test, pred_labels))
```

```
ax = data.plot(kind='scatter', x='cpu_sum', color='white', y='ram_used', alpha=1,
     fontsize = 18)
pyplot.xlabel('cpu_sum', fontsize=18)
pyplot.ylabel('ram_used', fontsize=18)
pyplot.title("Dataset with actual labels", fontsize=18)
ax.set_ylim((0.16, 0.23))
ax.set_xlim((0, 0.25))
ax.set_facecolor("white")
fig = pyplot.gcf()
fig.set_size_inches(18.5, 10.5)
ax.grid(color='w', linestyle='-', linewidth=0)
ax.scatter(f1, f2, c=f3, s=30, cmap='prism_r')
ax = data.plot(kind='scatter', x='cpu_sum', color='white', y='ram_used', alpha=1,
     fontsize = 18)
pyplot.xlabel('cpu_sum', fontsize=18)
pyplot.ylabel('ram_used', fontsize=18)
pyplot.title("Training set with Actual labels", fontsize=18)
ax.set_ylim((0.16, 0.23))
ax.set_xlim((0, 0.25))
ax.set_facecolor("white")
fig = pyplot.gcf()
fig.set_size_inches(18.5, 10.5)
ax.grid(color='w', linestyle='-', linewidth=0)
ax.scatter(X_train[:,0], X_train[:,1],
             c=y_train, s=30, cmap='prism_r')
ax = data.plot(kind='scatter', x='cpu_sum', color='white', y='ram_used', alpha=1,
     fontsize = 18)
pyplot.xlabel('cpu_sum', fontsize=18)
pyplot.ylabel('ram_used', fontsize=18)
pyplot.title("Test set with Actual labels", fontsize=18)
ax.set_ylim((0.17, 0.23))
ax.set_xlim((0, 0.25))
ax.set_facecolor("white")
fig = pyplot.gcf()
fig.set_size_inches(18.5, 10.5)
ax.grid(color='w', linestyle='-', linewidth=0)
ax.scatter(X_test[:,0], X_test[:,1],
             c=y_test, s=40, cmap='prism_r')
ax = data.plot(kind='scatter', x='cpu_sum', color='white', y='ram_used', alpha=1,
     fontsize = 18)
pyplot.xlabel('cpu_sum', fontsize=18)
pyplot.ylabel('ram_used', fontsize=18)
pyplot.title("Test set with Predicted labels", fontsize=18)
ax.set_ylim((0.17, 0.23))
ax.set_xlim((0, 0.25))
ax.set_facecolor("white")
fig = pyplot.gcf()
fig.set_size_inches(18.5, 10.5)
ax.grid(color='w', linestyle='-', linewidth=0)
ax.scatter(X_test[:,0], X_test[:,1],
             c=pred_labels, s=30, cmap='prism_r')
```

Table 5.2 Cluster errors for various cluster sizes

Cluster error	Number of clusters
434.000000	1
228.243097	2
87.053358	3
66.918779	4
49.961182	5
40.220119	6
33.986886	7
27.744551	8
24.332209	9
21.221772	10
17.753111	11
15.832128	12
13.973376	13
12.298085	14
11.188095	15
10.195367	16
9.510805	17
8.771753	18
8.111558	19
7.633717	20
7.269531	21
6.989808	22
6.428701	23
6.170228	24

The line in the code "print(data.shape)" produces the output (217,2). Here 2 refers to the number of features used, which are CPU usage and RAM usage and 217 refers to the total number of instances of CPU and RAM usage of the 10 applications. "plt.scatter" is used to plot the data points. To plot the scatter points in different colors, we made use of "cmap". It takes in values such as inferno, magma, viridis, cool, etc.

Elbow method is used to find an optimal value for k in k-means clustering algorithm. Here, we plot a graph for the value of k to the sum of squared errors for each value of k. Sum of squared error (cluster error) is a measure of variation within each cluster. It is measured as the difference between each observed cluster and the mean of the group to which it belongs to. In the elbow method where the graph looks like an arm, an optimal value for k is chosen where an abrupt drop is seen for the sum of squared errors. Out of the 217 data points, 145 data points were used for training. The cluster errors for different values of k are given in Table 5.2.

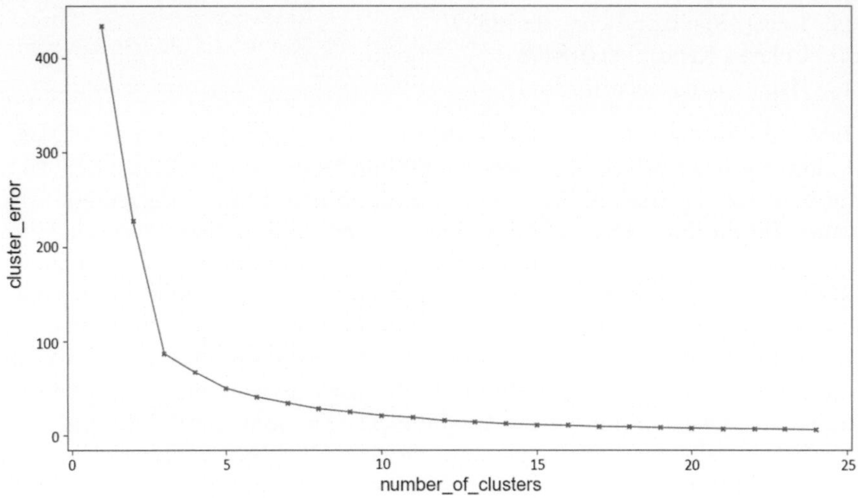

Fig. 5.6 Cluster errors for various cluster sizes

Figure 5.6 shows a graphical representation of the number of clusters to the corresponding cluster error. There is an abrupt reduction in the error rate when the number of clusters equals 2, 3, 4, and 5 from which we may conclude the probable values of k as one among them for an optimal clustering. Since we need to classify the data points as either goodware or malware only, we fixed the value of k as 2.

Out of the 217 data points, 145 data points were used for training and the remaining 72 were used for testing. The results obtained are given below.

1. The centroids are {(0.14157285, 0.19482979), (0.025885220.19022933)}
2. Actual labels of the test set are
   [110100101010100110101100011001000100000000100000101100100000000
   0001000100]
3. Corresponding set of predicted labels for the test set are
   [111111101101111111111111110111111111011011111111101111111111111
   101111111]
   By comparing the predicted labels to the actual labels, we can clearly see the difference. This is a clear indicator of misclassification.
4. Accuracy score: 0.638889
5. Precision score: 0.551954
6. Mean absolute error: 0.361111
7. F-score: 0.567934
8. Homogeneity: 0.000458
9. Completeness: 0.001
10. V-measure: 0.001

11. Jaccard similarity score: 0.638889
12. Cohen's Kappa: −0.018498
13. Hamming distance: 0.36111.

Table 5.3 shows the classification report, where 0 indicates the goodware class and 1 indicates the malware class. Support is the number of test samples that were taken for clustering analysis. An increase in clustering error causes a decrease in AUC value. There exists a trade-off between the true positive rate and false positive rate as we move off the threshold of the classifier. When the test is more accurate the ROC curve is closer to the left top border. Figure 5.7 shows the ROC curve plot for k-means clustering of the data. The area under the ROC curve is 0.49. Our classifier clearly aligns with the diagonal, indicating that the efficiency and accuracy of the classifier are very low. This proves that CPU–RAM usage statistics is not a good feature for clustering malware and goodware using k-means clustering algorithm.

The confusion matrix indicating the correlation between the actual labels and predicted labels is shown in Fig. 5.8. Confusion matrix is one of the optimal ways of determining the number of labels that were predicted true/ false and the number of labels that are actually true/ false. Here the positive class refers to the goodware, and the negative class refers to the malware. The following information can be inferred from the confusion matrix : true positive = 2, true negative = 44, false positive = 5, and false negative = 21.

Table 5.3 Classification results for k-means clustering

Labels	Precision	Recall	F1 score	Support
0	0.71	0.10	0.18	49
1	0.32	0.91	0.48	23
Avg/total	0.59	0.36	0.27	72

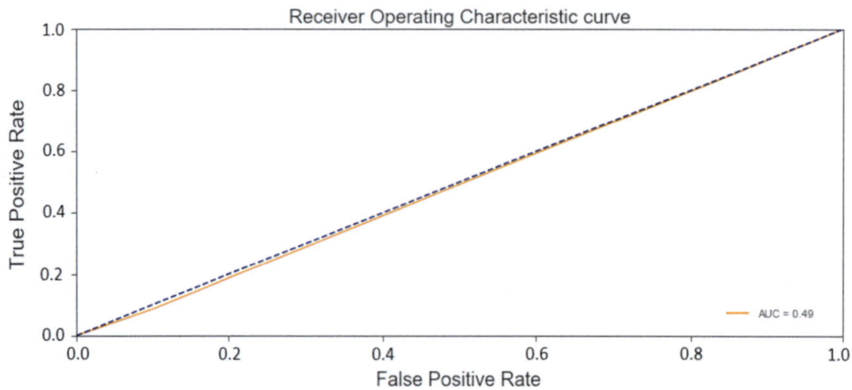

Fig. 5.7 ROC curve for k-means clustering

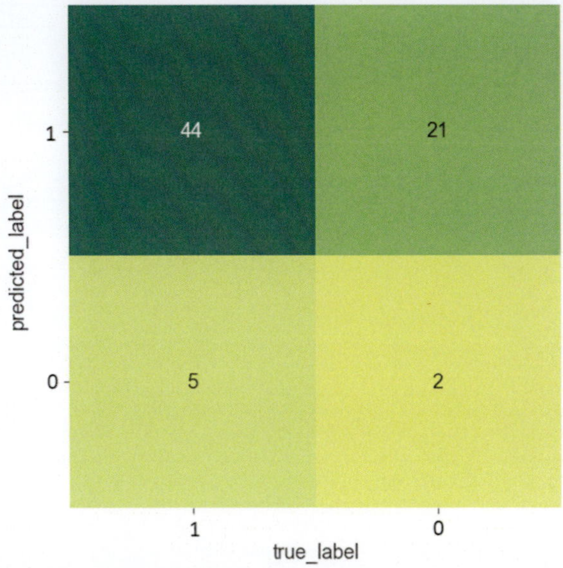

Fig. 5.8 Confusion matrix for k-means clustering

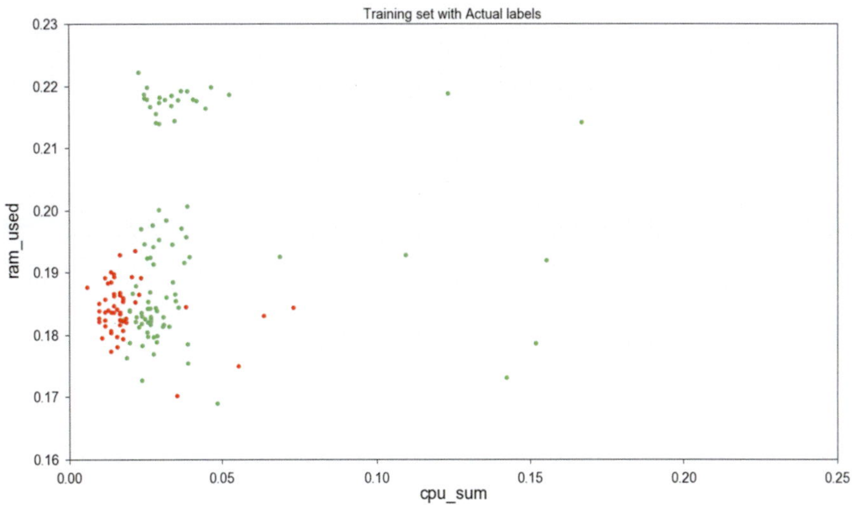

Fig. 5.9 Training dataset for k-means clustering

Figure 5.9 shows the set of data points used to train the classifier. It is based on this learning the classifier predicts the test data labels. There are chances of data getting misclassified during the prediction phase when the classifier is ill-trained during the training phase.

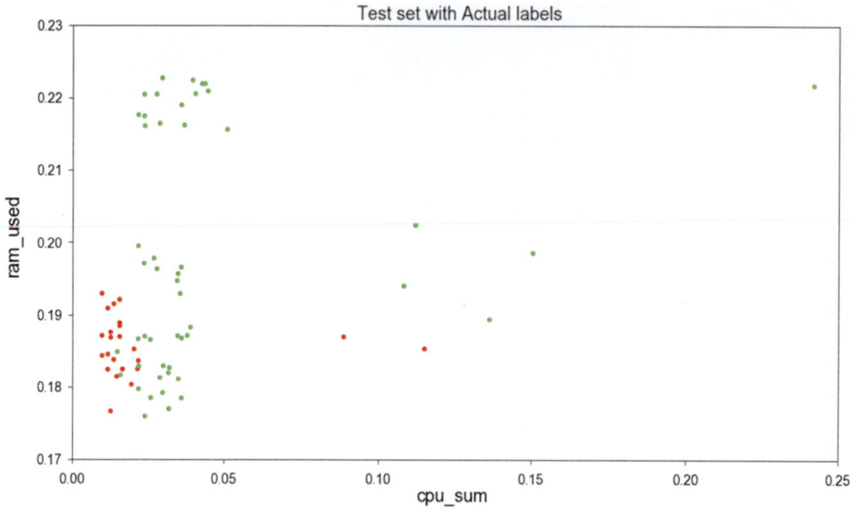

Fig. 5.10 Test dataset with actual labels for k-means clustering

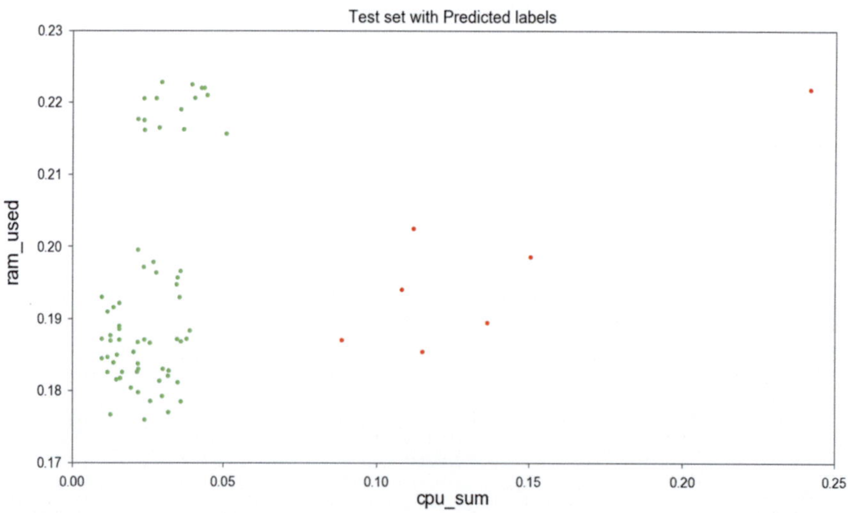

Fig. 5.11 Test dataset with predicted labels for k-means clustering

Figure 5.10 shows the test data with actual labels. Figure 5.11 shows the test dataset with predicted labels. It can be clearly seen in the figure that malware samples with features similar to that of goodware were labeled as goodware during the test phase.

5.6 Fuzzy C-Means Clustering

This is a kind of clustering in which each data point may belong to more than one cluster. To understand how fuzzy c-means clustering arranges similarly behaving samples in a malware–goodware collection, we shall take a look at its working mechanism. The mathematical derivation of fuzzy c-means clustering is given below, and its implementation details in python using sci-kit libraries are discussed below.

Consider a dataset with goodware and malware applications. Our aim is to cluster these data points based on fuzzy c-means clustering. Membership is assigned for each data point to a cluster by calculating the distance between the data point and the cluster centroid. The lesser the distance, the higher is its membership toward that cluster. By the term "membership", we mean the extent to which any data point belongs to a particular cluster. Points located on the boundary of a cluster would have less membership compared to those data points that are closer to the cluster centroid.

Consider a dataset having four clusters and two samples that are outliers which do not belong to either of the four clusters. A regular clustering algorithm searching will force these two points into any of the four clusters. This may cause distortion in the final solution. Fuzzy clustering, however, will assign a probability of about 0.25 to these outliers for belonging to each cluster. This equal membership probability indicates that these two points are outliers. Let the following notations are fixed.

- $N =$ Total number of data points.
- $X = \{x_1, x_2, \ldots, x_N\}$, the set of data points where each x_i is of dimension d.
- $c =$ Total number of clusters.
- $V = \{v_1, v_2, \ldots, v_c\}$, the set of centroids corresponding to the clusters.
- $m =$ The fuzziness index and $m \in [1, \infty)$.
- $\mu_{ij} =$ Membership of the data point x_i to the jth cluster.
- $U = \{\mu_{ij} : 1 \leq i \leq N, 1 \leq j \leq c\}$.
- $d_{ij} =$ The Euclidean distance between the data point x_i and the cluster center v_j .

The objective of fuzzy c-means algorithm is to minimize

$$J(U, V) = \sum_{i=1}^{N} \sum_{j=1}^{c} (\mu_{ij})^m ||x_i - v_j||^2, \quad \text{where } 1 \leq m < \infty. \tag{5.2}$$

The membership μ_{ij} is given by

$$\mu_{ij} = \frac{1}{\sum_{k=1}^{c} \left(\frac{||x_i - v_j||}{||x_i - v_k||} \right)^{\left(\frac{2}{m-1}\right)}}. \tag{5.3}$$

The cluster center v_j is given by

$$v_j = \frac{\sum_{i=1}^{N} \mu_{ij}^m x_i}{\sum_{i=1}^{N} \mu_{ij}^m}, \forall j = 1, 2, \ldots, c. \tag{5.4}$$

The iteration stops when $\max_{i,j} |\mu_{ij}^{(k+1)} - \mu_{ij}^{(k)}| < \varepsilon$, where ε is a termination criterion between 0 and 1, and k is the iteration index. The algorithm for fuzzy c-means clustering is given in Algorithm 5.2.

Algorithm 5.2 Fuzzy C-Means Clustering

Input: CSV file for each feature
Output: Clustered samples

```
Select 'c' number of clusters randomly
repeat
    Use the estimated means to classify the samples into clusters
    Calculate the fuzzy membership
    Then calculate the fuzzy centers
until the objective function is minimized
```

Fuzzy c-means clustering takes in a dataset as input and produces the optimal cluster centroids and membership grades for each data point as the output. Each data point can belong to more than one cluster. To implement fuzzy c-means clustering, we will be making use of numpy and peach packages. The starting values for memberships can be randomly chosen. The function that carries out clustering is

$$skfuzzy.cmeans(data, c, m, error, maxiter, init = None, seed = None),$$

where $data$ is the data to be clustered, c is the number of clusters, m is the array exponentiation applied to the membership function, $error$ is of float type and is the stopping condition, $maxiter$ is the maximum number of iterations allowed, $init$ is the initial fuzzy c-partitioned matrix, and $seed$ sets a random seed of $init$ and is mainly used for testing purposes.

The $cmeans()$ function returns the following: $cntr$, which is the cluster centers; u the final fuzzy c-partitioned matrix; u_0 the initial guess at fuzzy c-partitioned matrix which is either provided as $init$ or is a random guess; d the final Euclidean distance matrix; jm the objective function history; p the number of iterations and the fuzzy partition coefficient fpc.

5.7 Density-Based Clustering

Density-based clustering aims at grouping denser samples into single clusters. Unlike k-means clustering which clusters data points irrespective of the distance by which they are separated apart by finding centroids recursively, density-based clustering calculates a distance measure ε and data points that are lying within ε distance from a data point are only clustered together. That is, a cluster centered around p is given by

$$N_\varepsilon(p) = \{q|d(p, q) \leq \varepsilon\}. \tag{5.5}$$

Let p and q be two data points. Figure 5.12 shows a set of four data points out of which we consider two points p and q and an ε neighborhood is considered around them. The two circles drawn with a radius ε from p and q indicate that those points that fall within this boundary can be grouped into a single cluster. That is, the objects falling within the ε boundary are of high density and falls into the same cluster. Density at a point q refers to the fraction of data points that are included in the neighborhood of radius ε of the point q. The lesser is the value of ε, the smaller would be the neighborhood. Our aim is to identify highly dense neighborhoods containing most of the data points.

Mainly there are three different types of density-based clustering algorithms: density-based spatial clustering of applications with noise (DBSCAN), ordering points to identify the clustering structure (OPTICS), and density-based clustering (DENCLUE). In the following section, we shall take a look into the details of DBSCAN algorithm.

5.7.1 Density-Based Spatial Clustering of Applications with Noise (DBSCAN)

DBSCAN is one of the most popular density-based clustering algorithms. Unlike k-means algorithm which requires the number of clusters as a parameter, DBSCAN infers the number of clusters based on the input dataset and discovers clusters of

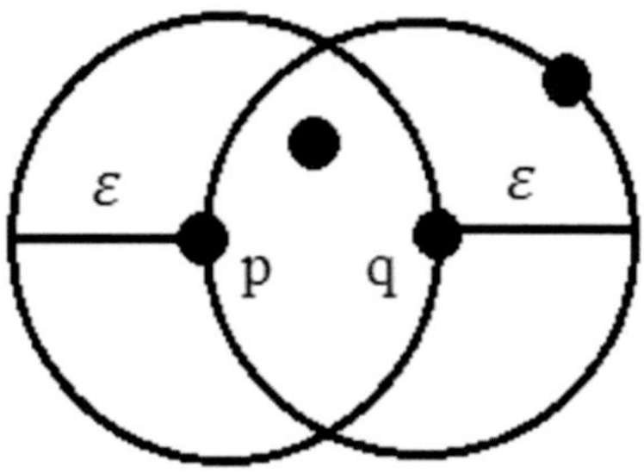

Fig. 5.12 Clustering p and q

arbitrary sizes. As discussed earlier, DBSCAN approximates local density using the ε-neighborhood by making use of the following two important parameters.

1. ε, the radius of neighborhood around any data point q.
2. minPts, the minimum number of data points needed in a neighborhood to define a cluster.

The DBSCAN algorithm identifies the data points in the sample space as three different types.

1. *Core Points*: A data point q is a core point if the ε-neighborhood of q contains at least minPts.
2. *Border Points*: A data point p is a border point if the neighborhood of p contains less than minPts data points, but p is reachable from some core point q.
3. *Outlier*: A data point o is an outlier if it is neither a core point nor a border point.

A data point p is said to be directly density reachable from a point q only if p is in the ε-neighborhood of q, while q is a core object. If a data point p is in the ε-neighborhood of q and q is in the ε-neighborhood of r and r is in the ε-neighborhood of s, then p is said to be indirectly density reachable from s.

Let dp be any data point in a dataset D. The DBSCAN algorithm requires two parameters to be specified: ε and min_samples. ε neighborhood indicates that objects within an ε radius from each data point are considered to determine whether a data point is a core point, non-core point, or an outlier. min_samples specifies the minimum number of samples any data point should have in its ε neighborhood to be a core point. The DBSCAN algorithm is given in Algorithm 5.3. The code for DBSCAN algorithm is given below.

Algorithm 5.3 DBSCAN Clustering

Input: CSV file for each feature
Output: Clustered samples

1: For every data point dp in the dataset find the number of its ε neighbors k.
2: **if** $k >$ min_samples **then**
3: The data point corresponding to k is a core point; hence, collect all objects density reachable from that data point and assign them to a new cluster.
4: **else if** The data point corresponding to k is an ε neighbor of some other core point. **then**
5: If the data point is an ε neighbor of the cluster, then assign it (also known as non-core point) to a nearby cluster.
6: **else**
7: The data point is an outlier.
8: **end if**

```
import pandas as pd
import sklearn
from sklearn.cluster import DBSCAN
import numpy as np
from matplotlib import pyplot as plt
from sklearn import metrics
```

```
from matplotlib import pyplot
from sklearn.metrics.cluster import homogeneity_score
from sklearn.model_selection import train_test_split
from sklearn.metrics import roc_curve, auc, roc_auc_score
import seaborn
pyplot.style.use('ggplot')
seaborn.set(style='ticks')
data = pd.read_csv('GM-cpu_ram-labeled.csv')
data = data[["cpu_sum", "ram_used", "labels"]]
f1 = data['cpu_sum'].values
f2 = data['ram_used'].values
f3 = data['labels'].values
class_names=[1,0]
X = np.array(list(zip(f1, f2)))
X_train, X_test, y_train, y_test = train_test_split(X, f3,
                              test_size=0.33, random_state=42)
dbsc = DBSCAN(eps = 0.04, metric = 'euclidean',
            min_samples = 4).fit(X_train,y_train)
pred_labels = dbsc.fit_predict(X_test)
core_samples = np.zeros_like(pred_labels, dtype = bool)
core_samples[dbsc.core_sample_indices_] = True
print("Predicted set of labels are : ")
print(pred_labels)
print("Actual set of labels are : ")
print(y_test)
fpr, recall, thresholds = roc_curve(y_test,pred_labels)
roc_auc = auc(fpr, recall)
pyplot.figure(figsize=(15,6))
pyplot.plot(fpr, recall, 'b', label='AUC = %0.2f' % roc_auc, color='darkorange')
pyplot.title('Receiver Operating Characteristic curve', fontsize=20)
pyplot.legend(loc='lower right')
pyplot.plot([0, 1], [0, 1], color='navy', linestyle='--')
pyplot.xlim([0.0, 1.0])
pyplot.ylim([0.0, 1.0])
pyplot.ylabel('True Positive Rate', fontsize=20)
pyplot.xlabel('False Positive Rate', fontsize=20)
pyplot.show()
print("Area under the ROC curve is ")
print(roc_auc_score(y_test, pred_labels))
fig = pyplot.gcf()
cnf_matrix = metrics.confusion_matrix(y_test, pred_labels)
print(cnf_matrix)
seaborn.heatmap(cnf_matrix.T, square=True, annot=True, fmt='d',
cbar=False, xticklabels=class_names, yticklabels=class_names,
cmap='summer_r',annot_kws={"size":20})
fig.set_size_inches(2,2)
pyplot.xlabel('true_label', fontsize=20)
pyplot.ylabel('predicted_label', fontsize=20)
na = np.array(data).astype("float")
n_clusters_ = len(set(pred_labels)) - (1 if -1 in pred_labels else 0)
print("Ignoring noise (if any) the total number of clusters = %d"
     % n_clusters_)
print("Homogeneity: %0.6f" % homogeneity_score(y_test, pred_labels))
print("Completeness: %0.3f" % metrics.completeness_score(y_test, pred_labels))
print("V-measure: %0.3f" % metrics.v_measure_score(y_test, pred_labels))
print("Jaccard Similarity score : %0.6f" %metrics.jaccard_similarity_score
     (y_test, pred_labels,normalize=True, sample_weight=None))
print("Cohen's Kappa : %0.6f" % metrics.cohen_kappa_score(y_test, pred_labels,
                                       labels=None, weights=None))
print("Hamming matrix : %0.06f" %metrics.hamming_loss(y_test, pred_labels,
                    labels=None, sample_weight=None, classes=None))
print("Accuracy Score : %0.06f" %sklearn.metrics.accuracy_score(y_test,
              pred_labels,normalize=True,sample_weight=None))
```

```
print("Precision Score : %0.06f" %sklearn.metrics.precision_score(y_test,
pred_labels,labels=None,pos_label=1, average='weighted', sample_weight=None))
print("Mean Absolute Error : %0.06f" %sklearn.metrics.mean_absolute_error
        (y_test, pred_labels, sample_weight=None,multioutput='raw_values'))
print("F-Score : %0.06f" %sklearn.metrics.f1_score(y_test, pred_labels,
      labels=None, pos_label=1,average='weighted',sample_weight=None))
print(metrics.classification_report(y_test, pred_labels))
ax = data.plot(kind='scatter', x='cpu_sum', color='white', y='ram_used', alpha=1,
     fontsize = 18)
pyplot.xlabel('cpu_sum', fontsize=20)
pyplot.ylabel('ram_used', fontsize=20)
pyplot.title("Labeled dataset", fontsize=20)
ax.set_ylim((0.16, 0.23))
ax.set_xlim((0, 0.25))
ax.set_facecolor("white")
fig = pyplot.gcf()
fig.set_size_inches(18.5, 10.5)
#ax.grid(color='w', linestyle='-', linewidth=0)
ax.scatter(f1, f2, c=f3, s=18, cmap='prism_r')
plt.xlabel('cpu_sum')
plt.ylabel('ram_used')
limit = len(X_test)
ax = data.plot(kind='scatter', x='cpu_sum', color='white', y='ram_used', alpha=1,
     fontsize = 20)
pyplot.xlabel('cpu_sum', fontsize=20)
pyplot.ylabel('ram_used', fontsize=20)
pyplot.title("Test dataset with actual labels", fontsize=20)
```

```
ax.set_ylim((0.16, 0.23))
ax.set_xlim((0, 0.25))
ax.set_facecolor("white")
fig = pyplot.gcf()
fig.set_size_inches(18.5, 10.5)
#ax.grid(color='w', linestyle='-', linewidth=0)
for i in range(0,limit):
    if(y_test[i] == 0):
        ax.scatter(na[i][0], na[i][1], c='red', s=20)
    elif(y_test[i] == 1):
        ax.scatter(na[i][0], na[i][1], c='green', s=20)
    elif(y_test[i] == -1):
        ax.scatter(na[i][0], na[i][1], c='black', s=20)
    elif(y_test[i] == 2):
        ax.scatter(na[i][0], na[i][1], c='yellow', s=20)
plt.xlabel('cpu_sum')
plt.ylabel('ram_used')
limit = len(X_test)
ax = data.plot(kind='scatter', x='cpu_sum', color='white', y='ram_used', alpha=1,
     fontsize = 20)
pyplot.xlabel('cpu_sum', fontsize=20)
pyplot.ylabel('ram_used', fontsize=20)
pyplot.title("Test dataset with predicted labels", fontsize=20)
ax.set_ylim((0.16, 0.23))
ax.set_xlim((0, 0.25))
ax.set_facecolor("white")
fig = pyplot.gcf()
fig.set_size_inches(18.5, 10.5)
#ax.grid(color='w', linestyle='-', linewidth=0)
for i in range(0,limit):
    if(pred_labels[i] == 0):
        ax.scatter(na[i][0], na[i][1], c='red', s=17)
    elif(pred_labels[i] == 1):
```

```
        ax.scatter(na[i][0], na[i][1], c='green', s=30)
    elif(pred_labels[i] == -1):
        ax.scatter(na[i][0], na[i][1], c='black', s=50)
    elif(pred_labels[i] == 2):
        ax.scatter(na[i][0], na[i][1], c='yellow', s=17)
```

Using DBSCAN, we obtain the labels as $[-1, 0, 1, 2, \ldots]$. In our case -1 indicates outliers, 0 indicates goodware, and 1 indicates malware. But there might be situations where more than two labels are used by the classifier. Thus $[-1, 0, 1, 2, \ldots]$ are just indicators of the labels. The number of classes the clustering results in depends on the eps (ε) value and the min_samples (minPts) of samples to be included in a cluster while clustering. We may modify the algorithm by finding the optimal value of eps.

Out of the 217 data points, 145 data points were used for training and the remaining 72 were used for testing. The results obtained are given below.

1. Actual labels of the test set are [110100101010100110101100011001000100000001000001011001000000000 001000100]
2. Corresponding set of predicted labels for the test set are [000000010010000000000000001000000000100100000000010000000000000 00 − 10000000]
3. Accuracy score : 0.638889
4. Precision score : 0.567165
5. Mean absolute error : 0.361111
6. F-Score : 0.569402
7. Homogeneity: 0.008635
8. Completeness: 0.015
9. V-measure: 0.011
10. Jaccard similarity score : 0.638889
11. Cohen's Kappa : -0.005911
12. Hamming matrix : 0.36111

Table 5.4 shows the classification report. Label 0 indicates the goodware class and 1 indicates the malware class. Support is the number of test samples that were taken for clustering analysis.

As discussed earlier, an increase in clustering error causes a decrease in AUC value. There exists a trade-off between the true positive rate and false positive rate

Table 5.4 Classification results for DBSCAN clustering

Labels	Precision	Recall	F1 score	Support
−1	0.00	0.00	0.00	0
0	0.68	0.90	0.77	49
1	0.33	0.09	0.14 8	23
Avg/total	0.57	0.64	0.57	72

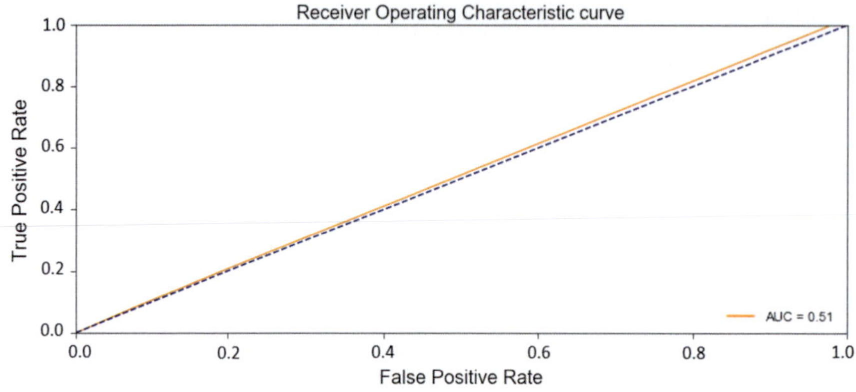

Fig. 5.13 ROC curve for DBSCAN clustering

Fig. 5.14 Confusion matrix for DBSCAN clustering

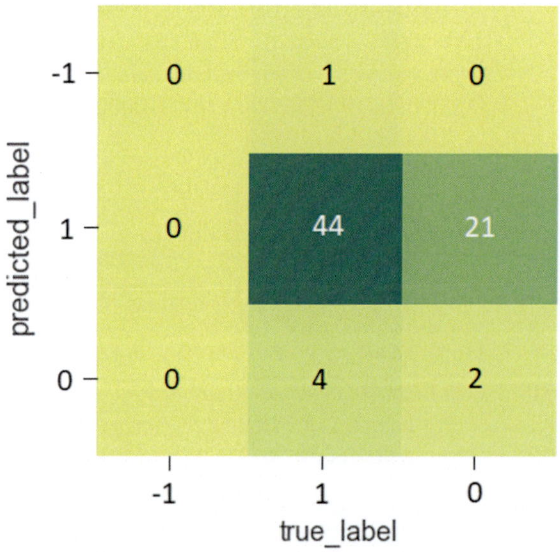

as we move off the threshold of the classifier. Figure 5.13 shows the ROC curve plot for DBSCAN clustering. The area under the ROC curve is 0.51.

The confusion matrix indicating the correlation between actual labels and predicted labels is as shown in Fig. 5.14. The following information can be inferred from the confusion matrix: True Positive = 2, True Negative = 44, False Positive = 5, and False Negative = 21. Confusion matrix is one of the optimal ways of determining the number of labels that were predicted true/ false and the number of labels that are actually true/ false.

The test dataset with actual labels is shown in Fig. 5.15, and test dataset with predicted labels is shown in Fig. 5.16. The black data point indicates outliers.

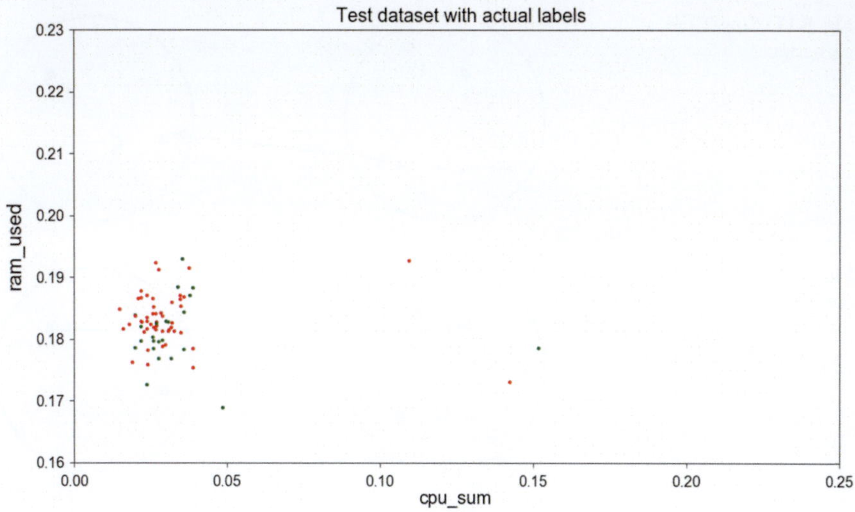

Fig. 5.15 Test dataset with actual labels for DBSCAN clustering

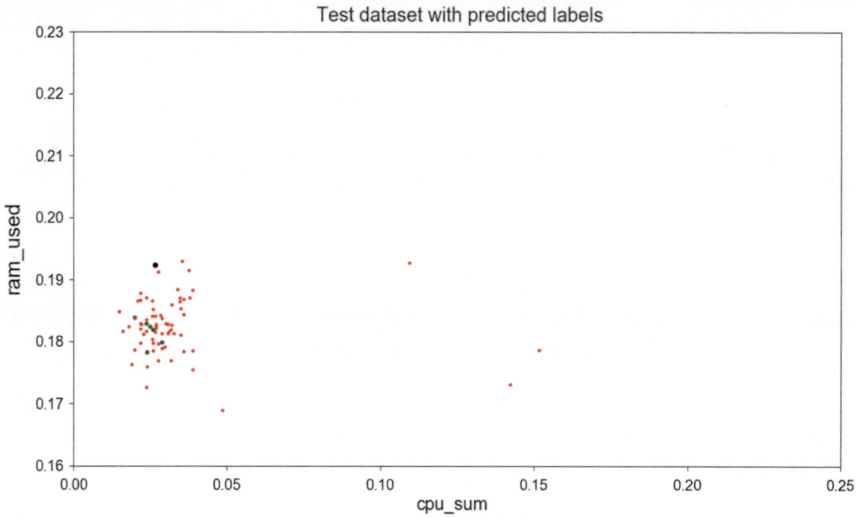

Fig. 5.16 Test dataset with predicted labels for DBSCAN clustering

5.8 Hierarchical Clustering

Hierarchical clustering involves building a cluster tree to represent the dataset. It has a tree-like structure with parent nodes linking to two or more child nodes which splits further. It is ordered either from bottom to top or from top to bottom. As mentioned in the beginning of this chapter, there are two different types of clustering, "divisive"

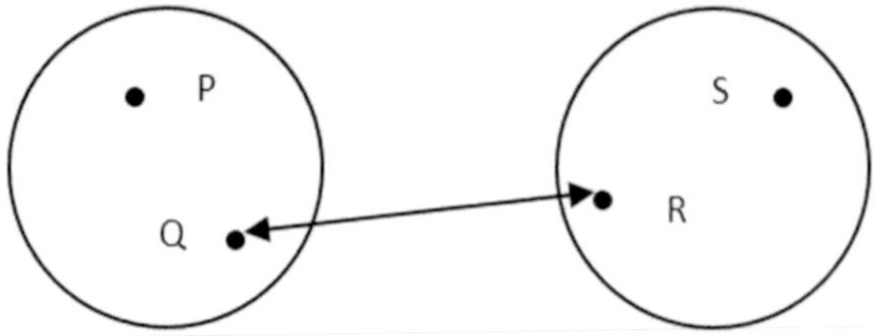

Fig. 5.17 Single-link clustering

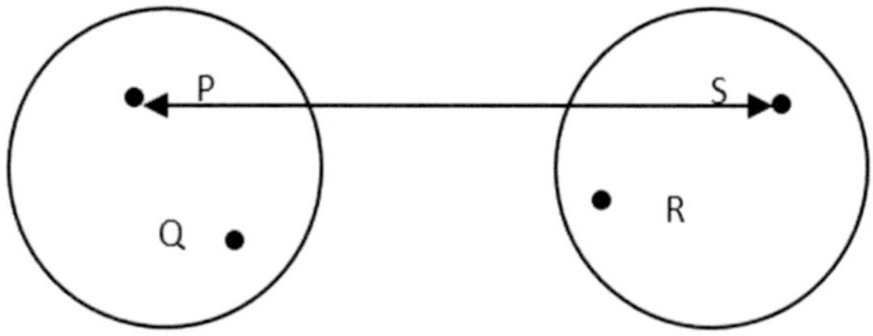

Fig. 5.18 Complete-link clustering

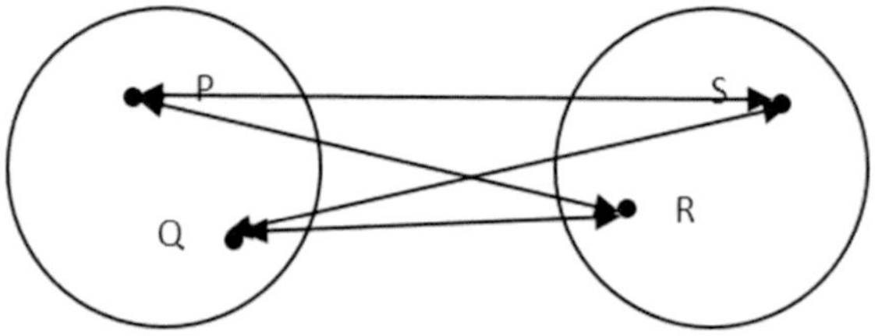

Fig. 5.19 Average-link clustering

and "agglomerative". In divisive clustering, the entire dataset is assigned to a single cluster which is then partitioned into two least similar clusters. Finally, each cluster is visited until each data point is assigned to a cluster. In agglomerative clustering, each element in the dataset is assigned to a separate cluster. The similarity between each of the clusters is computed, and then the two most similar clusters are joined to form a single cluster. The above two steps are repeated until there is only a single cluster left.

Hierarchical clustering considers each data point to be a singleton cluster and then merges them until a single cluster is formed. In single-link clustering, the distance between two clusters is equal to the distance between two closest members of the group. This is shown in Fig. 5.17.

In complete-link clustering, the distance between the farthest points is considered while clustering. Here, two points are clustered only if all observations in their union are relatively similar. This produces compact clusters of lesser diameter. This is shown in Fig. 5.18.

In average-linkage clustering, the average distance between all pairs is measured for clustering the data points. This is shown in Fig. 5.19.

The hierarchical clustering algorithm is given in Algorithm 5.4.

In hierarchical clustering, the relationship between similar data points and parent–child data points is represented using dendrograms. These dendrograms can either be

Algorithm 5.4 Hierarchical Clustering

Input: CSV file for each feature
Output: Dendograms indicating the clustered samples

Initialisation: Here we take each individual data point as a cluster. Given a set $\{x_1, x_2, \ldots, x_n\}$ of n data points and a distance function $d(,)$. Let $C = \{c_1, c_2, \ldots, c_n\}$ be the set of centroids.

for $i \leftarrow 1$ to n **do**
  Assign each data point to be the cluster center, $c_i = x_i$
end for
$l = n + 1$
while sizeof(C) $> l$ **do**
  for all $c_i, c_j \in C$ **do**
    $d(c_i, c_j)$ is the minimum distance between any two individual data points x_i, x_j
  end for
  Let (c_{min1}, c_{min2}) be the centroids corresponding to the minimal distance
  Remove the centroids c_{min1} and c_{min2} from C
  Combine both the centroids and add $\{c_{min1}, c_{min2}\}$ to C. By this step we combine those individual data points separated apart by a minimal distance.
  $l = l + 1$
end while

a column graph or a row graph. Each branch in dendrogram is called a clade, where each clade has one or more leaves: single or double or triple. Thus hierarchical clustering supports three different types of linkage: single, average, and complete. The code is given below.

```
from matplotlib import pyplot
from scipy.cluster.hierarchy import dendrogram, linkage
from scipy.cluster import hierarchy
import numpy as np
import pandas as pd
from scipy.cluster.hierarchy import cophenet
from sklearn.metrics.cluster import homogeneity_score
from scipy.spatial.distance import pdist
from sklearn.cluster import AgglomerativeClustering
from sklearn.cluster import SpectralClustering
from sklearn.model_selection import train_test_split
from sklearn.metrics import roc_curve, auc, roc_auc_score
from sklearn import metrics
import seaborn
from matplotlib.colors import rgb2hex, colorConverter
from collections import defaultdict
pyplot.style.use('ggplot')
seaborn.set(style='ticks')
pyplot.rcParams['figure.figsize'] = (16, 9)
pyplot.style.use('ggplot')
fig = pyplot.gcf()
# Importing the dataset
data = pd.read_csv('GM-cpu_ram-labeled.csv')
print(data.shape)
data.head()
f1 = data['cpu_sum'].values
f2 = data['ram_used'].values
f3 = data['labels'].values
X = np.array(list(zip(f1, f2)))
X = np.array(list(zip(f1, f2)))
```

```
X_train, X_test, y_train, y_test = train_test_split(X, f3, test_size=0.33,
     random_state=42)
ac = SpectralClustering(n_clusters = 2)
ac = ac.fit(X_train, y=None)
y_pred = ac.fit_predict(X_test)
ax = data.plot(kind='scatter', x='cpu_sum', color='white', y='ram_used', alpha=1,
     fontsize = 18)
pyplot.xlabel('cpu_sum', fontsize=18)
pyplot.ylabel('ram_used', fontsize=18)
pyplot.title("Testing set with predicted labels", fontsize=18)
ax.set_ylim((0.16, 0.23))
ax.set_xlim((0, 0.25))
ax.set_facecolor("white")
fig.set_size_inches(18.5, 10.5)
ax.grid(color='w', linestyle='-', linewidth=0)
ax.scatter(X_test[:, 0], X_test[:, 1], c = y_pred, s=50, cmap='prism_r')
n_clusters_ = len(set(y_pred)) - (1 if -1 in y_pred else 0)
print("Ignoring noise (if any) the total number of clusters = %d"
     % n_clusters_)
print("Homogeneity: %0.6f" % metrics.homogeneity_score(y_test, y_pred))
print("Completeness: %0.3f" % metrics.completeness_score(y_test, y_pred))
print("V-measure: %0.3f" % metrics.v_measure_score(y_test, y_pred))
print("Jaccard Similarity score : %0.6f" %metrics.jaccard_similarity_score
     (y_test, y_pred,normalize=True, sample_weight=None))
print("Cohen's Kappa : %0.6f" % metrics.cohen_kappa_score(y_test, y_pred,
                                        labels=None, weights=None))
print("Hamming matrix : %0.06f" %metrics.hamming_loss(y_test, y_pred,
                    labels=None, sample_weight=None, classes=None))
print("Accuracy Score : %0.06f" %metrics.accuracy_score(y_test,
              y_pred,normalize=True,sample_weight=None))
print("Precision Score : %0.06f" %metrics.precision_score(y_test,
y_pred,labels=None,pos_label=1, average='weighted', sample_weight=None))
print("Mean Absolute Error : %0.06f" %metrics.mean_absolute_error
        (y_test, y_pred, sample_weight=None,multioutput='raw_values'))
print("F-Score : %0.06f" %metrics.f1_score(y_test, y_pred,
      labels=None, pos_label=1,average='weighted',sample_weight=None))
print(metrics.classification_report(y_test, y_pred))
print("Predicted set of labels are : ")
print(y_pred)
print("Actual set of labels are : ")
print(y_test)
fpr, recall, thresholds = roc_curve(y_test,y_pred)
```

```
roc_auc = auc(fpr, recall)
pyplot.figure(figsize=(15,6))
pyplot.plot(fpr, recall, 'b', label='AUC = %0.2f' % roc_auc, color='darkorange')
pyplot.title('Receiver Operating Characteristic curve', fontsize=20)
pyplot.legend(loc='lower right')
pyplot.plot([0, 1], [0, 1], color='navy', linestyle='--')
pyplot.xlim([0.0, 1.0])
pyplot.ylim([0.0, 1.0])
pyplot.ylabel('True Positive Rate', fontsize=20)
pyplot.xlabel('False Positive Rate', fontsize=20)
pyplot.show()
print("Area under the ROC curve is ")
print(roc_auc_score(y_test, y_pred))
class_names = [1,0]
cnf_matrix = metrics.confusion_matrix(y_test, y_pred)
print(cnf_matrix)
seaborn.heatmap(cnf_matrix.T, square=True, annot=True, fmt='d',cbar=False,
       xticklabels=class_names, yticklabels=class_names, cmap='summer_r',
```

```
    annot_kws={"size":20})
fig.set_size_inches(2,2)
pyplot.xlabel('true_label', fontsize=18)
pyplot.ylabel('predicted_label', fontsize=18)

fig = pyplot.gcf()
Z = linkage(X, method='complete', metric='euclidean')
c, coph_dists = cophenet(Z, pdist(X))
hierarchy.set_link_color_palette(['m', 'c', 'y', 'k'])
pyplot.subplots(figsize=(15, 50))
den = hierarchy.dendrogram(Z, above_threshold_color='#bcbddc',no_plot=False,
                        leaf_font_size=13., orientation='right')
cluster_idxs = defaultdict(list)
for c, pi in zip(den['color_list'], den['icoord']):
    for leg in pi[1:3]:
        i = (leg - 5.0) / 10.0
        if abs(i - int(i)) < 1e-5:
            cluster_idxs[c].append(int(i))
            print("cluster_idxs is")
print(cluster_idxs)
pyplot.title('The Truncated Hierarchical Clustering Dendrogram')
pyplot.xlabel('distance', fontsize=18)
pyplot.ylabel('sample index', fontsize=18)
dendrogram(Z,truncate_mode='lastp',p=30,#shows only the last p merged clusters
leaf_rotation=90., leaf_font_size=15.,
show_contracted=True)# to get a distribution impression in truncated branches
pyplot.show()
```

1. Actual labels of the test set are [110100101010100110101100011001000100000001000001011001000000000001000100]
2. Corresponding set of predicted labels for the test set are [00000001001000000000000000010000000001001000000000100000000000000010000000]
3. Accuracy score: 0.638889
4. Precision score: 0.551954
5. Mean absolute error: 0.361111
6. F-score: 0.567934
7. Homogeneity: 0.000458
8. Completeness: 0.001
9. V-measure: 0.001
10. Jaccard similarity score: 0.638889
11. Cohen's Kappa: −0.018498
12. Hamming matrix: 0.361111

Table 5.5 shows the classification report. 0 label indicates the goodware class and 1 indicates the malware class.

Table 5.5 Classification results for hierarchical clustering

Labels	Precision	Recall	F1 score	Support
0	0.68	0.90	0.77	49
1	0.29	0.09	0.13 8	23
Avg/total	0.55	0.64	0.57	72

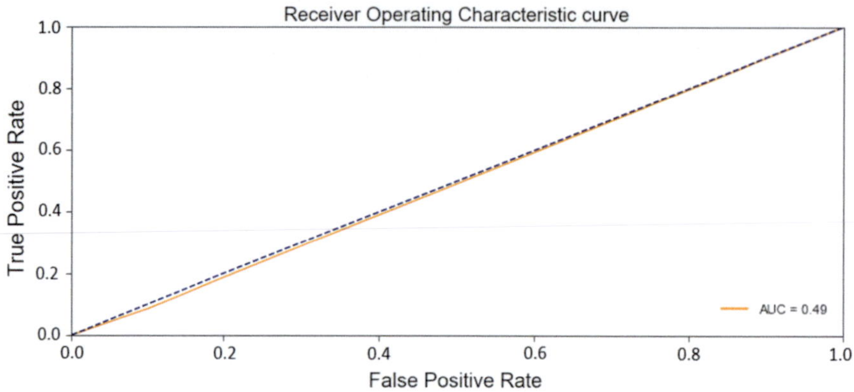

Fig. 5.20 ROC curve for hierarchical clustering

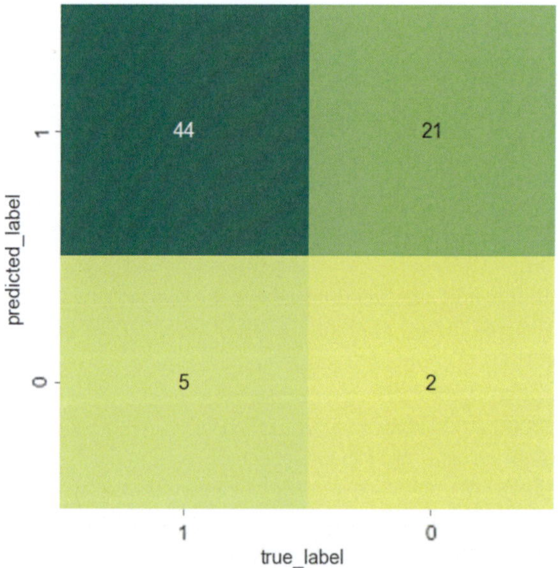

Fig. 5.21 Confusion matrix for hierarchical clustering

As discussed earlier, an increase in clustering error causes a decrease in AUC value. Figure 5.20 shows the ROC curve plot for hierarchical clustering. The area under the ROC curve is 0.49. Our classifier clearly aligns with the diagonal, indicating that the efficiency and accuracy of the classifier are very low. This further proves that CPU–RAM usage measure is not an efficient method for clustering malware and goodware.

The confusion matrix indicating the correlation between actual labels and predicted labels is as shown in Fig. 5.21. The test dataset with actual labels is shown

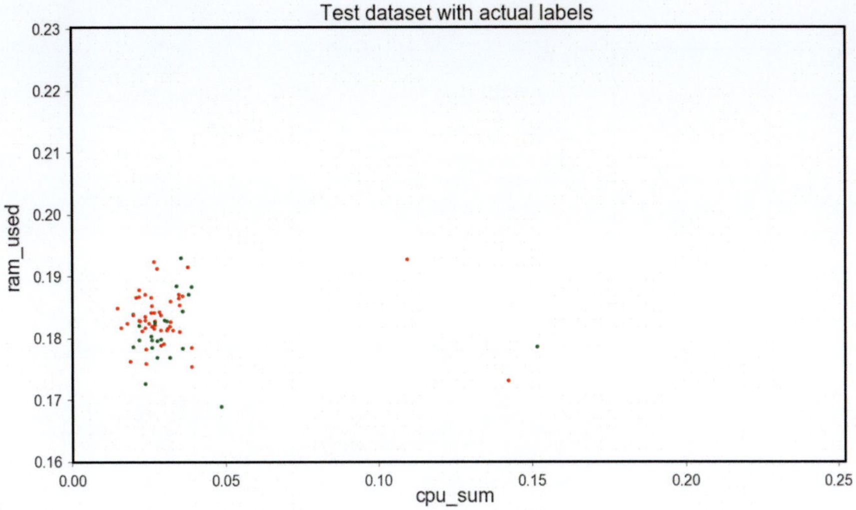

Fig. 5.22 Test dataset with actual labels for hierarchical clustering

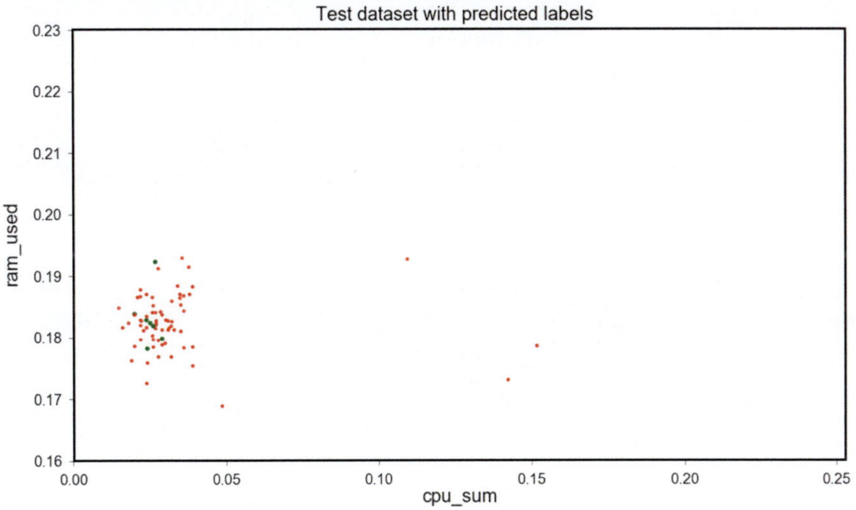

Fig. 5.23 Test dataset with predicted labels for hierarchical clustering

in Fig. 5.22, and test dataset with predicted labels is shown in Fig. 5.23. The black-colored data point are outliers.

Implementing single, complete, and average-linkage clustering gives us the output images shown in Figs. 5.24, 5.25, and 5.26, respectively. The dendrogram shown in Fig. 5.24 clearly indicates that all the objects are connected such that sum of distance (edge weights) is minimized. Two closest members of the clusters are connected and merged together. This is said to be the lightest weight edge. Single clustering is also called the nearest neighbor clustering.

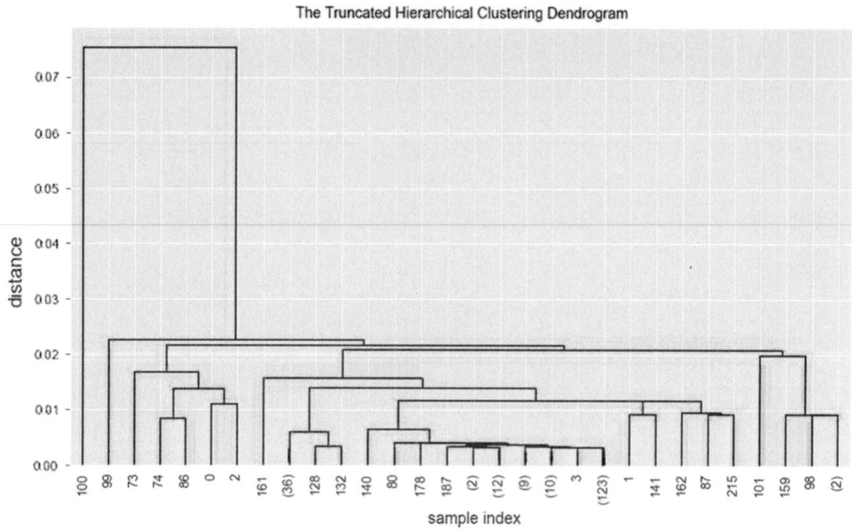

Fig. 5.24 Truncated dendrogram for single-link clustering

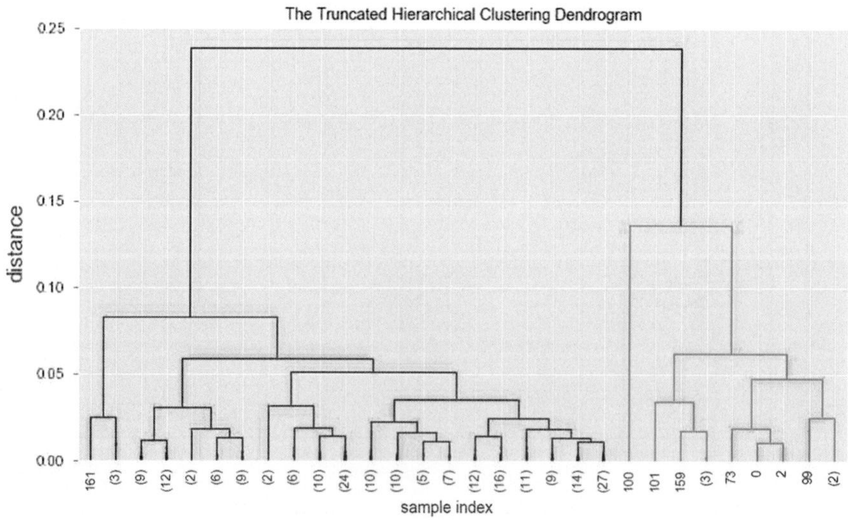

Fig. 5.25 Truncated dendrogram for complete-link clustering

Calculating the distance between the farthest points in the dataset gives the complete clustering as shown in Fig. 5.25

The truncate dendrogram for average-linkage clustering is shown in Fig. 5.26

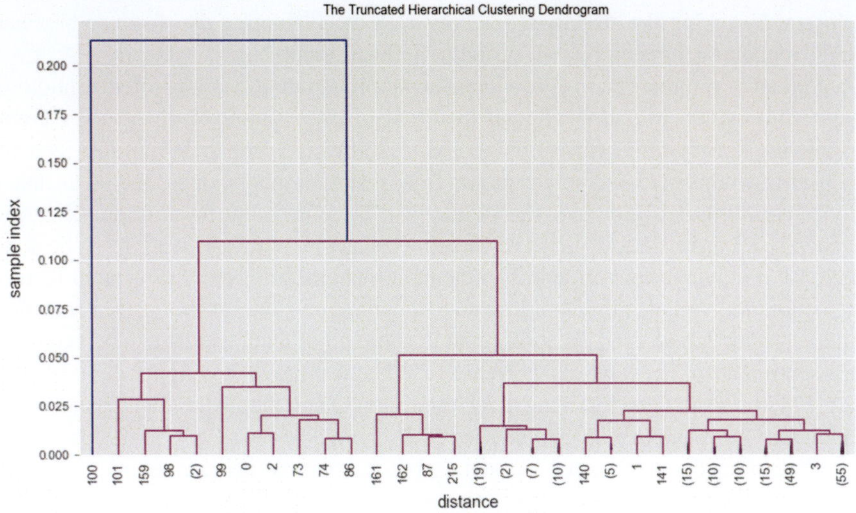

Fig. 5.26 Truncated dendrogram for average-linkage clustering

5.9 State of the Art of Clustering Applications

Clustering techniques can be used for malware detection, phishing web page identification, spam email filtering, and side-channel attack detection. In malware detection, clustering can also be used to identify different malware families such as Zbot, ZeroAccess, WinWebSec, etc.

Android malware can be detected using fuzzy c-means clustering. Malware samples from AndroidZoo dataset belonging to different families can be taken to capture the network traffic generated by each of them. Similarly, network traffic can be captured for goodware applications downloaded from Google Playstore as well. This would result in a massive dataset containing hundreds of thousands of network features. The three main features that can be extracted are the duration of each connection, size of a TCP packet, and the number of parameters in the GET/POST request. The degree of membership of each data point can be calculated by using fuzzy c-means clustering algorithm. If the degree of membership of a data point in the malicious class is high, then the data point gets labeled as malicious.

Clustering can also be carried out on HTTP network traffic generated by Windows executables (both malware and goodware). Some of the statistical features that can be extracted to construct the dataset are total number of HTTP requests, number of GET and POST requests, average length of the URL, average count of parameters in the request, average amount of data sent by the POST request, etc. After applying a suitable distance measure like Euclidean distance after standardizing the statistical features, a coarse-grained clustering can be implemented using single-linkage clustering algorithm. The coarse-grained cluster can be split into smaller fine-grained clusters by taking the structural features such as calculating the distance between GET requests generated by two different malware samples.

Spread of rumour news is growing at an alarming rate especially after technology started to evolve over time. Social media also has a nature of openness, thereby providing opportunities for people to create, share, and propagate rumours as well. Clustering helps in identifying rumours from that of authentic ones, and let us take a look at how this can be done in the Twitter platform. One of the best rumour detection systems at present does veracity verification task. A bit of preprocessing can be done here by removing the stop words, punctuation characters, etc. Chi-squared feature selection and variance threshold feature selection are some of the feature selection methods that can be used. In addition to it, some other features that can be extracted are sentiments of tweet words, presence of WH questions, checking for denial terms, etc. Finally, a suitable clustering algorithm can be implemented to find clusters so as to classify rumours from legitimate tweets.

Creating cyber profiles for Internet users by assessing the user behavior is a new area of research that includes data mining in big data and k-means clustering. This is done to understand the users' browsing behavior and hence applicable in digital forensics. Educational institution's cyber profile can be constructed by collecting data such as packets received and sent over the network traffic and websites accessed by the user. In the initial phase, clustering technique can be used to group the visitors of a website into three groups based on the visitor count as low, medium, and high.

Clustering algorithm can also be used to predict the locality that has a high probability for different kinds of crime occurrence. Clustering having the advantage of being an unsupervised machine learning technique helps in identifying similarly behaving patterns by observing the details of the type of crime and its corresponding geo-location.

5.10 Conclusion

The experimental results obtained prove that each clustering mechanism has its own way of creating clusters. A few clustering algorithms such as k-means clustering and density-based clustering can predict the labels of input data points, and thus they behave similar to supervised machine learning techniques. However, other clustering techniques like hierarchical and fuzzy c-means clustering are not capable of predicting labels, and thus they behave similar to unsupervised machine learning techniques. While k-means clustering requires the number of clusters to be specified in the beginning, hierarchical clustering does not. Even though clustering alone does not help us to identify a benign or malicious application, it groups similarly behaving samples into same clusters. These clustered data may further be classified using support vector machines or other classification algorithms. Hence, we may conclude that clustering may be used as an intermediate step in malware detection.

Chapter 6
Nearest Neighbor and Fingerprint Classification

6.1 Introduction

Nearest neighbors (NN) is a supervised machine learning technique. The basic principle of a NN algorithm is to find the neighbors located near to each data point in the test dataset and then assign it to a class that is most represented by the neighbors. NN classifier works by taking into consideration the maximum number of nearest neighbors belonging to the similar class. NN is a simple algorithm that stores all available cases and predicts the numerical target based on a similarity measure, which is a distance function.

NN is an instance-based learning. It does not attempt to construct a general model; instead, it stores instances of the training data. The data point is classified and labeled based on the label of its neighboring data points. For instance, NN could be used in the areas of pattern recognition such as malware detection by identifying the system call patterns, intrusion detection systems (IDS) by observing the incoming and outgoing network packets by capturing the *pcap* files, fingerprint recognition, and so on. In all the above cases, the basic principle of NN remains the same. The application of NN in classifying images is an interesting area of research. We shall see, in the last section of this chapter, more about how to obtain some useful information about each type of fingerprint pattern and classify them accordingly. Similar to clustering, NN invokes different distance measures to determine how far the data points are separated apart. Nearest neighbors are mainly of two different types: k-nearest neighbors (k-NN) and radius-based nearest neighbors.

As the name indicates, k-NN considers k number of neighbors surrounding the data sample to be classified. The basic principle of a k-NN algorithm is to find the k neighbors located near to each data point in the test dataset and then assign it to a class that is most represented by the neighbors. Classification is solely dependent on the value of k. Larger k may suppress the noise effects but may make the classification boundaries to overlap. In k-NN, the value of k solely depends on the type of dataset. Thus, if the value of k equals 5 in the case of malware classification, k may or may not be equal to 5 in the case of fingerprint classification. The major difference

T. Thomas et al., *Machine Learning Approaches in Cyber Security Analytics*, https://doi.org/10.1007/978-981-15-1706-8_6

between the symbol k in k-means clustering and k-NN is that k indicates the number of clusters in the former and the number of neighbors to be considered to categorize a sample from an unknown class in the latter.

Radius-based nearest neighbors are used in those cases where the data is not uniformly sampled. Here, the nearest neighbors are determined by finding the neighboring points surrounding the test data to be classified within a radius r of the test data. A specific radius r is chosen, and those nearest neighbors that fall within the boundary are considered for classification. In high-dimensional spaces, this method performs poorly, due to the curse of dimensionality.

NN is a nonparametric and lazy learning algorithm. It uses a dataset in which the data points are separated into several classes to predict the classification of a new data point. A technique is said to be nonparametric if it does not make any assumptions on the underlying data distribution and the model structure is determined from the data itself. This is pretty useful, because in many cases most of the data does not follow any typical theoretical distribution. Therefore, NN could be one of the first choices for a classification study when there is little or no prior knowledge about the distribution of the data. NN is also a lazy algorithm (as opposed to an eager algorithm). This means that it does not use the training data points to do any generalization. That is, there is only a minimal or no explicit training phase. This makes the training phase pretty fast.

The k-NN graph of any dataset is obtained by connecting each data point in the set to its k closest neighbors in the dataset, where any distance calculating measure determines the closeness. When it becomes impractical to find such k neighbors while handling data of higher dimension, we adopt data structures like ball tree, k-d tree, etc. to do the nearest neighbor search so as to classify the point of interests in the test dataset. Predictions are made for a test data point by searching through the entire training set for the k-most similar instances (the neighbors) and finding the classes to which those k instances belong to.

NN is used to tackle both classification and regression problems. In solving classification problems, input points are placed into appropriate categories that are already known, whereas regression involves predicting a relationship between input points and the rest of the data points.

Using k-NN for solving classification problems involves calculating the label with highest number of occurrences (or frequency) from the k nearby instances. The probability of each class (or label) is calculated as the normalized frequency of k-most similar samples of a test data point that belong to each class. The choice of k defines the locality of k-NN. For large k, the classifier generalizes ignoring small agglomerations of patterns. In the case of large datasets, k-NN has to search for the k-nearest patterns in the whole space but can yield a good approximation based on the k-nearest neighbors in a scanned subset. While classification experiments are conducted, cross-validation is employed to choose the best value for k. This is also to avoid over-fitting. Cross-validation is done, to split-up the dataset to be classified into training, validation, and test set.

k-NN is also used for solving multi-class classification problems, as in pattern recognition. When k-NN is used for regression problems, the prediction is based on the mean or the median of the k-most similar instances.

6.2 NN Regression

In NN regression, the labels are not classes, instead are real values or discrete values. Let $\{(x_i, y_i)\}$ be an example training set, with x_i being the ith data point and y_i being the corresponding label which is a discrete or real value. The NN regression algorithm is given in Algorithm 6.1.

Algorithm 6.1 NN Regression Algorithm

1: Compute the distance $d(x, x_i)$ for every sample x_i in the training dataset to the test data x.
2: Select k instances x_{i_j} for $1 \leq j \leq k$ from the dataset where $d(x, x_{i_j})$ are the least. Let $y_{i_1}, y_{i_2}, \ldots, y_{i_k}$ be their corresponding labels.
3: Calculate the label y of x as the mean of the k labels, $y = \frac{1}{k} \sum_{j=1}^{k} y_{i_j}$

6.3 K-NN Classification

Proper identification of the neighbors that surround a data point is necessary in classification. NN is an instance-based machine learning. In a usual k-NN search, k number of neighbors lying close to the data sample to be classified are considered. The closeness of k closest instances are determined by a distance metric. In higher dimensional spaces, this can be computationally inefficient. One of the major problems of high-dimensional data is the determination of nearest neighbors/closest points. Thus, it is necessary to speed up the performance by finding the k closest neighbors by sorting the samples based on some data structure such as ball tree or KD tree. These algorithms mainly aimed at reducing the number of computations required to be made to calculate the distance among the samples in the dataset.

Consider a two-dimensional dataset. The simplest way to classify the data points using k-NN is to first calculate the distance from the data point to be classified to every other point in the training dataset. During classification, the data point to be classified is considered to belong to that class which contains the majority of neighbors surrounding the point of interest. This is called brute force method. The brute force k-NN classification algorithm is given in Algorithm 6.2.

Consider a training dataset containing n number of samples of dimension d, then the runtime complexity of brute force algorithm is given by $O(dn^2)$. Brute force works well with a good performance when the dataset size is small and the samples are of lesser dimension. However, the performance of brute force algorithm

Algorithm 6.2 Brute Force k-NN Classification Algorithm

1: Compute the distance $d(x, x_i)$ for every sample x_i in the training dataset to the test data x.
2: Select k instances x_{i_j} for $1 \leq j \leq k$ from the dataset where $d(x, x_{i_j})$ are the least. Let $y_{i_1}, y_{i_2}, \ldots, y_{i_k}$ be their corresponding labels.
3: Assign the label y of x as the majority of the labels $y_{i_1}, y_{i_2}, \ldots, y_{i_k}$.

drops significantly and becomes practically useless with increase in dataset size and dimension.

6.4 Preparing Data for K-NN

The methods that may be used to best prepare data for k-NN are given below:

1. Normalization: Data scaling is very much important when it comes to classification of data using nearest neighbors. k-NN is always found to perform well if the data has the same scale. It is better to normalize the input data in the range of [0, 1]. This is done when we have numeric input data.
2. Dimensionality reduction techniques: Though k-NN works on high-dimensional data, its performance is seen to reduce tremendously in those instances. k-NN better suits lower dimensional data, and thus can benefit from good feature selection techniques, thereby reducing the dimensionality of the input data points.

In the case of fingerprint recognition, instead of extracting all features from the entire image, it is better to crop the desired section and extract features from the cropped section alone. This helps in removing unnecessary noise and unwanted sections in the fingerprint.

6.5 Locality-Sensitive Hashing (LSH)

Locality-sensitive hashing (LSH) is a dimensionality reduction technique, used to eliminate the duplicate samples which also includes data points that may not be exactly similar. When malware detection is carried out on very large datasets, there are chances for samples belonging to the same family to have similar set of permissions and API calls. In such situations, locality-sensitive hashing technique helps in reducing the dataset for easy and precise clustering. Similar elements are mapped into the same bucket. Locality-sensitive hashing is defined only for the following distance metrics: Cosine similarity, Jaccard similarity, Hamming distance, and Euclidean distance.

Let Q be a query point such that LSH searches for the approximate nearest neighbor points of Q from a set of data samples in the Euclidean space. The hash function used by LSH ensures that points located near to each other are stored in the same bucket with a higher probability and points located far apart are stored in the same bucket with a lower probability. In this case, the LSH only needs to search points within the bucket corresponding to Q. In addition, LSH uses multiple hash functions to reduce the probability that a point near to Q goes unnoticed. LSH has proved its efficiency in both theory and experiments for high-dimensional data.

6.6 Algorithms to Compute Nearest Neighbors

Proper identification of the neighbors that surround a data point is necessary in classification. As mentioned earlier, nearest neighbor is an instance-based machine learning. In a usual k-nearest neighbor search, k number of neighbors lying close to the data sample to be classified is considered. The closeness of k closest instances is defined by a distance metric. In higher dimensional planes, this can be computationally inefficient. Thus, it is necessary to speed up the performance by finding the k closest neighbors by sorting the samples based on some data structure such as ball tree or KD tree. We shall take a look at different algorithms that are used for finding the nearest neighbors.

6.6.1 Brute Force

Consider a two-dimensional dataset. The simplest way to classify the data points using k-nearest neighbor is to calculate the distance from the data point to be classified called the point of interest, to every other point in the training dataset. During classification, the data point to be classified is considered to belong to that class which contains the majority of neighbors surrounding the point of interest. This is called brute force method.

Consider a dataset containing n number of samples of dimension d, then the runtime complexity is given by $O[dn^2]$. Brute force works fine with a good performance when the dataset size is small and the samples are of lesser dimension. But the performance of brute force drops tremendously and becomes unfeasible with increase in dataset size and dimension.

6.6.2 KD Tree

KD tree stands for K-dimensional tree. It generalizes different tree structures such as binary tree, quad-tree, oct-tree, etc., where each node in the tree will have K number of nodes: 2 in case of binary trees, 4 in case of quad-trees, 8 in the case of oct-trees, etc. It is a sorted hierarchical data structure. It is used to find the nearest neighbors in higher dimensional spaces. One of the major problems of high-dimensional data is the difficulty in finding nearest neighbors.

The computational cost of KD tree is $O[dn \log N]$ indicating that the performance of KD tree algorithm will be very high for a higher value of N. But for a higher value of dimension D, this algorithm takes more time which is also termed as the curse of dimensionality.

6.6.2.1 KD Tree Construction

The two basic steps involved in the construction of a KD tree are to find a median after traversing the whole tree and then to split the dataset along the median. Just as we construct a binary search tree data structure to classify a dataset constituting data points of d-dimension, a K-dimensional tree partitions data points of dimension d. KD trees recursively partition a region of space, creating a binary space partition at each level of the tree.

To start with, take a set of two-dimensional dataset, our aim is to build a data structure by picking any random dimension, find the median, and split the dataset along the median. This data structure would organize the dataset as a binary search tree, and then to find the nearest neighbors of the query point it would navigate down the tree starting from the root node. In binary search trees, the binary partition of the real line is at each internal node and is represented by a "point" on the real line. Similarly, the binary partition of a two-dimensional Cartesian plane at each internal node in the case of KD tree is represented by a line in the plane. Thus, any line passing through the point represented by the internal node partitions the two-dimensional Cartesian plane.

1. For a two-dimensional dataset, choose the dimension having the greatest spread of values, and find the median of that attribute.
2. Use the median to split the dataset evenly (if possible).
3. Next, choose median of the y attribute of this subset.
4. Whenever a median of the x attribute is chosen, draw a line perpendicular to x-axis. Similarly, for each median chosen for the y-axis, a line is drawn perpendicular to the y-axis.
5. The depth of the tree can never be greater than $log_2 N$, where N is the total number of elements in the dataset. This is because the tree is going to end up with singleton sets if the depth increases than $log_2 N$.

A non-leaf node in KD tree divides the space into two parts, known as half-spaces. Points to the left of this space are represented by the left sub-tree of that node, and points to the right of the space are represented by the right sub-tree. For a given query point q, the search is done by traversing the tree from the root node. Once the search encounters the leaf region containing the query, simple linear search is used to find and store the k-nearest neighbors of the query point from among the points in that region. This tree can be used to find the nearest neighbors of any test data point.

6.6.3 Ball Tree

Ball tree, a nested set model, works by partitioning data points into hierarchical sets (or nested sets) of hyperspheres in a multidimensional space so as to make it convenient for nearest neighbor search in a much more organized way. Ball tree construction algorithm aims in addressing the computational inefficiency of KD tree algorithm in higher dimensions by assuming the data to be in a multidimensional space. It then creates nested hyperspheres. The time complexity for querying is $O[dlog(n)]$. While KD tree make use of lines parallel to the Cartesian plane, ball trees make use of hyperspheres to classify data. In ball tree algorithm, the entire dataset n is taken to be the root node and may be represented as in Fig. 6.1.

More hyperspheres are constructed such that no two hypersphere contains the same data point. In Fig. 6.1, each "**x**" represents a data point. Root node is indicated by the outer bigger circle, and each smaller circle indicates a hypersphere.

In a ball tree data structure, each node of the binary tree would be a hypersphere with exactly two data points. The hyperspheres may or may not overlap but each data point can only belong to a single node. Every hypersphere has a predefined radius R and a centroid C. Calculating the distance of the data point to the center of the ball would help us decide that ball of which the data point would belong to. The data point always belongs to that ball for which the distance to the centroid is the least. If the distance of the data point to both the centroids happens to be the same, it may belong to any one of the balls in the intersection. Balls in the tree data structure may or may not intersect, and are defined by the leaf nodes in the tree. The data points are always enumerated within the ball. This explanation of how a data point can be categorized iterates the fact that a ball tree is a hierarchical structured

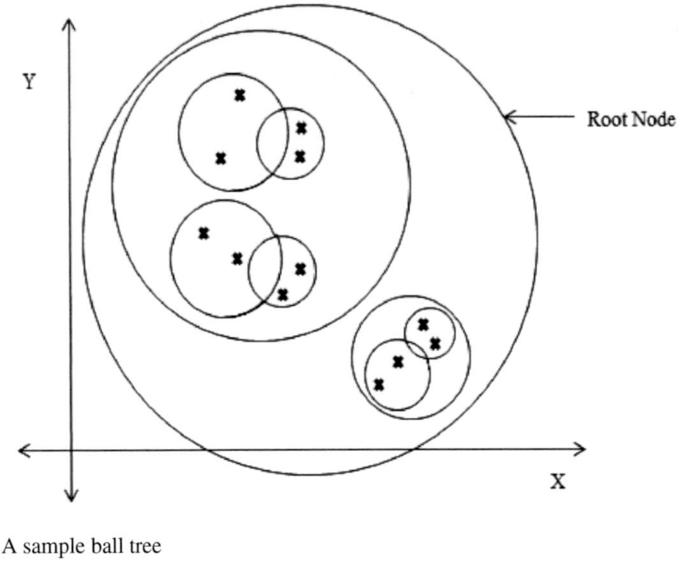

Fig. 6.1 A sample ball tree

binary tree. Each node in a ball tree defines the smallest ball that contains all the data points in its sub-tree. One of the most important properties of a ball tree is that the distance of a test data point t to any other data point in ball B within the tree is either equal to or greater than the distance from the ball to t.

To begin with, two ball-like structures called clusters are created. Any data point to be classified will belong to either of the clusters but not both. The ball tree defines a radius R and centroid C to recursively divide the dataset into various nodes, such that each data point in the node lies within the hypersphere defined by R and C. According to the triangle inequality $|m| + |n| \geq |l|$, sum of any two sides is always greater than the third side of the triangle. The triangle inequality is used to reduce the number of candidate points while doing a neighbor search, it also helps in reducing the search time. Thus it is enough to calculate the distance between a test data point and the centroid of a ball to determine the upper bound and lower bound on the distance to all data points within the node. Remembering the fact that ball tree is a binary tree, each ball thereby created is further subdivided into two subclusters. These subclusters resemble a ball, implying that it has a centroid and distance from the subcluster to the centroid decides whether the data point belongs to the ball or not. The sub–sub-balls are again divided until it reaches a predefined depth. To find the nearest neighbors of a test data point and subsequently the class to which it might belong to, the primary step is to include it in any of the nested balls in the ball tree. We assume that the data points lying within this nested ball are the ones more closer to the target point (test data point). A non-leaf node does not contain any data point and thus points to two child nodes. Though ball tree construction takes a lot of time and memory initially, identification of nearest data points becomes much easier once nested hyperspheres are created.

6.6.3.1 Nearest Neighbor Search Using Ball Tree

Nearest neighbor often require the construction of a graph so as to enable a quicker search. As said earlier, no two data points can belong to more than one hypersphere. As a primary step, construct a ball tree data structure and carry out a nearest neighbor search in the ball tree. While the data points are split by plotting lines parallel to the Cartesian axes in KD tree, ball trees split data into a set of hyperspheres, with two close set of data points belonging to the same hypersphere. The hyperspheres may intersect, but each data point belong to either of the hypersphere. This is based on the distance of that data point from the ball's centroid. Each leaf node in the tree enumerates all the data points inside that ball. For any given data point t, the distance to any data point in a hypersphere B in the tree is greater than or equal to the distance from t to the hypersphere. While searching for the nearest neighbors of a test data point t in a ball tree data structure, assume that we come across a data point p that appears to be close to t; then, all those sub-trees whose child nodes are further from t than p are ignored for the rest of the search.

Nearest neighbor search is done in ball trees using depth-first order search. The depth-first order search starts at the root node and traverses all the necessary nodes.

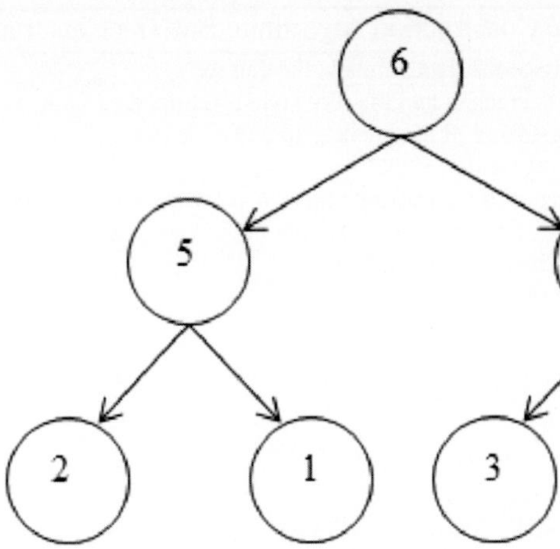

Fig. 6.2 An example heap tree

Fig. 6.3 Priority queue array, *arr*

6	5	4	2	1	3
[1]	[2]	[3]	[4]	[5]	[6]

One of the most important applications of ball trees is to use it to query every data points using the nearest neighbor technique using some distance metric. During the search, the algorithm maintains a max-first priority queue. The queue is implemented using a heap. There are different data structures using which a priority queue can be implemented (Fig. 6.2).

An array is starting at position 1 is maintained to create the priority queue. Figure 6.3 shows the priority queue constructed from the heap tree.

1. $arr[1]$ has the root node of the heap tree.
2. $arr[2]$ has the left child of the node.
3. $arr[3]$ has the right child.
4. A node at position $arr[k]$ has its left child in array $arr[k \star 2]$ and right child in array $arr[k \star 2 + 1]$.
5. If a node is in array $arr[k]$ then it would have its parent in array $arr[k/2]$.

Now let us take a look at the algorithm to construct a ball tree data structure.

The property followed by a maximum heap tree is as follows: *The value of a node is always less than or equal to the value of its parent node.* A heap tree is not a sorted tree structure and hence is considered to be partially ordered. Thus, there is no relationship between nodes in the different levels and same level. While inserting a new element to a heap tree, it is initially appended to the end of heap tree. Based on the heap property, the elements of the tree are rearranged so that the newly added element would be placed in its exact index position. Consider a scenario where a new node *N* when inserted into a tree causes imbalance. Pivot node is said to be that

Algorithm 6.3 Ball Tree Construction Algorithm, BallTreeConstruct()

Input: N: an array consisting of the data points in the dataset
Output: BT: The Ball Tree is created, and the root node is returned
Initialization: d is the dimension of the greatest spread of points,
p is the median of points along d,
L is the set of points lying to the left of p along c, R is the set of points lying to the right of p along c

if a single point remains **then**
  Create a node BT, that contains the only data point in N
  Return BT
else
  Create BT with two children, where
  $BT.pivot$ is the median
  The function $BallTreeConstruct(L)$ and $BallTreeConstruct(R)$ is invoked to create the children
  return BT
end if

imbalanced node found on the path traversed from root node to the leaf node such that p is farthest from the root node.

Now let us take a look at the algorithm to understand how a nearest neighbor search is done in a ball tree data structure.

Algorithm 6.4 KnnSearch(t, k, Q, B)

Input: k: maximum number of nearest neighbors to be searched for
t: Test data point to be classified
Q: max-first priority queue containing all the k points
B: any node (or hypersphere) in the tree
Output: Q: max-first priority queue containing k-Nearest Neighbors of t

$c1$ is the child node closest to the test data point t
$c2$ is the child node farthest from the test data point t
if distance between t and current node B is greater than the distance between t and the furthest point in Q **then**
  Return Q without any change
else if B is a leaf node **then**
  for each data point p in the node B **do**
    if distance between t and p is less than the distance between t and the first element of Q **then**
      add the data point p to the priority queue Q
      if the total number of elements in the priority queue Q exceeds the maximum limit k **then**
        Eliminate the furthest element of Q
      end if
    end if
  end for
else
  do $KnnSearch(t, k, Q, c1)$
  do $KnnSearch(t, k, Q, c2)$
end if

In situations where the dimensions of datasets are very high, ball tree data structure proves to be an efficient technique.

6.7 Radius-Based Nearest Neighbor

Radius-based nearest neighbor algorithm attempts to find all the neighbors separated from a data point to be classified at a specific radius. When too a small radius is used so that there are no neighbors for a test sample, code crashes.

In Fig. 6.4, R represents the radius hyperparameter, X indicates a sample taken from the test dataset and the all *dots* within the circle and the observations that lie inside the radius which vote to predict the class. If a sample that has to be classified using radius-based nearest neighbors, then a circular area is considered around the data point to be classified to find those training samples similar to it. In k-NN, the distance measure is considered that the sample to be classified is given the label of the maximum number of neighbors that surround the point of interest at a defined distance. Here we specify the radius to find the family into which a neighbor observation belongs to. Some parameters that are considered are

1. radius hyperparameter and
2. outlier label.

It decides what label to give a data point that has no other data points within a radius (a useful tool/strategy for identifying outliers).

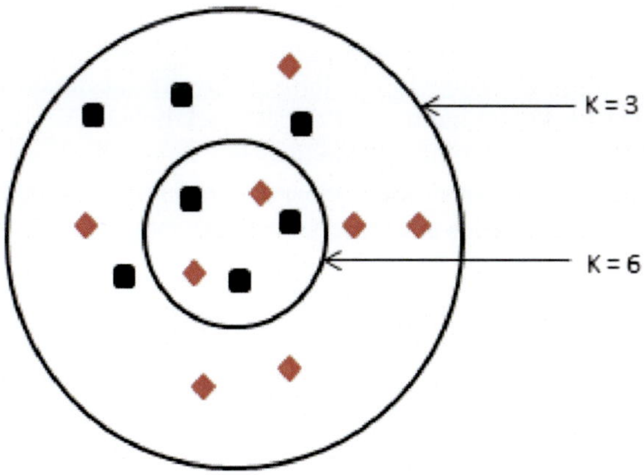

Fig. 6.4 A sample radius-based Nearest Neighbor representation

6.8 Applications of NN in Biometrics

In this section, we will examine the application of NN in fingerprint biometrics. NN are mostly used in solving classification problems, and thus can be used to classify images. Fingerprint is one of the oldest biometric modalities and is still used widely. Each and every human being is assumed to have unique fingerprints. With the growing use of biometric authentication systems, it has become important to detect fraudulent fingerprints. As it is very easy to spoof fingerprints using gelatin, silicon, wood glue, paper print, etc., it has become very essential to have a safe fingerprint detection system so as to successfully distinguish spoofed fingerprints from authentic fingerprints.

Detecting fake from original fingerprints is out of scope of this chapter. Instead, we will be concentrating on fingerprint classification based on their patterns. Fingerprint matching is of prominence in crime scenes. Most of the criminal cases demand fingerprint matching as one of the criteria for identifying the criminal. An investigation department would hence have a huge fingerprint database of previously known criminals and suspects. It would be impractical to search for a suspects fingerprint by testing a one-to-one match on the entire database. This is where classification algorithms like NN find relevance. Each fingerprint pattern has a unique orientation. Different methods are adopted to find the orientation of fingerprints, and NN algorithm is used to find the class to which the suspects fingerprint may belong to. Once the class is identified, a perfect match can be checked with the fingerprint samples belonging to that particular class.

For the purpose of conducting experiments, we used a CSD200 model "Single Finger Livescan Capture Device without Membrane" manufactured by the 3M company. Ten unique fingerprints of each finger acquired from ten people (100 fingerprints in total) are taken. Minutiae points are local ridge characteristics that are found at ridge endings and ridge bifurcations. A fingerprint can be seen as a pattern of valleys (bright lines) and interleaved ridges (dark lines). They run in parallel or may bifurcate. Ridges are the thin visible lines in a fingerprint image, and the space between two ridges is called a valley. A clear understanding of minutiae is necessary in image processing, as it gives a detailed knowledge about the different features that fingerprints posses.

Although there are numerous generic and specific classes for fingerprints, we shall only consider the following most prominent fingerprint patterns here: *Tented Arch, Arch, Whorl, Right Loop, Left Loop*, and *Double Loop* as shown in Fig. 6.5. Fingerprints belonging to a class differ from other classes based on their ridge patterns, number of core and delta points, etc. Core refers to the innermost point of a loop in a fingerprint, and delta refers to a ridge pattern that resembles the Greek letter Δ. While arch has no core and delta point, whorl has a single core point where the ridges are found to converge in a spiral fashion. Tented arch has one or more delta points. Both right loop and left loop can either have a core point alone or can also have both a core point and delta point. Figure 6.6 shows a right loop fingerprint with $\circ$ indicating the core and Δ indicating the delta.

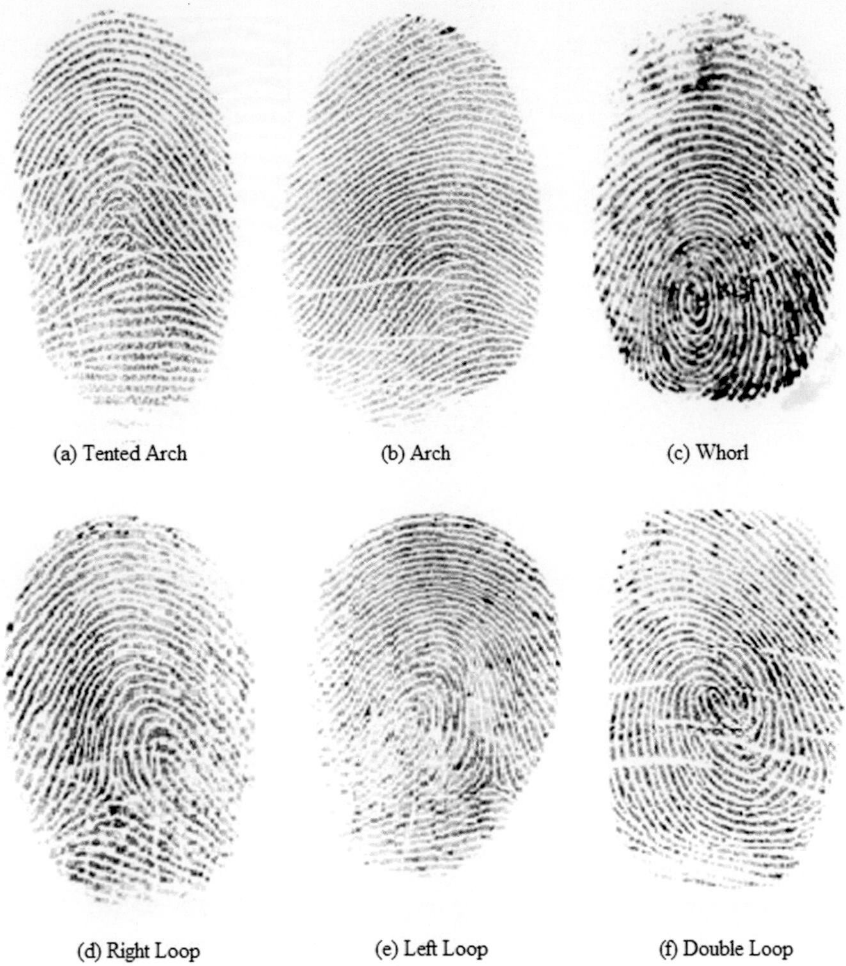

Fig. 6.5 Fingerprint classes

A few other variations seen in the classes are shown in Fig. 6.7. The highlighted rectangular box in (a) shows a fingerprint print feature called island which is a small line type of ridge that stands alone; (b) has two core points (indicated by red circles) resembling a double loop, but also has a delta point (indicated by a red-colored triangle); (c) is a whorl like fingerprint having two delta points and one core point. The classification process is shown in Fig. 6.8.

Matlab uses a function *level = grraythresh(I)* to compute a global threshold value of an input image I, which is later used to convert an intensity image to a binary image. *im2bw(I, threshold_level)* converts a grayscale image I to a binary image. It is necessary to convert fingerprint images into binary images to facilitate easy processing. It replaces all pixels in the input image with a pixel value greater than

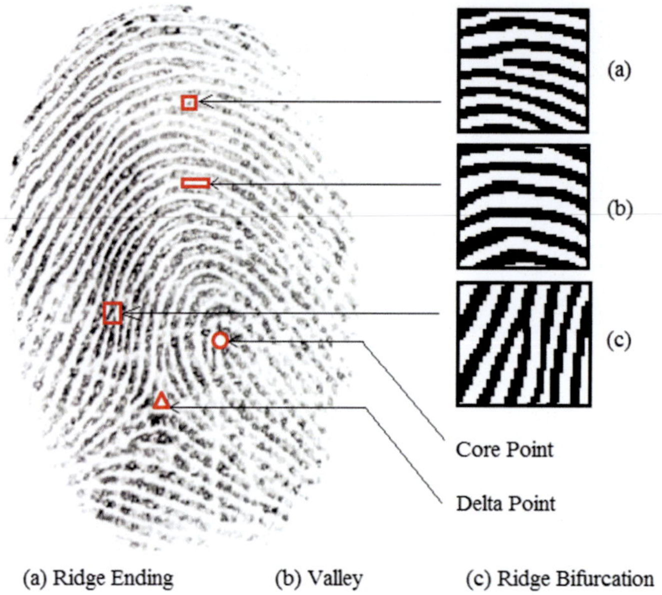

Fig. 6.6 Fingerprint features

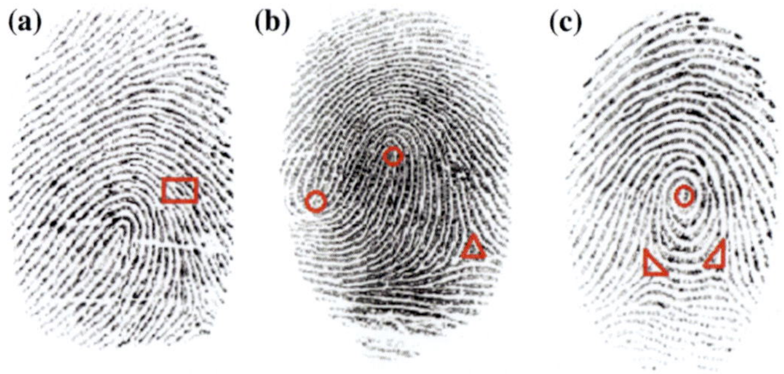

Fig. 6.7 Fingerprint classes

a particular *threshold value* with 1 (white) and replaces all other values of pixels with 0 (black). Basically, images are represented in Matlab as an $m \times n$ array, where each cell of the array represents the pixel value. *graythresh* aims in minimizing the intra-class variance of the black and white pixels. For this purpose, *graythresh* makes use of the Otsu's method. Otsu's threshold is used to convert a grayscale images into a monochrome image. In monochrome images, each pixel is stored as a single bit either "0" or "1", whereas in grayscale images each pixel is stored as a byte (any value between "0" and "255").

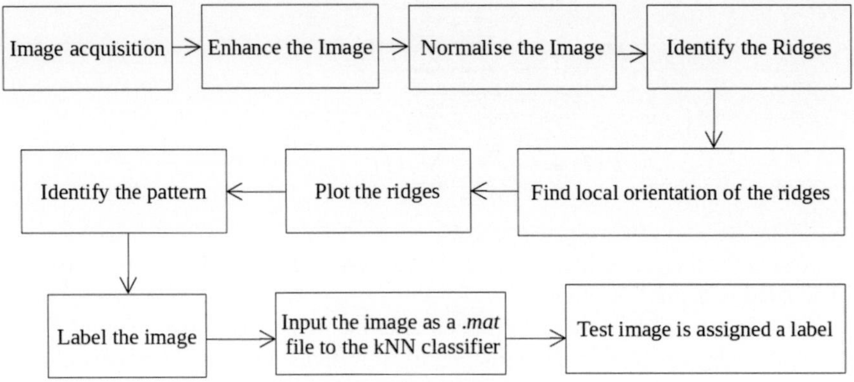

Fig. 6.8 Pattern recognition and classification of fingerprints

Binarization helps to improve the contrast between the ridges and valleys, thereby facilitating efficient minutiae extraction. Minutiae extraction is a vital part of fingerprint detection, and the feature extraction purely depends on the image quality. It is in order to obtain ridges of improved quality, enhancement algorithms are used. The inspiration behind using an enhancement algorithm is to improve the clarity of the ridges in a fingerprint, so that the essential minutiae points can be extracted. The success rate of the enhancement algorithm is determined by examining the spurious ridges, which when enhanced gives a fingerprint from which no relevant information can be inferred.

Let I be a grayscale fingerprint image defined as an $m \times n$ array, and $I(i, j)$ represent the intensity of a pixel at ith row and jth column. Then the orientation image O is defined as an $m \times n$ array where $O(i, j)$ is the local ridge orientation of a pixel at ith row and jth column.

Oriented filters are used to enhance the fingerprint image which thereby reduces the creation of fake ridges to an extent. First, the fingerprint image is normalized to a desired value of mean and variance. This is to rescale the image so that the minimum value is 0 and the maximum value is 1.

The intensity values in an image are standardized by normalization. The gray-level values are adjusted to lie within a desired range of values. Let $N(i, j)$ represent the normalized gray-level value at pixel (i, j), $I(i, j)$ represents the gray-level value at pixel (i, j), M and V be the estimated mean and variance, and M_0 and V_0 be the desired mean and variance, respectively. Then the normalized image is given by

$$N(i, j) = \begin{cases} M_0 + \sqrt{\frac{V_0(I(i,j)-M)^2}{V}} & \text{if } I(i, j) > M, \\ M_0 - \sqrt{\frac{V_0(I(i,j)-M)^2}{V}} & \text{otherwise.} \end{cases}$$

The mean and variance are given by

$$M(I) = \frac{1}{b^2} \sum_{i=\frac{-b}{2}}^{\frac{b}{2}} \sum_{j=\frac{-b}{2}}^{\frac{b}{2}} I(i, j)$$

$$V(I) = \frac{1}{b^2} \sum_{i=\frac{-b}{2}}^{\frac{b}{2}} \sum_{j=\frac{-b}{2}}^{\frac{b}{2}} (I(i, j) - M(I))^2,$$

where I is the image, (i, j) are the pixel locations, and b is the block size (explained in detailed in the next section).

The ridge orientations are determined after identifying the ridge regions. To calculate the ridge orientation of an image, first it is divided into $b \times b$ nonoverlapping blocks, and a single local ridge orientation is found for each block. The block is taken to be a part of the image only if its standard deviation is above the threshold value set. Here, the method used for finding the orientation image corresponding to a fingerprint image is *least mean square estimation algorithm*. The steps involved in the algorithm are as follows:

1. Divide the image I into $b \times b$ nonoverlapping blocks.
2. Calculate the gradients $\partial_x(i, j)$ and $\partial_y(i, j)$ for each pixel in the block at (i, j). This is to aid the gradient orientation estimation, and finally to plot the ridge orientation.
3. Now estimate the local orientation of each block b by fixing the center pixel (i, j). After plotting the orientation of a fingerprint image, assign it a label (any number between 1 and 6). For instance, 1 is the label for left loop, 2 for right loop, and so on.

$$L_x(i, j) = \sum_{u=i-\frac{b}{2}}^{i+\frac{b}{2}} \sum_{v=j-\frac{b}{2}}^{j+\frac{b}{2}} 2\partial_x(u, v)\partial_y(u, v)$$

$$L_y(i, j) = \sum_{u=i-\frac{b}{2}}^{i+\frac{b}{2}} \sum_{v=j-\frac{b}{2}}^{j+\frac{b}{2}} (\partial_x^2(u, v)\partial_y^2(u, v))$$

$$\theta(i, j) = \frac{1}{2} \tan^{-1}(\frac{L_y(i, j)}{L_x(i, j)})$$

Here, $\theta(i, j)$ is the least square estimate of the local ridge orientation at the block which has (i, j) as the center pixel, and L_x, L_y are the directional orientations of ridges in each block.

6.8.1 *Brute Force Classification*

Let us take a look at how fingerprints will be classified using the brute force method. Our aim is to label the unknown incoming test fingerprint images I_{test} through brute

Fig. 6.9 Test fingerprint image

force method. The primary step is to create a training dataset, containing images I_{train} with appropriate class labels. We take the image shown in Fig. 6.9 as the test image I_{test} to assign an appropriate label.

A desired portion of the image $f \times f$ is cropped by selecting it using the tool *imcrop* in Matlab such that $f < \min\{m, n\}$, where m and n are the actual dimensions of the image. This is done so that we will have uniformly sized training and test images. This is shown in Fig. 6.10. The binarized image is shown in Fig. 6.11.

The ridge orientation looks as shown in Fig. 6.12. Images with different patterns were identified, while the experiment was done. The image with its corresponding binary image and ridge orientation are shown in Figs. 6.13, 6.14, 6.15, 6.16, and 6.17.

Once the ridge orientation images corresponding to I_{train} and I_{test} are obtained, the images are further cropped such that the core point remains in the center. This step may be skipped for images with no core point (as in Arch class). The array corresponding to the new set of orientation images is the multidimensional feature vector that is used for finding the nearest neighbors. For labeling the training images, we assign class labels to each of I_{train} by visually observing them. To find the nearest neighbors of I_{test}, the distance between I_{test} and each of the I_{train} in the training set of images is calculated. Any distance calculating function such as Euclidean, Mahalanobis, etc. can be used to measure the distance between the corresponding pixels of I_{test} and I_{train}. I_{test} is assigned the class of the majority of I_{train} which are more closer to it.

Fig. 6.10 Selecting the image to be cropped

6.8.2 State of the Art Applications of Nearest Neighbor

With the growing number of IoT devices, an increasing number of attacks such as replay attack, DoS attack, false routing information attack, etc. are seen. Nearest neighbors can be used to model an IDS to detect intrusions in a wireless sensor network.

Android malware detection can be done by extracting various features such as permissions, API calls, CPU–RAM usage, system calls, etc. Among them, one of the most efficient techniques is malware detection using kernel-level API calls. The dynamic API calls captured are stored within a CSV file. Calculating the nearest neighbors of API calls corresponding to a particular application (might be a malware or a goodware) helps to identify the similarly behaving samples. The resulting dataset can then be used to train nearest neighbor classification algorithm.

An approach that can be adopted to detect attacks targeting IoT devices is to monitor the energy consumption and analyze the characteristics of the energy data to identify the type of attack. Collect the energy consumption data from normally behaving devices and attacked devices, for about 2 hours length. As the captured signals would be too noisy, any suitable filter can be used to obtain clear

Fig. 6.11 Binary image

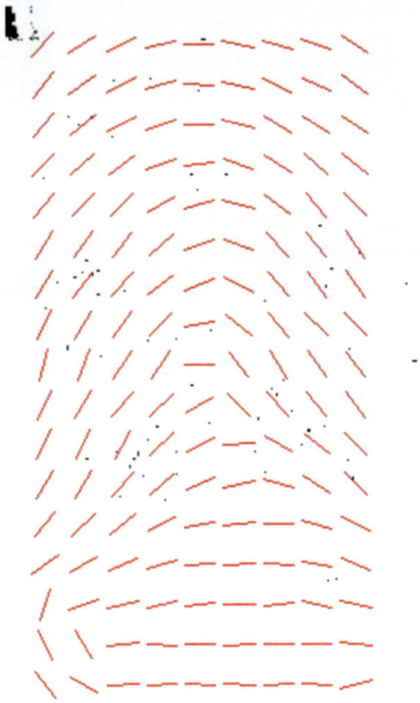

Fig. 6.12 Ridge orientation

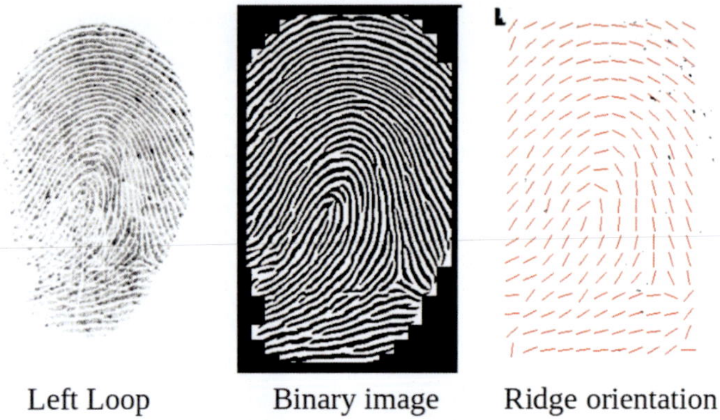

Fig. 6.13 Left loop

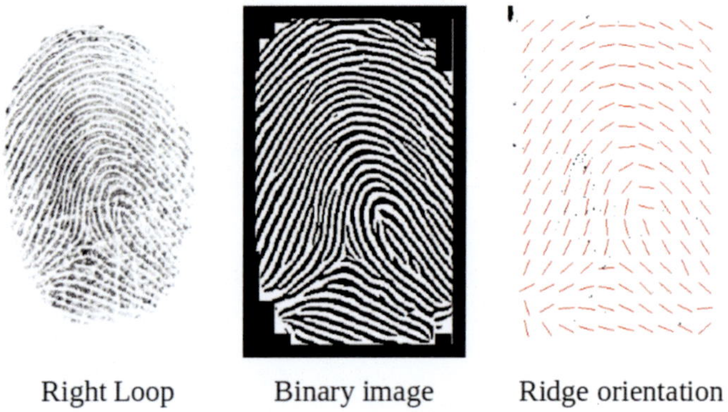

Fig. 6.14 Right loop

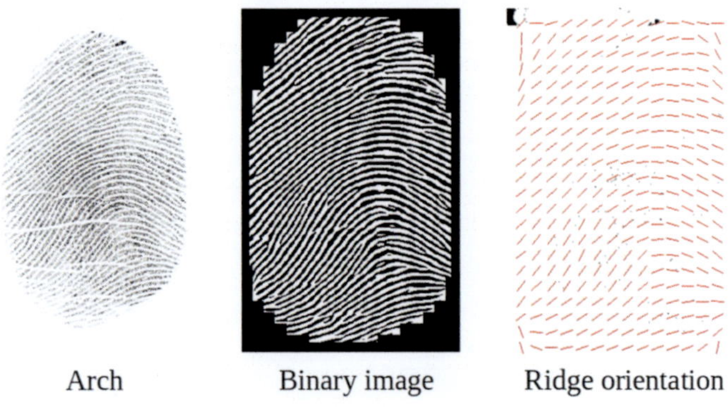

Fig. 6.15 Arch

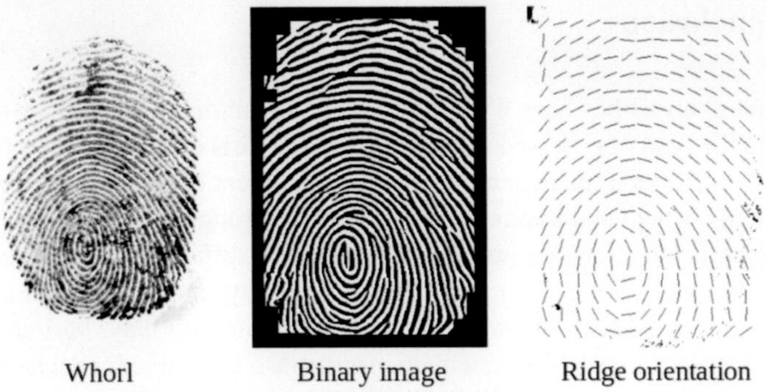

Fig. 6.16 Whorl

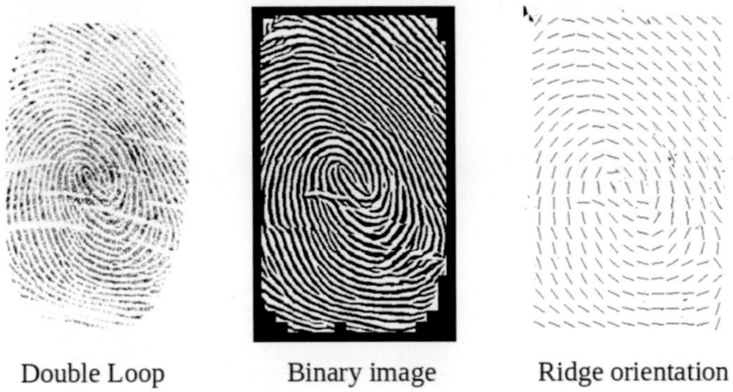

Fig. 6.17 Double loop

and smooth signals within a sliding time window. The features that can be extracted for each windowed signal are minimum and maximum value, cumulative sum, and the real part of the fast Fourier transform (FFT). Nearest neighbor algorithm can then be used to distinguish the feature distribution so as to prepare the dataset for classification.

Nearest neighbors can be used to filter spam emails from legitimate ones as they have been proved to have high F-score value. Specific set of words and phrases helps in identifying spam emails. Spearman's correlation coefficient when used as distance measure has proved to give higher accuracy when compared to traditional distance calculation measures such as Euclidean distance. The class is determined by finding the neighbors lying closest to a point in the test dataset and assigning the text point the class of its nearest neighbors. The dataset for this purpose can be downloaded from the UCI machine learning repository. Recent studies also show that nearest neighbors can be combined with deep learning to improve the robustness of nearest neighbor algorithm against adversarial attacks.

6.9 Conclusion

Fingerprint analysis has been a very important technique in the history of forensic science. In the field of cybersecurity, face or palm or iris or fingerprint or finger vein, recognition has a vital role when it comes to authentication. One of the biggest security problems is the unauthorized entry of people through impersonation. Although biometric authentication systems are believed to be difficult to be cracked or intervened, an increase in the rate of spoofing of these systems for unauthorized entry has been on rise. This is where ML techniques come into play. Various ML techniques can be used to help the system learn and make it capable for decision-making. NN technique as discussed in the earlier sections is a classification-cum regression technique.

Chapter 7
Dimensionality Reduction and Face Recognition

7.1 Introduction

Dimensionality reduction is used to reduce the number of features under consideration, where each feature is a dimension that partly represents the data objects. Dimensionality reduction methods make sure that all the relevant information remains intact while mapping data from a higher dimension to a lower dimension. If more features are added, the dimensionality increases resulting in very sparse dataset and the analysis can suffer from the curse of dimensionality. Further, it is easier and efficient to process smaller datasets. Dimensionality reduction can be carried out using the following two different methods:

- feature selection: selecting significant features from the existing features;
- feature extraction: extracting new features from the existing features.

The mathematical approaches for dimensionality reduction include diffusion maps (DM), principal component analysis (PCA), and random projection (RP). In this chapter, we will focus on PCA. PCA is applied to reduce the complexity of problems faced in the field of cybersecurity such as multi-modal biometrics, face recognition, anomaly detection, intrusion detection, etc. It is one of the most common mechanisms used to identify patterns in higher dimensional data.

7.2 About Principal Component Analysis (PCA)

Being a popular dimensionality reduction technique, PCA aims in finding a linear subspace of dimension m lower than the dimension of the dataset n such that the data points mainly lie in this linear subspace. The PCA aims to find the best linear transformation that reduces the number of dimensions with a minimum loss of information while maintaining most of the variability of the data. The information that was lost may be regarded as noise that does not contribute to the fact we are

T. Thomas et al., *Machine Learning Approaches in Cyber Security Analytics*, https://doi.org/10.1007/978-981-15-1706-8_7

trying to model. The final output is a subspace of much lower dimension which tries to maintain most of the unevenness in the data. We may define the linear subspace using "principal components," which is a newly formed coordinate system on the basis of m orthogonal vectors. There can be no more than n principal components as it is a linear transformation of the original data points and is orthonormal.

PCA aims to approximate $m < n$ number of principal components so as to approximate the space spanned by the original data points. The principal components are determined such that, for a given set of data points $Z = \{z_1, z_2, \ldots, z_t\}$, the m principal components are those orthonormal vectors onto which the variance retained under projection is maximal.

Suppose that all centered observations are stacked into the columns of a $n \times t$ matrix $X = Z - \bar{Z}$, where each column corresponds to an n-dimensional observation and there are t observations. The m dominant (normalized) eigenvectors $U = \{U_1, \ldots, U_m\}$ of the covariance matrix XX^T determine the first m principal components. Another advantage of PCA is that the projection onto the principal subspace minimizes the squared reconstruction error.

7.2.1 PCA Algorithm

The PCA algorithm is given below:

1. Computing the principal components: Calculate XX^T, where $X = Z - \bar{Z}$ and Z is training data matrix. Let $U = \{U_1, \ldots, U_m\}$ be the eigenvectors of XX^T corresponding to the top m eigenvalues.
2. Encoding the training data: Compute $Y = U^T X$ where Y is a $m \times t$ matrix of encodings of the original data.
3. Reconstructing the training data: $\tilde{X} = UY$.
4. Encoding the test data: $y = U^T x$.
5. Reconstructing the test data: $\tilde{x} = Uy$.

7.2.2 Capturing the Variability

In order to capture as much of the variability as possible, we choose the first principal component, U_1, to have the maximum variance. Let the first principal component be a linear combination of X defined by coefficients (or weights) $w = [w_1, \ldots, w_n]$. In matrix form

$$\begin{aligned} U_1 &= w^T X \\ var(U_1) &= var(w^T X) = w^T S w, \end{aligned} \tag{7.1}$$

where S is the $n \times n$ sample covariance matrix of X. Clearly, $var(U_1)$ can be made arbitrarily large by increasing the magnitude of w. Therefore, we choose w to maximize $w^T Sw$ while constraining w to have unit length. That is, we have the optimization problem,

$$\max w^T Sw \quad \text{subject to} \quad w^T w = 1.$$

To solve this optimization problem, a Lagrange multiplier α_1 is introduced,

$$L(w, \alpha) = w^T Sw - \alpha_1(w^T w - 1). \tag{7.2}$$

Differentiating with respect to w gives n equations,

$$Sw = \alpha_1 w. \tag{7.3}$$

Premultiplying both sides by w^T, we have

$$w^T Sw = \alpha_1 w^T w = \alpha_1. \tag{7.4}$$

Thus, $var(U_1)$ is maximized if α_1 is the largest eigenvalue of S. Clearly, α_1 and w are an eigenvalue and an eigenvector of S. Differentiating with respect to the Lagrange multiplier α_1 gives us back the constraint:

$$w^T w = 1. \tag{7.5}$$

This shows that the first principal component is given by the normalized eigenvector with the largest associated eigenvalue of the sample covariance matrix S. A similar argument can show that the d dominant eigenvectors of covariance matrix S determine the first d principal components.

7.2.3 Squared Reconstruction Error

Another property of PCA, is that the projection onto the principal subspace minimizes the squared reconstruction error, $\sum_{i=1}^{t} ||x_i - \tilde{x}_i||^2$. In other words, the principal components of a set of data in $\mathbf{R}^n$ provide a sequence of best linear approximations to that data, for all ranks $d \leq n$. Consider the rank-d linear approximation model as

$$f(y) = \bar{x} + Uy. \tag{7.6}$$

This is the parametric representation of a hyperplane of rank d. For convenience, suppose $\bar{x} = 0$ (otherwise, the observations can be simply replaced by their centered versions). Under this assumption, the rank-d linear model would be $f(y) = Uy$, where U is an $n \times d$ matrix with d orthogonal unit vectors as columns and y is a vector of parameters. Fitting this model to the data by least squares leaves us to minimize the reconstruction error:

$$\sum_{i}^{t} ||x_i - U y_i||^2. \tag{7.7}$$

By partial optimization for y_i, we obtain $y_i = U^T x_i$. The orthogonal matrix U can be obtained as

$$\min_{U} \sum_{i}^{t} ||x_i - U U^T x_i||^2. \tag{7.8}$$

Define $H = UU^T$. H is a $n \times n$ matrix which acts as a projection matrix and projects each data point x_i onto its rank-d reconstruction. In other words, Hx_i is the orthogonal projection of x_i onto the subspace spanned by the columns of U. A unique solution U can be obtained by finding the singular value decomposition (SVD) of X. The solution for U can be expressed as singular value decomposition of $X = U \sum V^T$, since the columns of U in the SVD contain the eigenvectors of XX^T.

In order to apply PCA, all the data points need to be processed beforehand in order to compute the projection. This can be very costly if the dataset is very large. In those cases, a non-adaptive alternative to PCA is needed that chooses the projection before actually using the data. A simple method that tends to work well is to project the data onto a random subspace. In particular, if the data points are $x_1, x_2, \cdots \in \mathbf{R}^n$, we can obtain a random projection by multiplying the data with a random matrix $A \in \mathbf{R}^{m \times n}$ to obtain $Ax_1, Ax_2, \cdots \in \mathbf{R}^m$.

7.3 Compressed Sensing

Compressed sensing is a dimensionality reduction technique which assumes that the original vector is sparse. It is a technique that simultaneously acquires and compresses the data, resulting in a random linear transformation that can compress x without losing information. A signal is called sparse or compressible, if it can be represented with very few coefficients—compared to the signal dimension—while losing exactly no or nearly no signal information. Representing data by these coefficients is called sparse approximation, which forms the foundation of transform coding schemes that exploit signal sparsity and compressibility, including the JPEG, MPEG, and MP3 standard. Consider a vector $x \in \mathbf{R}^d$ that has at most s nonzero elements. That is,

$$||x||_o \stackrel{def}{=} |\{i : x_i \neq 0\}| \leq s. \tag{7.9}$$

x can be compressed through representing it with the help of s (index, value) pairs. As x can be exactly reconstructed from s (index, value), this compression is completely lossless. The main premises of the compressed sensing are the following:

1. It is possible to reconstruct any sparse signal fully if it was compressed by $x \to Wx$, where W is a matrix which satisfies a condition called the restricted isoperimetric property (RIP). A matrix that satisfies this property is guaranteed to have a low distortion of the norm of any sparse representable vector.
2. A linear program can be solved to calculate the reconstruction in polynomial time.
3. A random $n \times d$ matrix is likely to satisfy the RIP condition provided that n is greater than an order of $s \log(d)$.

7.4 Kernel PCA

We have seen that PCA is capable of performing transformations on linearly separable data. Since data in the real world is nonlinear in most of the cases, we might require transforming such data into higher dimensional planes. Kernel PCA makes use of the kernel trick to find the principal components in a higher dimensional space. Kernel PCA is a nonlinear version of PCA.

PCA can be used to model only linear variabilities in high-dimensional data by mapping into a linear subspace. However, in many situations, the datasets have a nonlinear nature. In these cases, the high-dimensional data lie on or near a nonlinear manifold instead of a linear subspace, and therefore PCA cannot model the data correctly. Kernel PCA is designed to address the problem of nonlinear dimensionality reduction. In Kernel PCA, through the use of kernels, the principal components can be computed efficiently in high-dimensional feature spaces. Kernel PCA finds principal components which are nonlinearly related to the input data by performing PCA in a space produced by a nonlinear mapping, where the low-dimensional latent structure is easier to discover.

7.5 Application of PCA in Intrusion Detection

Two major approaches in intrusion detection systems (IDS) are anomaly detection and signature detection. Anomaly detection relies on flagging behaviors that are abnormal, whereas signature detection relies on flagging behaviors that are close to some known intrusion signature pattern. In signature detection, the intrusion patterns are modeled through the construction of a database of attack signatures. Incoming intrusion patterns that match with signatures in the database are labeled as attacks. Some similarity measure is employed in detecting the close match. In anomaly detection, the normal behavior of the system is modeled and incoming intrusion patterns that differ substantially from normal behavior patterns are labeled as attacks.

An IDS can be either network-based or host-based. A network-based IDS, which runs on a single host, is responsible for an entire network, or some network segment, whereas a host-based IDS is only responsible for the host on which it resides.

One of the advantages of using PCA for the detection of network traffic anomalies is its ability to operate on the space of input feature vectors directly without the need to transform the data into another output space.

7.6 Biometrics

As today's technology has sneaked into every nooks and corners of modern living, protection of personal data has become more crucial. Furthermore, the increase of security breaches in networks and identity thefts have clearly indicated the need for a stronger authentication mechanism. This corner stoned the advent and flourishing of biometric-based authentication technology which is an effective method for personal authentication. Biometric technology uses our body as a natural identification system through the application of statistical analysis to physiological or behavioral data.

The practice of using biometric technology for person identification and authentication has its roots in the Babylonian age. In the nineteenth century, a method called Bertillonage used anthropometric measurements to identify criminals. Later, police started using fingerprint identification techniques, developed by Richard Edward Henry of Scotland Yard. This was followed by an evolution of biometric authentication and identification technologies based on different biometric traits such as face, iris, voice, etc. However, automated biometric systems became available only in the last few decades. Now we are in the age of a technological revolution in the field of biometrics with wide range of research and product developments taking place to utilize the complete benefits of this exciting technology in its entirety.

Biometrics deal with measuring the physiological or behavioral information to verify an individuals identify, and hence it is accurate and reliable. Physiological characteristics pertain to visible parts of the human body. These include fingerprint, finger vein, retina, palm geometry, iris, facial structure, etc. Behavioral characteristics are based on what a person does. These include voiceprints, signatures, typing patterns, keystroke pattern, gait, and so on.

A biometric system is a pattern recognition system that functions by acquiring biometric data from an individual, extracting a feature set and comparing this feature set against the template set stored in the database. The two different phases involved in any biometric system are enrolment (registration) and verification (authentication). Users' biometric data is collected for future comparison during enrolment phase, and the collected biometric data (biometric template) is stored in the database. In the verification phase, a user provides his/her biometric data template to the system and the system compares this template with the corresponding template of the user in the database. The verification process aims to establish someone's claimed identity. If a positive match is established, the user will be provided with privileges or access to the system or service. In the case of person identification, the entire database needs to be searched against the query biometric template. As the template can belong to anyone in the database, a one-to-many matching is needed to be examined. A good example of a person identification system is automated fingerprint identification services (AFIS), which is used by many law enforcement agencies to identify and track known criminals.

The biological characteristic used for identification or authentication should be quantifiable or measurable, as only quantifiable characteristic can be compared to obtain a boolean result (match or non-match). The different components in a generic biometric system are sensors or data acquisition module, preprocessing and enhancement module, feature extraction module, matching module, and the decision-making module. Capturing users biometric trait for authentication is performed by the data acquisition module and most of the time the captured data will be in the form of an image. The quality of the acquired biometric data need to be improved for better matching performance in the preprocessing stage. The salient features are then extracted from the enhanced biometric data in the feature extraction stage. The resulting feature template is stored in the database, and it is used for future comparison with query biometric templates in the matching stage. The final decision of the comparison is taken by the decision module based on the match score obtained.

Biometric-based authentication or person identification is currently used in various applications in our life. Biometric systems offer significant advantages over traditional methods of access control such as passwords or tokens in many aspects. Main advantages include the following:

1. Biometric systems are based on who a person is or what a person does, not on what a person knows (password, PIN) or what a person has (token, smart card).
2. Biometrics use a physiological or behavioral characteristic for authentication; it is unique and accurate, and the duplication of a person's biological characteristic is comparatively difficult.
3. Stealing of the biometric data and its re-usage is difficult. Users are relieved from the need to remember passwords and forgery can be minimized as biometric features cannot be shared.

Selecting the appropriate trait suitable for designing a biometric system from the various biometric modalities such as fingerprint, iris, vein, face, etc. is very important. This selection is usually done based on the performance requirements of the target application and different performance aspects of the biometric trait. Different characteristics of the biometric trait are required to be analyzed, and certain metrics need to be evaluated while designing a biometric system.

Biometric systems based on different biometric traits show variations in measuring human characteristics or behavior. A measure of variation is embedded into these systems which can be translated in technical language as false rejection (Type I) error and false acceptance (Type II) error. False rejection causes frustration, whereas false acceptance causes fraud. The setting of the error tolerance is critical to the performance of the system.

Other than the performance metrics, there are some important characteristics of biometric traits which need to be analyzed before fixing the appropriate biometric trait to be used in a given application. The different characteristics of a biometric trait which need to be taken under consideration are as follows:

1. Uniqueness: The selected trait should be sufficiently unique across individuals;
2. Universality: The selected trait should be possessed by almost all the individuals;
3. Permanence: The selected trait should be invariant for sufficiently long duration;
4. Circumvention: It should be computationally hard for an adversary to spoof the selected trait;
5. Inter/intra-class Performance: There should be sufficiently enough distinctiveness between the inter-class templates (templates of two different individuals). Intra-class templates (templates of same individual) should only possess a minimum amount of distinctiveness;
6. Collectability: It should be easy to collect the biometric template of the selected trait from users;
7. Acceptability: The target population should be willing to reveal the selected biometric template to the biometric system and the user interface of the system should be as simple as possible;
8. Cost: The infrastructure cost and the maintenance cost of the system which can process the selected trait should be minimal.

Low values are preferred for the circumvention and the cost, whereas high values are preferred for the other characteristics.

7.7 Face Recognition

Face is one of the most commonly used biometric modalities to recognize people. Face recognition or face biometrics has received much attention from researchers due to various security applications in automatic person identification from a distance. Compared to other biometric traits such as palm print, iris, fingerprint, etc. face biometrics can be non-intrusive. They can be taken even without user's knowledge and further can be used for security-based applications such as criminal identification, face tracking, airport security, and surveillance systems.

Face recognition involves capturing a face image from a video or image. The captured image is then compared with the images stored in the database. Face biometrics involves training known images, classifying them into known classes, and then storing into a database. When a test image is given to the system, it is classified and compared with the images stored in the database. Face biometrics is a challenging field of research due to various issues such as variations in head pose, change in illumination, facial expression, aging, occlusion due to accessories, etc.

Automatic face recognition involves face detection, feature extraction, and face recognition. Face recognition algorithms are broadly classified into two classes: image template based and geometric feature based. The template-based methods compute correlation between face and one or more training templates to determine the face identity. Face templates are constructed using principal component analysis (PCA), linear discriminate analysis (LDA), kernel methods, etc. The geometric feature-based methods use explicit local features and their geometric relations. Multi-resolution mechanisms such as contour lets and ridge lets are useful for analyzing information content of images. Curvelets transform is used for texture classification and image de-noising.

7.8 Application of PCA in Face Recognition

In this section, we shall see the basics of how PCA can be used to reduce the facial features and thereby minimize the time required for facial recognition. PCA has proven to be an effective dimensionality reduction technique for facial images. For a feature vector having numerous variables correlated to each other, PCA can reduce its dimensionality.

Facial detection is a computer vision technology that determines the location and size of human faces. It aims in identifying the facial features alone. Facial recognition is the task of identifying a previously known/unknown face and determining whose face it exactly is. In this case, the facial image is searched for a match in the database.

7.8.1 Eigenfaces of Facial Images

One of the aims of PCA is to reduce the size of an image database. Though dimensionality reduction indirectly implies information loss, the principal components (the best features) determine the best low-dimensional space.

PCA is a dimensionality reduction technique whose primary aim is to represent a face as a linear combination of a set of basis images. Consider a training dataset that consists of a total of t images. Then PCA is used to reduce the dimensionality of each image. In order to carry out this dimensionality reduction, PCA uses orthogonal transformation to convert the set of t images into a set of m uncorrelated variables called eigenfaces. The first eigenface will always have the most dominant features of all the training images. Each succeeding eigenface will show the next most relevant features and so on. Thus, only a first few eigenface is selected and the rest of the eigenfaces are discarded. For easy calculation of the eigenfaces, first the dimension of the original training dataset is reduced.

The eigenfaces depict the most relevant features of the training images. Hence, we may conclude that each training face is made up of proportions of these m eigenfaces. The proportions are the weights associated with each eigenface for a particular training face. The combination of weights corresponding to each eigenface that helps in reconstructing a particular facial image is called the weight vector of that image. Facial recognition is done by calculating the shortest distance at which the weight vector corresponding to the test image lies from the weight vector of an appropriate training face.

7.8.2 PCA Algorithm for Facial Recognition

Let us see how the feature reduction is done in facial images. As we have seen earlier, our aim is to represent a facial image as a linear combination of eigenfaces.

Suppose an unknown facial image comes for recognition. Now this image can also be represented in terms of the selected m eigenfaces. We calculate the weight vector of the test image (i.e., the unknown image) and then find its distance to the weight vectors corresponding to each image in the training set. If the distance is above a particular threshold, then the unknown face is recognized. A few requirements of PCA eigenfaces are as follows:

1. Each pixel in an image is considered to be a separate dimension. Thus an image of size $n \times n$ will have n^2 dimensions.
2. The size of all facial images in the training set should be the same. Thus each image of only random size $r \times s$ is transformed into $n \times n$ size.
3. PCA does not work directly on images and thus it needs to be converted into a vector. That is, a test image of size $n \times n$ is converted to a vector of dimension n^2.

For example, consider an image of dimension 4×5. In Fig. 7.1, we can see that a 4×5 image has been transformed into a 20-dimensional vector. This image can be regarded as a point in a 20-dimensional space.

Let t be the total number of faces in the training set and let each image be of dimension n^2 after vectorization. We can now create a matrix A of dimension $n^2 \times t$ with each column corresponding to each image vector. Let I be the training dataset, where $I = (I_1, I_2, \ldots, I_t)$. Then $A = [I_1 I_2 \ldots I_t]$.

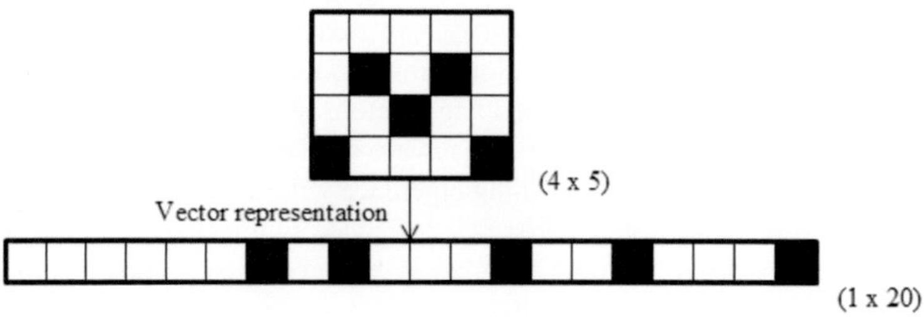

Fig. 7.1 Vectorization

7.9 Experimental Results

For the purpose of demonstration, we took six facial images belonging to the same person as the training data. The dataset comprising of six equal-dimensional facial images of a test person is shown in Fig. 7.2.

The primary step of normalization is the calculation of the mean $\bar{I}$ also known as the average face vector. It is given by

$$\bar{I} = \frac{1}{t}\sum_{i=1}^{t} I_i. \tag{7.10}$$

The average face is as shown in Fig. 7.3. It depicts the average features of all the training images in the dataset, and through normalization we remove all the common features shared by the entire set of training images.

The next step is to subtract each original image from the average face image vector (shown in Fig. 7.4). That is

$$\tilde{I}_i = I_i - \bar{I}, \quad \text{for } i = 1, 2. \ldots, t. \tag{7.11}$$

The aim of a covariance matrix is to show how the data changes in any dataset. Let B be a matrix with each column as the normalized face vector $\tilde{I}_i$ corresponding to each training image. That is

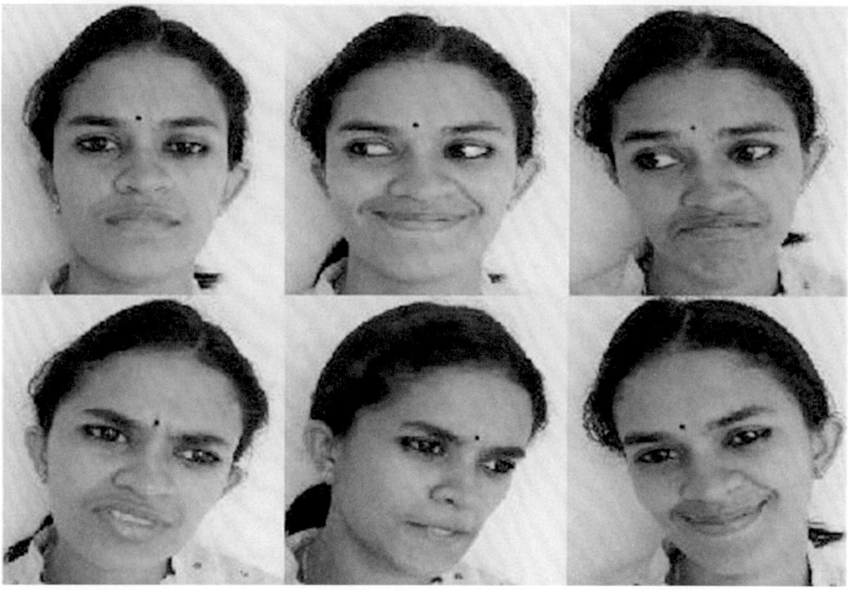

Fig. 7.2 Training dataset

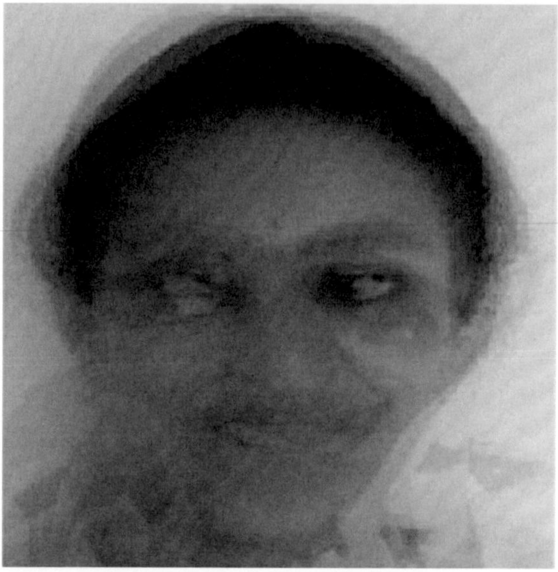

Fig. 7.3 Average face

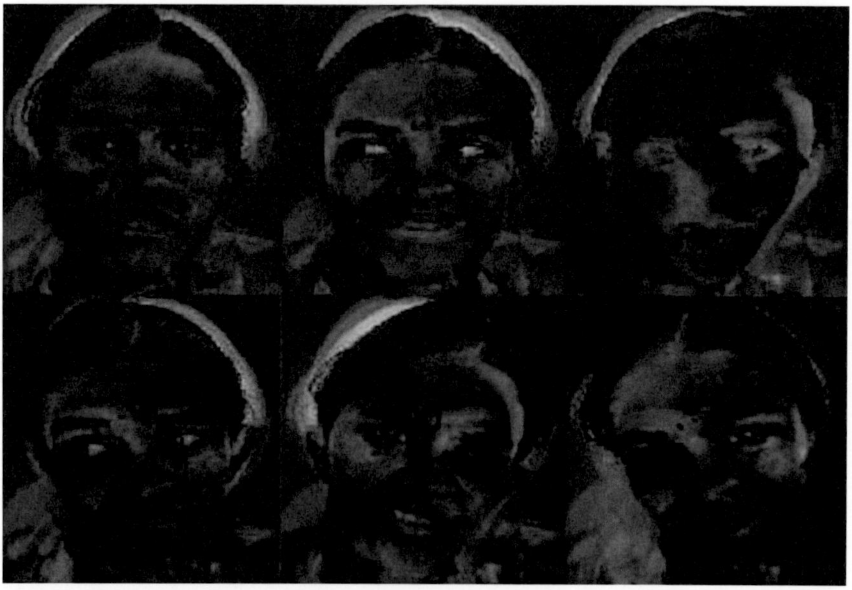

Fig. 7.4 Average face subtracted from individual training faces

$$B = [\tilde{I}_1, \tilde{I}_2, \ldots, \tilde{I}_t]. \tag{7.12}$$

Then the covariance matrix C is given by $C = BB^T$. Since B is a $n^2 \times t$ matrix, C is a $n^2 \times n^2$ matrix.

Now we calculate the eigenvectors and eigenvalues of the covariance matrix. From the previous step, it follows that the covariance matrix is going to be of very large dimension. For an image of dimension 50×50, the dimension of the covariance matrix is 2500×2500. This means that the covariance matrix has n^2 eigenvectors. As we had said earlier our aim is to generate m relevant eigenfaces (vectors). Now let us try to reduce the dimension by reducing the noise in the eigenvectors, for which we calculate the covariance matrix $C = B^T \times B$. This make the covariance matrix $t \times t$ dimensional. We compute the m most significant eigenvectors from the altered covariance matrix. Let the number of eigenvectors returned by the new covariance matrix be equal to 100 in our case. After finding the reduced eigenvector, we map the 100×1-dimensional eigenvector to 2500×1 so as to save the computation time.

Multiplying B $(n^2 \times t)$ with the eigenvector in the lower dimensional space $(t \times 1)$ will give us the eigenvector in the original dimension $(n^2 \times 1)$. This will give us the m eigenfaces in the higher dimension. The eigenfaces are shown in Fig. 7.5.

Fig. 7.5 Eigenfaces

7.10 Conclusion

Biometrics has always proven to be one of the most effective techniques for ensuring authenticity. Aadhaar, the unique identity card issued to all the citizens of India by the government, has recently started using face recognition also for verification. This is in addition to the iris and fingerprint recognition that the aadhar system uses at present.

Politicians, celebrities, and other eminent personalities often fall prey to morphing. Face recognition can be used to detect morphed faces (both in images and videos) and uses feature reduction techniques for easy computation. PCA has always proven to be effective in face recognition, detection, and tracking.

Chapter 8
Neural Networks and Face Recognition

8.1 Introduction

Deep neural network also known as deep learning, an unsupervised machine learning technique, is an extension of neural networks with multiple hidden layers. Neural network has only a single hidden layer. The concept of deep learning was introduced to elevate the efficiency of neural nets by increasing the number of intermediate processing so as to increase the output prediction accuracy. The growing interest in automating tasks such as facial recognition, video surveillance, handwritten character recognition, voice recognition and other computer vision activities such as automated cars, IoT devices, etc. have led to tremendous research in deep learning.

Let us take a look at what makes deep learning stand out from all other machine learning techniques that we have previously dealt with. Deep learning requires a large amount of training data to train the classifier, while other ML techniques can efficiently train the classifier with less number of training data. Deep learning demands more time to train the data and makes use of a high performing GPU for the same. Feature extraction is done manually for other ML techniques but not for deep learning, which makes it more feasible to work with big data. Deep learning is an optimal technique for image processing. Deep learning has improved since its advent, and today it has reached a point where it has started to outperform humans in different tasks such as image processing, malware detection, driverless cars, etc. In real-time scenarios, images are large-sized, and hence it is mandatory to use a machine learning technique for its recognition and classification.

8.2 Artificial Neural Networks (ANN)

Artificial neural networks with more than one hidden layer are called deep neural networks. To understand what deep learning is, we need to first get an idea of how a simple neural network works.

T. Thomas et al., *Machine Learning Approaches in Cyber Security Analytics*, https://doi.org/10.1007/978-981-15-1706-8_8

Neural networks have an activation function and a set of weights. If the set of weights range from any positive value to some negative value, then it is necessary to transform all the weights to a range within which the activation function is limited to vary. A sigmoid function does this transformation. This sigmoid function is given by

$$\sigma(x) = \frac{1}{1 + e^{-x}}. \tag{8.1}$$

The sigmoid is applied to the sum of product of weights and activations. If $w_1, \ldots, w_n$ are the weights and $a_1, \ldots, a_n$ are the activations, we compute

$$\sigma(w_1 a_1 + w_2 a_2 + \ldots + w_n a_n). \tag{8.2}$$

If we wish a particular neuron to be inactive (or to not light) for some value of the activation function, then we might need a bias. Bias determines whether neurons are inactive or not. So in short the weights in the first layer determine which pattern of input points will be lit in the second layer. Thus to obtain a proper learned neural network, the system needs to find the correct bias and weights. Let 0 be the input layer 1 be the first hidden layer, then

$$a^{(1)} = \sigma(wa^{(0)} + b), \tag{8.3}$$

where w is the weight, $a^{(0)}$ and $a^{(1)}$ are the activations in layer 0 and layer 1, respectively, and b is the bias.

8.2.1 *Learning by the Network*

Cost function calculates the sum of squares of the difference between actual output activation and predicted output activations. For instance, consider a facial image recognition system. If the neural network fails to identify an image to be recognized, then we need to subtract zero from the predicted activation function value for all output neurons except for the neuron that should have been activated. Activation function for the neuron in the final layer with the expected output will be 1. The sum if small indicates that the network has classified the number correctly and the sum is found to be large when the misclassification is high. Then the average cost is calculated for all training samples.

To converge to a local minima of the cost function, we calculate the gradient descent. The adjustment made to some weights will have more impact on the cost function than adjustment made to some other weights. We calculate the derivative of the loss function, which is nothing other than the slope of the function at any given point. One thing to be understood is that when the output activation function gives an error or fails to detect the intended image, then we need to adjust the weights and biases. Consider the neuron whose activation function is to be increased to match the output. We take the weights that were assigned to the second last layer's activation function and try to adjust them. For this, we consider those neurons that have the greatest weights and thus more influence on the activation of the neuron corresponding to our desired output. Along with increasing the activation function for the desired output neuron, the activation for other neurons should be decreased. This is called backpropagation and is done for each element in the training dataset. As this might be little time-consuming, we divide the entire training dataset into specific number of groups and calculate each of the above steps for each group. Stochastic gradient is used to find the local minima.

8.3 Convolutional Neural Networks (CNN)

Neural network as seen in the earlier section is a fully connected network and hence is unsuitable for image recognition and classification. This is because of the fact that real-life images are not small in size. The pixel representation is $m \times n \times c$, where m and n are the number of rows and columns, respectively, and c is the number of channels present in the image, which is 3 in the case of RGB images and 1 for $grayscale$ images. An image of size $22 \times 22 \times 3$ will have 1452 weights per neuron in the first hidden layer, whereas a facial image of size $230 \times 230 \times 3$ will have 158700 weights per neuron in the first hidden layer. Each hidden layer can have more than one neuron too. Processing these many parameters would require lot many neurons which would eventually lead to over-fitting. This makes fully connected neural networks unsuitable for image classification.

Convolution neural network or CNN is a multilayer neural network with multiple hidden layers. When traditional image matching algorithms do pixel-by-pixel matching, a convolutional neural network aims in creating filtered images. Unlike neural networks where each neuron is connected to every other neuron in the preceding layer, in CNN the neurons of a layer are connected only to a few neurons of the previous layer. A CNN basically consists of the following four different layers:

1. Convolution,
2. Rectified linear unit,
3. Pooling, and
4. Fully connected.

Facial images of a person can have lot many variants with each image differing in pose, expression, angle, etc. In all these cases, it is mandatory for the CNN to identify all the images as corresponding to a single person.

Filters or features or neurons are selected from the base image, thereby making it more convenient for image recognition. Filters are parts of the image that are chosen to identify other images that might belong to the same class. An image can have multiple filters. These filters are used to construct the convolution layer. The steps involved in constructing the convolution layer are as follows:

1. Multiply each pixel in the image with the corresponding pixel in the filter chosen;
2. Add the products obtained;
3. Divide the sum by the total number of pixels in the filter.

Move the filter throughout the image and repeat the above steps for all pixels in the image. The output is the convolution performed on the image with every other filter chosen in the beginning. Thus determining the size of filters used would play an important role in deciding the efficiency of CNN. The term "convolution" in CNN indicates finding the possible match by recursively applying the filter after traversing the entire image (through each and every pixel). A "convolution layer" is a stack of such filtered images.

Now let us see what is pooling in CNN. For carrying out pooling, we need to pick a window and a stride of fixed sizes, and then move the window in strides across the filtered set of images. Stride controls how the filter moves over the input image. It is the leap taken by the filter while moving around the image. The shift of the filter takes place based on the stride. In other words, stride indicates how long the filter jumps to analyze the next set of data. Padding is the process where zeroes are added to the image so as to aid the stride, when the filter window's size is not able to properly match the image size. The padding data is added around the entire input, and its size is given by *width of the padding data* = *width of the filter* − 1. Padding is done around the edge of the image.

Pooling is done for all the filtered images in the convolution layer to obtain a shrunken image. Pooling reduces the size of an image by only selecting the highest valued pixel in a predefined sized window. The end result of pooling is a smaller sized image stack (or convolution layer). So each value in the output of the pooled layer indicates the region that is pulled over using the max operation. This step helps in down-sampling the image and thereby reducing the size of the feature map. Another step is normalization. This is done by changing the negative pixel values in the image to zero, which gives us another stack of images with no negative values. This is known as rectified linear unit layer. Thus, rectified linear unit layer activates a neuron only if a pixel of the input image is above a particular threshold. That is, the output is zero when the input is below zero. This helps in removing the zeros of the images in the convolutional layer. Finally, we take the convolution layer, rectified linear unit layer, and the pooling layer, and club them together so that they become a single stack and the output of one layer becomes input of the other.

These three sets of steps can be repeated as many times as required. Passing images through multiple convolution layers would lead to more filtered images while multiple pooling would give more smaller sized images. The final layer is a fully connected layer where each pixel value would aid in determining the output value. We can find certain pixel values to be high for a particular kind of input and certain pixel values to be low for some other kinds of input. Those pixels that are seen higher for an input image indicate how strong it predicts that input image. To predict an input test image, it traverses through all layers in the CNN. Based on the pixel values of the final output layer and the corresponding weights, we determine the class to which the input test image would belong to.

8.4 Application of CNN in Feature Extraction

In this section, we demonstrate how CNN can be used to identify the facial image features which further can be used for facial image recognition. CNN can be implemented on both grayscale images and RGB images. Here, we have made use of grayscale facial images. Kaggle dataset available for facial feature competition is made use to train and test the network. The objective of this task is to predict key point positions on face images. This can be used to track faces in videos and images, analyze facial expressions, etc. The training datasets taken from Kaggle have facial images with key points detected in prior. The key points are specified by a (x, y) real-valued pair in the space of pixel indices.

Identifying the key points is the primary step of image processing. Facial recognition requires the face to be detected at first and next the important features (also called as key points) to be identified. We had seen how a feature reduction technique called PCA is used to reduce the dimensionality of facial features in the previous chapter. In this chapter, we shall understand how efficient is deep learning in identifying the important features of a facial image. "Key points" in this context indicate those features of a facial image which when identified proves the presence of human faces in any image provided as input. Here, we make use of CNN to extract features. The neural network is trained using the Kaggle dataset that contains a maximum of 15 key points for a single image. Facial key point detection is a challenging problem as the facial features can vary from one person to the other. A person can also have multiple images that vary in size, position, and pose.

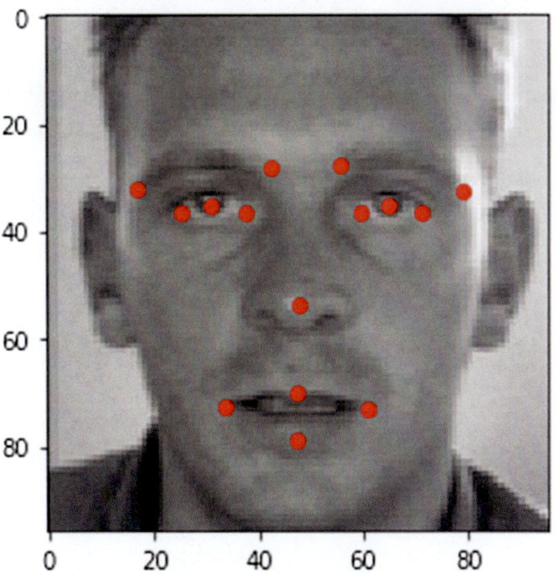

Fig. 8.1 Sample facial image with key points

The dataset consists of grayscale images with 96×96 resolution and 15 key points. Figure 8.1 shows a training image from the Kaggle dataset with four key points for the mouth, one for the nose, and five for each eye position.

8.4.1 Understanding the Dataset

The training CSV file consists of 7049 images, and the test CSV contains 1783 test images. Each row in the test.csv contains an ID and a list of pixels of the test images. Once the dataset is downloaded from Kaggle, it is saved to any location in the local system. A set of random images from training dataset is shown in Fig. 8.2.

Fig. 8.2 Training dataset

The contents of the dataset are read using pandas. The 15 key points to be searched in a test image, along with their x- and y-coordinates are as follows:

- left_eye_center_x, left_eye_center_y, right_eye_center_x, right_eye_center_y;
- left_eye_inner_corner_x, left_eye_inner_corner_y, left_eye_outer_corner_x, left_eye_outer_corner_y;
- right_eye_inner_corner_x, right_eye_inner_corner_y, right_eye_outer_corner_x, right_eye_outer_corner_y;
- left_eyebrow_inner_end_x, left_eyebrow_inner_end_y, left_eyebrow_outer_end_x, left_eyebrow_outer_end_y;
- right_eyebrow_inner_end_x, right_eyebrow_inner_end_y, right_eyebrow_outer_end_x, right_eyebrow_outer_end_y;
- nose_tip_x, nose_tip_y;
- mouth_left_corner_x, mouth_left_corner_y, mouth_right_corner_x, mouth_right_corner_y;
- mouth_center_top_lip_x, mouth_center_top_lip_y, mouth_center_bottom_lip_x, mouth_center_bottom_lip_y.

The last column of the dataset is the input image and consists of pixels ranging from 0 to 255 that corresponds to each training image. The key point positions are missing for a few images in the training dataset, mainly due to poor quality of images and thus can be ignored. The x- and y-coordinates of the key points corresponding to each image are extracted from the *training.csv* file to plot the key points over these training images. The output is shown in Fig. 8.3.

As said earlier, a few images are of high resolution while some are of low resolution. For images with less resolution, the key points detected are less. The statistics of key points is shown in Fig. 8.4 and can be plotted using the code snippet given here.

```
df.describe().loc['count'].plot.bar()
```

8.4.2 Building a Keras Model

In this section, we shall take a look at how Keras is used to build a convolutional neural network model to predict key points for the test images. Pipelining helps in making it easier to repeat the commonly occurring steps while constructing our machine learning model. Pipelining helps to fit the training data and apply the result to the test data. As machine learning techniques demand a sequence of transformations to be performed such as feature generation, feature reduction, optimal feature selection, etc., pipelining is always advised. A pipeline constructor allows to encapsulate

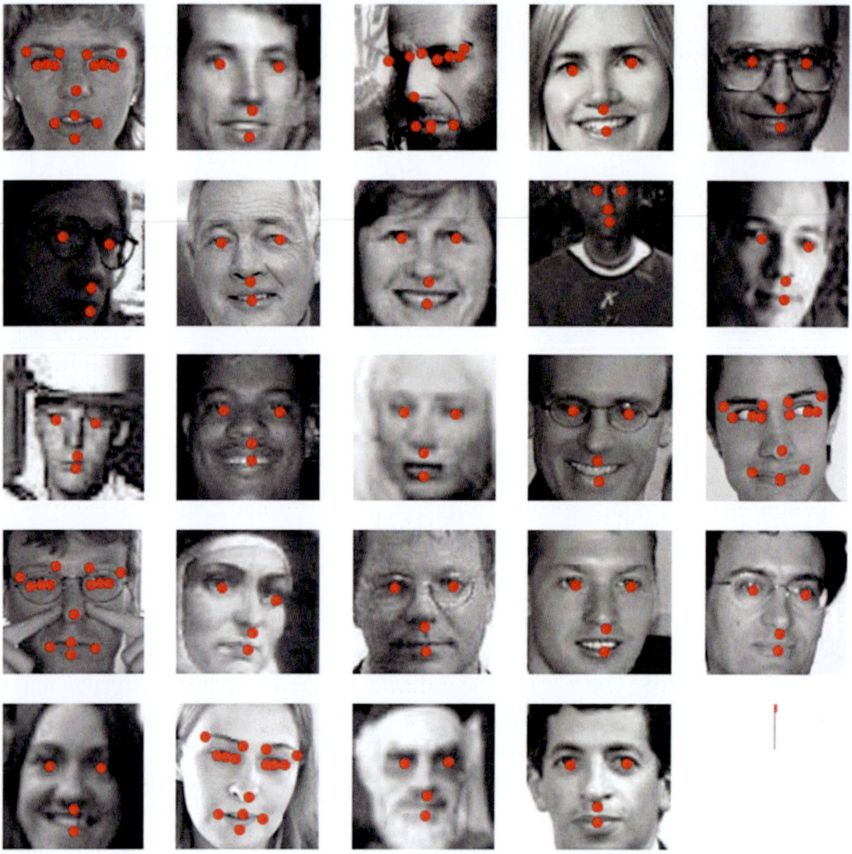

Fig. 8.3 Key points extracted

transformers and estimators that would function as a single unit. The transformers and estimators can be feature selection measures, regression, etc. Pipeline enables data transformation to be performed in the correct order and prevents data leakage during cross-validation. Scaling is done to transform the features to a given range. Both the steps are implemented with the below code snippet.

```
output_pipe = make_pipeline(MinMaxScaler(feature_range=(-1, 1))).
```

A function *vstack* is used to vertically stack the image pixel arrays for processing. Building a convolutional neural network with multiple layers is done by the below code snippet. Here, we make use of seven layers excluding the input layer. As Keras is used to construct CNN, there is not any need to specify the weights and bias.

```
model = Sequential()
# input layer
model.add(BatchNormalization(input_shape=(96, 96, 1)))
model.add(Conv2D(24, (5, 5), kernel_initializer='he_normal'))
model.add(Activation('relu'))
model.add(MaxPooling2D(pool_size=(2, 2), strides=(2, 2)))
model.add(Dropout(0.2))
# layer 2
model.add(Conv2D(36, (5, 5)))
model.add(Activation('relu'))
model.add(MaxPooling2D(pool_size=(2, 2), strides=(2, 2)))
model.add(Dropout(0.2))
# layer 3
model.add(Conv2D(48, (5, 5)))
model.add(Activation('relu'))
model.add(MaxPooling2D(pool_size=(2, 2), strides=(2, 2)))
model.add(Dropout(0.2))
# layer 4
model.add(Conv2D(64, (3, 3)))
model.add(Activation('relu'))
model.add(MaxPooling2D(pool_size=(2, 2), strides=(2, 2)))
model.add(Dropout(0.2))
# layer 5
model.add(Conv2D(64, (3, 3)))
model.add(Activation('relu'))
model.add(Flatten())
# layer 6
model.add(Dense(500, activation="relu"))
# layer 7
model.add(Dense(90, activation="relu"))
# layer 8
model.add(Dense(30))

sgd = optimizers.SGD(lr=0.1, decay=1e-6, momentum=0.95,
    nesterov=True)
model.compile(optimizer=sgd, loss='mse', metrics=['accuracy'])
```

Different functionalities that are used in modeling the convolutional neural network are as follows:

1. Sequential(): The sequential model is a linear stack of layers which is used to initialize the network. The list of different layers can be passed via the $.add()$ method. Keras models can have two forms—sequential and functional. Sequential models allow to easily stack the layers in the network from input to the output.
2. BatchNormalization: The $BatchNormalization$ layer normalizes the input to the activation function. $input\_shape = (96, 96, 1)$ is used in designing our model, where 96×96 is the dimension of our image and 1 is the number of color channel.

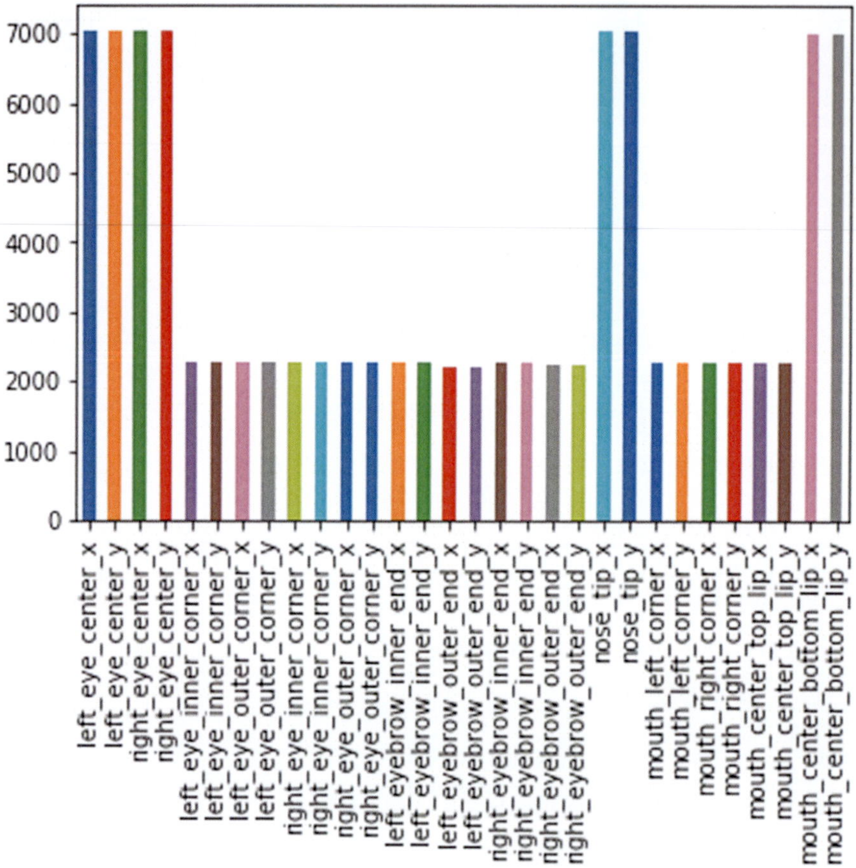

Fig. 8.4 Key point statistics

3. Conv2D: Convolution2D is a two-dimensional convolution layer. The function is used to filter windows for two-dimensional inputs. The keyword $input\_shape$ is used along with this layer if it is used as the first layer. The first argument of $Conv2D$ is the number of output channels of that layer. The next two arguments are the size of the filter window. For example, in $Conv2D(36, (5, 5))$, 36 is the number of output channels and 5×5 is the window size.
4. Activation (Relu): Relu is the rectified linear unit. This is to define the type of activation function to be used. The different kinds of activations are tanh, selu, softplus, etc. The $Relu$ activation function helps in treating image classification as a nonlinear problem.
5. MaxPooling2D: This layer is used to add pooling layers to the neural network model. $MaxPooling2D(pool\_size = (2, 2), strides = (2, 2))$ indicates that the size of pooling is $(2, 2)$ in x- and y-directions, and strides in the x- and y-directions is $(2, 2)$.

6. DropOut: It is a way to prevent the problem of over-fitting. It is implemented by randomly selecting the nodes with a certain probability to be dropped out (or deactivated) while training a model.
7. Flatten(): The *Flatten* function converts the pooled feature map to a single column so that it can be passed to the fully connected layer.
8. Dense: *Dense* helps in adding the fully connected layer to the convolutional neural network.
9. Optimizers.SGD: Stochastic gradient descent optimizer includes momentum, learning rate, decay, and Nesterov's momentum. The learning rate is decided by experimenting over a range of values.
10. Compile: Prior to training a model, the learning process needs to be configured. This is done using the *compile*() method. The method has the following arguments: *Optimizer* which specifies the optimization algorithm to be used, a loss function that the model will try to minimize, and a list of metrics such a

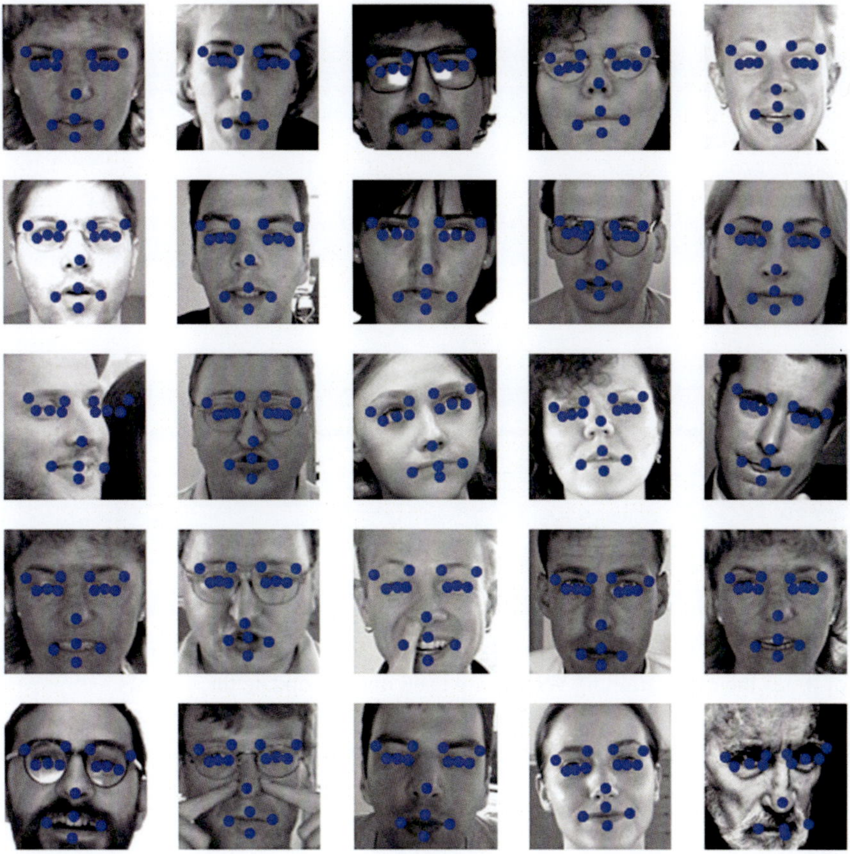

Fig. 8.5 Predicted key points

Accuracy which is mandatory for any classification problem. The loss function that we have made use is the "mean squared error." Other loss functions are mean absolute error, mean absolute percentage error, cosine proximity, etc.

The final output of the model is the predicted key points plotted in the test image and is as shown in Fig. 8.5.

Training and compiling the model give the following output.

```
Epoch 1/50
1712/1712 [==============================] - 53s 31ms/step -
    loss: 0.0389 - acc: 0.3002 - val_loss: 0.0704 - val_acc:
    0.0327
Epoch 2/50
1712/1712 [==============================] - 51s 30ms/step -
    loss: 0.0352 - acc: 0.3289 - val_loss: 0.0705 - val_acc:
    0.0327
Epoch 3/50
1712/1712 [==============================] - 51s 30ms/step -
    loss: 0.0347 - acc: 0.3324 - val_loss: 0.0685 - val_acc:
    0.0327
Epoch 4/50
1712/1712 [==============================] - 51s 30ms/step -
    loss: 0.0312 - acc: 0.3732 - val_loss: 0.0598 - val_acc:
    0.1051
Epoch 5/50
1712/1712 [==============================] - 51s 30ms/step -
    loss: 0.0253 - acc: 0.4007 - val_loss: 0.0543 - val_acc:
    0.1519
.
.
.
.
.
Epoch 49/50
1712/1712 [==============================] - 56s 33ms/step -
    loss: 0.0064 - acc: 0.6297 - val_loss: 0.0246 - val_acc:
    0.3458
Epoch 50/50
1712/1712 [==============================] - 54s 32ms/step -
    loss: 0.0064 - acc: 0.6419 - val_loss: 0.0246 - val_acc:
    0.3154
```

The loss of the model is plotted in Fig. 8.6. An epoch is a measure of the number of times the entire training vectors are used once to update the weights.

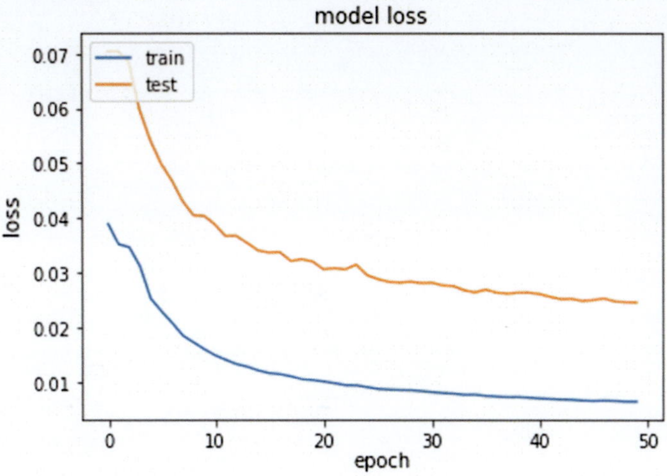

Fig. 8.6 Loss function

8.5 Conclusions and Directions for Research

The experiments conducted in this chapter aim to give an idea on how neural networks, specifically convolutional neural networks, can extract features from facial images. There has been increasing popularity in carrying out research in image processing nowadays. Though there are numerous types of neural networks such as recurrent neural networks, feedforward neural networks, self-normalizing neural networks, etc, CNN has been proved optimal for image processing. Neural networks is one of the most commonly used ML techniques used today due to the fact that it is unsupervised. The concept that we discussed in this chapter can be extended for facial recognition in videos as well. Other neural network techniques such as autoencoders can be used to extract features from malware sample. Neural networks are not confined to images alone but can be used to address many other cybersecurity problems such as early detection of malware.

Chapter 9
Applications of Decision Trees

9.1 Introduction

Decision tree is a machine learning technique for solving both classification and regression problems. They help in identifying the relationship among data points in a dataset by constructing tree structures. These tree-like structures are used to make accurate predictions about unseen data. The dataset is split into multiple subsets, thereby resulting in each decision node branching to more decision nodes. The very first decision node from which the split begins is called the root node, and the final decision nodes which do not split further anymore are called the leaf nodes. Decision trees are constructed as a top-to-down structured model in the divide-and-conquer fashion. A sample decision tree structure is shown in Fig. 9.1. It is a graph-like structure which is capable of representing an algorithm containing conditional control statements in the form of a flowchart-like structure. Decision trees are trained by passing the training data down from the root node to the leaves. The data is repeatedly split according to predictor variables so that the child nodes are more homogeneous in terms of the outcome variable. We select an attribute as the root node and construct branches for every other attribute. A decision tree in general has the following key elements:

1. Rules applied at nodes, to split the data based on the value of the node for any particular variable;
2. Stopping rule, to decide when the nodes turn out to be terminal nodes;
3. A leaf node assigned to a particular label.

The decision trees partition the dataset recursively creating subsets during each split at each step. The term *rules* indicates the path taken from the root node to reach the leaf node of the decision tree. A high-level algorithm for decision tree is given below:

1. Select the best attribute and assign it to the root node.
2. Next, split the training set into subsets in such a way that the data within a subset has the same value for a particular attribute.

T. Thomas et al., *Machine Learning Approaches in Cyber Security Analytics*, https://doi.org/10.1007/978-981-15-1706-8_9

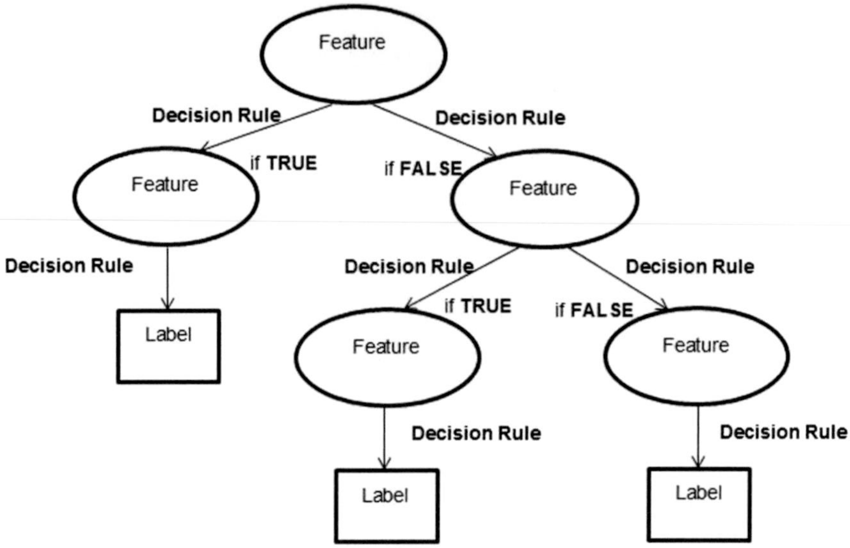

Fig. 9.1 A generic decision tree model

3. Continue till further split is not possible.

The leaf nodes of the decision tree represent the labels, and the internal nodes represent the attributes. Attribute selection is very important when it comes to selecting the root node. Criteria such as entropy, information gain, and Gini index are calculated for each and every attribute, thereby helping in determining the best attribute. That attribute with the highest value is placed at the root node. Specific rules are used to divide the dataset through numerous levels of decisions. The sequence of rules used is represented in a tree structure, consisting of root nodes, decision function, and leaf nodes. A decision tree becomes a classification tree when discrete class labels are to be chosen for the input dataset; it becomes a regression tree when a range of continuous values are to be chosen for the dataset.

Decision trees are more easy to handle categorical features, interpret and extend to more multi-class classification, do not require feature scaling, and hence are widely used. Other tree construction algorithms such as boosting and random forests are widely used and more preferred for regression and classification tasks. Few terminologies associated with decision trees are given below:

1. Hypothesis class is the set of all possible functions that can be mapped from the input space to the output space.
2. Concept is the function that maps an input to the output.
3. Target concept is the optimal function that efficiently maps an input to the output.
4. Splitting is the process of dividing a node into two or more sub-nodes based on some criteria.

5. Root node is that sample which is chosen as primary node for further split of the dataset into two or more homogeneous sets.
6. Decision node is that node of a decision tree which further splits into sub-nodes.
7. Pruning is the removal of sub-nodes from a decision node.
8. Leaf nodes are those nodes which do not split further indicating that the decision tree has terminated.
9. Gini impurity is a measure of how often a randomly chosen element from a set would be incorrectly labeled if it was randomly labeled according to the probability distribution of labels in the set.
10. Information gain is the amount of information gained about a random variable from observing another random variable.

Decision trees differ depending on the kind of algorithm that is used to construct it. Each algorithm differs in the criteria made use of to split the dataset. This finally results in a tree model that predicts the label of a sample by making use of decision rules inferred from the attributes of the dataset. While learning is carried out using decision trees, a sample to be classified is passed through a number of tests which finally determine the class to which the sample might belong to. The steps involved in finding the label of each sample are organized into a hierarchical structure called a decision tree.

In most of the cases, decision trees split data until we obtain singleton subsets as its leaf nodes. But this is not as efficient as we think it is, because the decision tree may fail when it has to classify a sample which it has not seen before.

In machine learning, over-fitting is a phenomenon in which the learning system tightly fits the given training data so much that it would be inaccurate in predicting the outcomes of the test data. In decision trees, over-fitting occurs when the tree is designed so as to perfectly fit all the training samples. Thus it ends up with branches with strict rules of sparse data. This affects the accuracy when predicting test data that are not part of the training set. One of the methods used to address the over-fitting problem in decision tree is called pruning which is done after the initial training is completed. In the next section, we discuss the details of pruning in decision trees.

9.2 Pruning in Decision Trees

Pruning is a solution to the problem of over-fitting in decision trees. It helps in reducing the tree size by eliminating those branches that do not play any significant role in labeling unknown samples. In pruning, the branches of the tree are trimmed by removing the decision nodes starting from the leaf node in such a way that the overall accuracy is not affected. This is done by segregating the actual training set into a training dataset and a validation data set. The decision tree is constructed using the segregated training dataset. Then, trimming is carried out on the tree to optimize the accuracy of the validation dataset. Some of the pruning algorithms are the following:

1. Minimal cost-complexity pruning (CCP) in CART,
2. Error-based pruning (EBP) in C4.5,
3. Minimum error pruning (MEP),
4. Reduced error pruning (REP),
5. Pessimistic error pruning (PEP),
6. MDL-based pruning, and
7. Classifiability-based pruning.

Pruning are of two types, pre-pruning and post-pruning. Pre-pruning is stopping the tree from growing when attributes are found to be irrelevant. Post-pruning a bottom-up approach is a process of cutting short the decision trees by traversing the tree from its leaf nodes after its construction. Basically, there are three pruning strategies as follows:

1. No pruning;
2. Minimum error, where the tree is pruned until the cross-validation error is minimum;
3. Smallest tree, where the tree is pruned a little further than the cross-validated error.

In the next section, we shall take a look at the different mathematical measures used in decision tree construction, after which we shall deal with different decision tree algorithms.

9.3 Entropy

Entropy is one of the decision factors depending on which the decision tree carries out a split. As the definition says entropy is a measure of uncertainty of a random variable. That is lower the entropy, lesser the information content. Entropy is used to calculate the homogeneity of a sample in the dataset; this is when the dataset has more than one record with similar set of values. The entropy is said to be "zero" when the samples are entirely homogeneous and the entropy is said to be "one" when the data points are equally divided. Entropy is calculated as

$$Entropy(D) = -\sum_{i=1}^{k} P(L_i) \times \log_2(P(L_i)), \tag{9.1}$$

where D is the dataset for which the entropy is calculated and $P(L_i)$ is the proportion of the number of data points in class L_i to the total number of elements in D. Entropy characterizes data using the probability distribution of any sample drawn from the dataset. Thus entropy is defined as the negative logarithm of the probability distribution of every sample's occurrence in the dataset. $Entropy(D) = 0$ indicates that the dataset is correctly classified. This implies that all data points of D now belong to the same class.

9.4 Information Gain

From the definition of entropy, we understand that the entropy changes with the change in the root node chosen (with change in the attribute that represents the root node). Thus constructing a decision tree is about finding the best attribute that returns the highest information gain. First, we calculate the entropies as follows:

1. First the entropy of the dataset is calculated;
2. Next, split the dataset on different attributes and calculate the entropy for each branch thereby generated;
3. Finally, calculate the total entropy of the resultant decision tree.

Subtracting the resulting entropy from the entropy calculated before carrying out the split gives the information gain. Thus information gain is a measure of the difference in entropy of the dataset and its entropy after it is split on an attribute. The information gain can be computed as

$$IG(A, D) = Entropy(D) - \sum_{i=1}^{k} P(T_i)Entropy(T_i), \tag{9.2}$$

where D is the dataset, A is the attribute chosen for the split, T_i are the subsets created from D after splitting with A, and $P(T)$ is the proportion of the number of elements in T_i to the number of elements in D.

Information gain is the most important measure used by decision tree algorithms for constructing tree models. The branch with entropy zero is a leaf node, and if the entropy is greater than zero then it would require further splitting. After choosing the optimal attribute using information gain for carrying out a split, we recursively construct decision tree subsets. The tree constructed will never contain the same attribute twice in any root to leaf path. Next, let us see how to construct a decision tree from the sample dataset shown in Table 9.1.

For easy calculation and the purpose of demonstration, we do not take the actual values of these features from the dataset. Suppose the training set has three features X, Y, Z and two classes $1, 2$. Then to build a decision tree the first step is to take any one of the features and calculate the information gain for it, and then repeat the process for rest of the features. Let us take an example to understand the concept

Table 9.1 Sample data

X	Y	Z	Category
1	1	1	1
1	1	0	1
0	0	1	2
1	0	0	2

Fig. 9.2 Split done on feature X

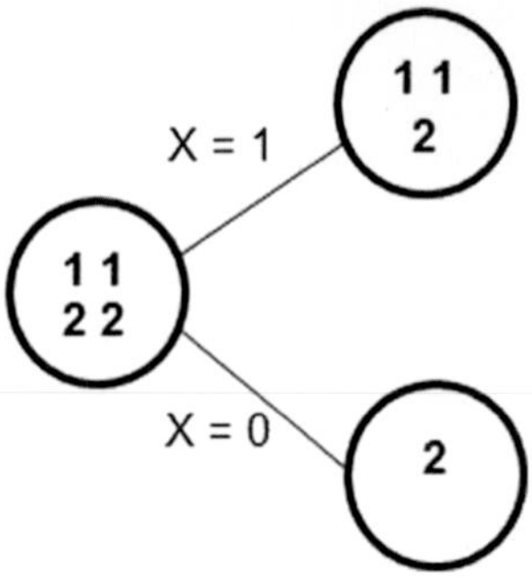

of splitting in more detail. Here, our aim is to find the best attribute that splits the dataset D by calculating the information gain. We calculate the information gain on splitting the data with respect to the features X, Y and Z as follows:

1. Splitting the dataset on feature X (Fig. 9.2).
   Entropy of the root node is calculated as

$$E_{root} = -[1/2 \times \log_2(1/2) + 1/2 \times \log_2(1/2)] = (-1) \times (-1) = 1. \tag{9.3}$$

   Entropies of the two child nodes are calculated as

$$\begin{aligned} E_{child_1} &= -[2/3 \times \log_2(2/3) + 1/3 \times \log_2(1/3)] = 0.916. \\ E_{child_0} &= -[1 \times \log_2(1)] = 0. \end{aligned} \tag{9.4}$$

   Thus the information gain of the entire tree is

$$\begin{aligned} IG(X, D) &= E_{root} - P(child_1) \times E_{child_1} - P(child_0) \times E_{child_0} \\ &= 1 - (3/4) \times (0.916) - (1/4) \times (0) = 0.313. \end{aligned} \tag{9.5}$$

2. Splitting the dataset on feature Y.

$$\begin{aligned} E_{child_1} &= -[1 \times \log_2(1)] = 0 \\ E_{child_0} &= -[1 \times \log_2(1)] = 0. \end{aligned} \tag{9.6}$$

   Thus information gain of the tree is given by (Fig. 9.3)

$$\begin{aligned} IG(Y, D) &= E_{root} - P(child_1) \times E_{child_1} - P(child_0) \times E_{child_0} \\ &= 1 - (1/2) \times [-(-1) \times 0 + 0] = 1. \end{aligned} \tag{9.7}$$

3. Splitting the dataset on feature Z (Fig. 9.4).

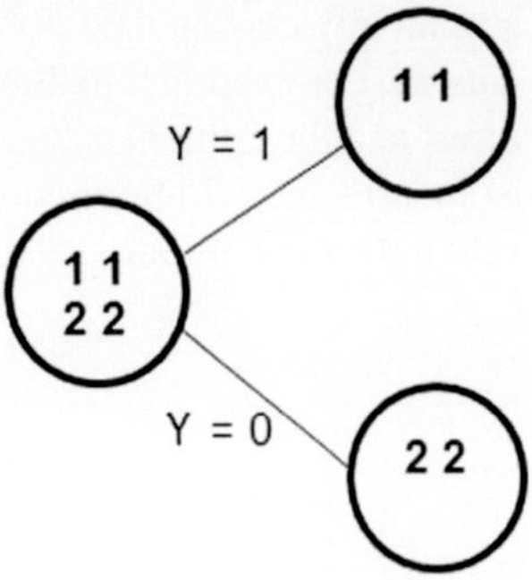

Fig. 9.3 Split done on feature Y

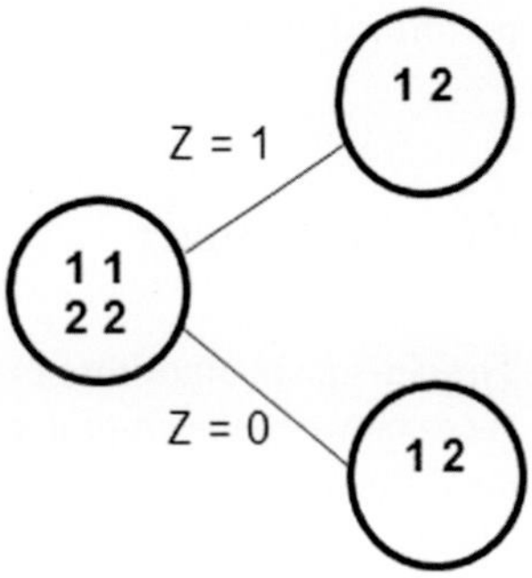

Fig. 9.4 Split done on feature Z

$$\begin{aligned} E_{child1} &= -[1/2 \times \log_2(1/2) + 1/2 \times \log_2(1/2)] = 1 \\ E_{child2} &= -[1/2 \times \log_2(1/2) + 1/2 \times \log_2(1/2)] = 1. \end{aligned} \tag{9.8}$$

The information gain of the tree is

$$\begin{aligned} IG(Z, D) &= E_{root} - P(child_1) \times E_{child_1} - P(child_0) \times E_{child_0} \\ &= 1 - [(1/2) \times [-((1/2) \times -1 + (1/2) \times -1)]] = 0. \end{aligned} \tag{9.9}$$

Thus, it is clear from the above computations that the information gain is maximum when the dataset is split on the feature Y. Thus, the values corresponding to the feature Y are a perfect choice for the root node. Also, it can be seen that when the dataset is split using the attribute Y, the leaf nodes contain only the target variable. Thus, further split is not required.

9.5 Gini Index

Gini index or Gini impurity is a measurement of how often a randomly selected data point would be wrongly classified. It is widely used in simple classification and regression decision trees. Gini index, is the probability of incorrect classification of a randomly chosen data point if it is labeled based on the label's distribution in the dataset. For example, in Table 9.1, let X, Y, and Z represent any three malware features, and the column *category* represents the labels of the samples. The probability of incorrectness in predicting the label of each sample in the dataset based on X is said to be the Gini impurity for the feature X. That is,

$$\text{Gini}(X) = 1 - \sum_{i=1}^{n} P_i^2, \tag{9.10}$$

where P_i is the relative frequency of the ith class in X. That attribute with the lowest Gini index is preferred for constructing a decision tree. Only binary splits are performed using Gini indices, and hence it is mainly used by the CART algorithm.

9.6 Chi-Square

The chi-square algorithm is used to find the statistical significance among the differences between the child nodes and parent node. Chi-square is the sum of squares of the differences between the observed and expected frequencies of a target variable. That is,

$$\chi^2 = \sum_{i} \frac{(Observed_i - Expected_i)^2}{Expected_i}. \tag{9.11}$$

The larger the value of chi-square, the greater the statistical significance (or probability) of the difference between the child node and the parent node. For each observed node in the tree, its chi-square is calculated by finding the deviation of success and failure. For each split carried out in the decision tree construction, chi-square of the split is the sum of all chi-square of success and failure of each node of the split. The chi-square algorithm generates a chi-squared automatic interaction detector (CHAID) tree. Mainly chi-square is used to estimate whether further split of a node will improve the performance either over the entire dataset or only on a particular sample of the training dataset. The selection of features does not depend on any specific machine learning algorithm. We calculate feature scores using different statistical calculations for its correlation with the output variable. When it comes to decision trees, we calculate feature scores from class counts after the data is split, where chi-square is used to measure the correlation. The algorithm decides the feature to be chosen by calculating its scores and the probability value associated with the scores. The feature with maximum score is considered for tree construction.

9.7 Gain Ratio

The information gain measure is used to select the test attribute at each node of the decision tree. The information gain measure prefers to select attributes having a large number of values.

Let S be a set consisting of s data samples with m distinct classes. The expected information needed to classify a given sample is given by

$$Info(S) = -\sum_{i=1}^{m} p_i \times \log_2 p_i,$$

where p_i is the probability that an arbitrary sample belongs to class C_i and is estimated by s_i/s.

Let an attribute A has n distinct values. Let s_{ij} be the number of samples of class C_i in a subset S_j. S_j contains those samples in S that have value a_j of A. In other words, $S_1, S_2, \ldots, S_n$ are the sub-trees created as a result of the split of S using A. The entropy, or expected information based on the partitioning into subsets by A, is given by

$$Info(A, S) = -\sum_{i=1}^{m} Info(S_i)\frac{s_{1,i} + \cdots + s_{m,i}}{s}. \tag{9.12}$$

Our next aim is to find the most efficient attribute in carrying out the split in S. We then rank these attributes in the order of its gain. The encoding information that would be gained by branching on A is

$$Gain(A) = Info(S) - Info(A, S).$$

From the formula for $Gain()$, it is clear that $Gain(A)$ equals the difference between the information required to classify a data point in S and the gain in information after the dataset S is split using A. The information generated by splitting the training data set S into n partitions corresponding to n outcomes of a test on the attribute A is given by

$$SplitInfo(A, S) = -\sum_{i=1}^{n} \frac{|S_i|}{|S|} \log_2 \frac{|S_i|}{|S|}. \tag{9.13}$$

$GainRatio(A, S)$ is the proportion of information generated by the split. That is,

$$GainRatio(A, S) = \frac{Gain(A)}{SplitInfo(A, S)}. \tag{9.14}$$

The element with the highest gain ratio is the root node, and the dataset is split on the basis of the root node. Further, information gain is calculated for each sub-node and the process is continued until prediction is complete. If an attribute A

in the training set S has distinct records for each sample, then $Info(A, S) = 0$ and $Gain(A, S)$ is maximum.

9.8 Classification and Regression Trees (CART)

CART which also stands for Classification and Regression Trees is a simple decision tree algorithm, in which classification tree produces categorical target variables and identifies their labels. Regression on the other hand produces continuous target variables and predicts their values. The CART model is represented as a binary tree. CART algorithm makes use of stopping conditions iff

1. minimum number of records in the dataset has been traversed,
2. majority of the entire records in the dataset have been assigned to nodes, and
3. splitting has been done for maximum number of levels.

Splitting becomes impossible when just a single case remains in a node, dataset has duplicate entries of records and the node is entirely pure.

CART Algorithm

The three major steps of the algorithm are as follows:

1. Find the best split for each feature. If there exists k different values for each feature in the training dataset, then the possible number of splits can be $k - 1$.
2. Once the best split is found for each feature, find that split which maximizes the splitting criterion.
3. Split the node using the best splitting criterion found in Step-2 and repeat from Step-1 until the stopping criterion is satisfied.

CART uses Gini impurity as the splitting criterion. Some of the advantages and the disadvantages of the CART algorithm are given below.

1. CART algorithm is very easy to interpret in general.
2. Outliers in the input variables never affect CART significantly.
3. It makes use of testing and cross-validation to accurately construct a decision tree.
4. One variable can be used more than once in different parts of the tree to reveal complex interdependencies between different sets of variables.
5. It can be used to select input variables when used along with other predictive machine learning techniques.
6. It does not demand data transformation.
7. Tree construction is possible with input datasets containing categorical as well as continuous variables.
8. It can be used as ensemble methods, for instance, decision trees can input selected variables to a neural network.

9. The trees created by CART are generally unstable. Slight changes made to the input data can have a major influence on the tree structure. As decision trees are hierarchical in nature, errors that occur in the beginning might affect the entire tree.
10. One of its major disadvantages is that the predictions made by CART are less accurate compared to other models.

Pruning in CART

CART algorithm produces decision trees that are grown larger than what is required. Hence, it is pruned back to find the optimal tree. CART uses test data or X-fold cross-validation to determine the best tree that efficiently classifies unknown incoming samples. To validate the tree using test dataset, the tree is scored by making use of samples that were not used by the tree during its training phase. Cross-validation evaluates the tree by training the decision tree model on certain number of samples from the distribution. Pruning can be done as follows:

1. Split the training data randomly into X folds.
2. Train X trees on different combinations of $X - 1$ folds, and find the estimated error for the Xth fold each time.
3. Find the accuracy of the decision tree by making use of the mean of the X error measurements.
4. Make use of parameters such as complexity penalty to minimize the error in Step-3. Complexity parameter controls the size of the tree and selects the optimal tree. The tree stops building if another variable is added at the current node position to the decision tree and the cost is more than the value of the complexity parameter.
5. Now refit the tree using the data and parameters obtained from Step-4.

9.9 Iterative Dichotomizer 3 (ID3)

ID3 that stands for iterative dichotomizer 3 is an algorithm that is used to generate decision trees from any dataset. It was developed by Ross Quinlan in the year 1983. It follows top-to-bottom greedy search through the dataset, in which each attribute at every node of the tree is tested to find the best. That is on every iteration the algorithm chooses the best attribute for split using different metrics such as entropy and information gain. Entropy measures the amount of uncertainty in the dataset, and information gain measures the reduced uncertainty of the dataset after the dataset is split on a particular attribute. The ID3 algorithm is used to produce a decision tree from a training dataset D which is then stored in the memory. The decision tree classifies a test data sample by traversing the tree in bottom-up fashion which finally tells the class to which the test dataset belongs to.

To construct an optimal decision tree, it is essential to minimize the depth of the tree. For the same, certain functions such as entropy and information gain are necessary to ensure balanced splitting. Entropy as discussed earlier helps in measuring the homogeneity of the training dataset. Now let us take a look at the ID3 algorithm.

ID3 Algorithm

1. Assign the dataset D as the root node.
2. For every iteration, the algorithm calculates the entropy and information gain for each unused attribute of the dataset D.
3. Select the attribute with either the smallest entropy or the highest information gain.
4. Now split the dataset using the selected attribute, which subsequently will generate subsets of the dataset.
5. For all attributes never used earlier, continue the above steps for each subset.

Leaf nodes of the tree also known as terminal nodes represent the label of the subset of this branch, while the nonterminal nodes represent the selected attribute for carrying out the split. Though ID3 algorithm can easily be implemented in python sci-kit by importing the *ID3Estimator* function, it is important to understand the steps involved within.

Entropy Calculation

1. First calculate the size of the dataset, indicating the total number of samples present in the dataset.
2. Retrieve the labels of samples into a dictionary.
3. For every label L_i, calculate its probability $P(L_i)$.
4. Calculate the entropy and return the final entropy of the dataset.

Selecting the Best Attribute for the Split

1. Find the number of features in the dataset.
2. Call the entropy calculation function and initialize the information gain variable to zero.
3. For each feature in the feature set, store all the values corresponding to that feature in an array.
4. Using set() function, get the unique values from the feature set. Set is an ordered collection of items where every element is unique.
5. Initialize two variables entropy and entropy_attribute to zero.
6. Perform the split on the dataset using each attribute from the feature set and calculate the probability of the currently created sub-tree. Also, calculate the entropy of the attribute used for the split.
7. Calculate the information gain and return the attribute with maximum information gain.

Splitting the Dataset

1. To split the dataset, we make use of that dataset, attribute Index, and the value of the attribute. The attribute_index and attribute_value correspond to the attribute with maximum information gain.
2. Split the dataset using the chosen attribute by iterating through every record in the dataset.

Finally, save the tree in a list structure and return it. To build the decision tree, integrate all the above processes, after which the decision tree can be used to predict the labels for unseen samples.

ID3 builds a smaller decision tree in less time, creation of the decision tree ends with the leaf nodes, thereby making the tree created to be pruned during testing. Over-fitting is one of the biggest problems of ID3 algorithm, in addition to which it consumes a lot of time as it only takes in a single attribute during decision-making in a node. Though ID3 usually produce small trees, it does not produce the smallest possible tree. ID3 also makes classification of continuous data very tedious, since it requires lot many trees to be generated to find where the data loses its continuity. As ID3 can get stuck in local optimums during the tree construction, it never guarantee an optimal solution. C4.5 algorithm a successor to ID3 was introduced with various improvements.

9.10 C4.5

C4.5 also developed by Ross Quinlan is an extension of ID3 algorithm which make use of gain ratio to construct the decision tree. Though C4.5 and ID3 algorithms are both accurate and efficient, they often face the problem of over-fitting. But unlike ID3 algorithm, C4.5 supports pruning to rectify the problems that occur due to over-fitting. C4.5 is a classification algorithm whose major advantage over ID3 is that it is capable of classifying continuous as well as discrete values. Let us take a look at some of the advantages and disadvantages of C4.5 algorithm.

1. It is easy to implement and much easier to interpret.
2. It deals with missing values and over-fitting very efficiently.
3. It is easy to manipulate the trees constructed using C4.5 algorithm by introducing slight variations in the input data.
4. C4.5 does not work well for a small training dataset.

C4.5 could carry out classification on both discrete and continuous attributes. It can easily deal with datasets have missing attributes as well as with attributes having differing costs. One of the similarities between ID3 and C4.5 is that both make use of entropy measure as their splitting function.

9.11 Application of Decision Trees to Classify Windows Malware

As we have dealt with the theoretical concepts of how decision tree works, it is important that we approach any cybersecurity problem practically too. Here, we intend to demonstrate how decision tree algorithms can be used to differentiate Windows malware from goodware. The experiments done in the following sections make use of datasets that were provided on request from Cardiff University Research portal.

Though malware detection has always been a topic of research interest for many, it continues to face problems when it comes to early detection. Malware continually evolves and thus finding a suitable technique for its early detection is necessary. Malware analysis can be of two types: static and dynamic. Static malware analysis can be done either by decompiling (to convert the machine code to any programming language) or reverse engineering an application to understand what the application is capable of doing and how it does it. As static code is susceptible to code obfuscation, dynamic behavior of an executable should be observed for details regarding its execution. Also, automatic malware detection is the only solution to protect a computer system from alien intrusion.

9.11.1 Learning More About the Datasets

Malicious and benign executables are run in a system with Windows 7 operating system installed. The behavior data of an executable is captured by observing the API calls made to the operating system kernel. Samples are run in a virtual machine using Cuckoo sandbox with a custom package written in Python library to capture the machine's activity. The CSV file already created by researchers at Cardiff University observes the execution of each executable for 5:05 min. For our purpose, we have normalized the values observed so that each sample only has one record for each feature. They have used a VM with specifications: 2 GB RAM, 25 GB storage, and a single-core CPU with Windows7:64-bit. A total of 594 benign and malicious samples are used for this experiment. Let us take a look the details of the CSV file.

1. sample_id: An identifier for each sample.
2. vector: It is the time in seconds after the file starts to execute.
3. malware: Indicates the label, 1 denotes a malware and 0 denotes a goodware.
4. cpu_system: Indicates the percentage of CPU used by the programs running in the kernel.
5. cpu_user: Indicates the percentage of CPU used by the programs running in the user space.
6. memory: Bytes currently used in the memory.
7. swap: Bytes used in the swap memory.
8. total_pro: Total number of processes running.
9. max_pid: Maximum process id held by a process.
10. rx_bytes: Number of bytes received.
11. tx_bytes: Number of bytes sent.
12. rx_packets: Number of packets received.
13. tx_packets: Number of packets sent.

14. test_set: An indicator of which sample belongs to the training set and which sample belongs to the test set. "True" indicates that the sample belongs to the test set, and "false" indicates that the sample belongs to the training dataset.

9.11.2 *Implementing CART Classification Using Python*

1. Let us import the necessary libraries.

```
import pandas as pd
from sklearn import metrics
from matplotlib import pyplot
from sklearn.metrics import roc_curve, auc, roc_auc_score
from sklearn import tree
from sklearn.metrics import classification_report,
    confusion_matrix
import seaborn
import graphviz
import os
from sklearn.cross_validation import train_test_split
```

2. The next step is to load the dataset.

```
data = pd.read_csv('data_1Normalised-final.csv')
y = data['malware']
X = data.drop('malware', axis=1)
```

3. Now carry out the split and make use of the classifier to classify the samples.

```
X_train, X_test, y_train, y_test = train_test_split(X,
    y, test_size=.7,random_state=None)
cls = tree.DecisionTreeClassifier()
cls.fit(X_train, y_train)
pred_labels = cls.predict(X_test)
print(confusion_matrix(y_test, pred_labels))
print(classification_report(y_test, pred_labels))
```

4. To plot the ROC curve and calculate area under the ROC curve.

```
fpr, recall, thresholds = roc_curve(y_test,pred_labels)
roc_auc = auc(fpr, recall)
pyplot.figure(figsize=(15,6))
pyplot.plot(fpr, recall, 'b', label='AUC = %0.2f' %
    roc_auc, color='darkorange')
pyplot.title('Receiver Operating Characteristic curve',
    fontsize=20)
pyplot.legend(loc='lower right')
pyplot.plot([0, 1], [0, 1], color='navy', linestyle='--')
pyplot.xlim([0.0, 1.0])
pyplot.ylim([0.0, 1.0])
```

```
pyplot.ylabel('True Positive Rate', fontsize=20)
pyplot.xlabel('False Positive Rate', fontsize=20)
pyplot.show()
print("Area under the ROC curve is ")
print(roc_auc_score(y_test, pred_labels))
```

5. Export the decision tree as a graph.

```
dot_data = tree.export_graphviz(cls, out_file=None)
graph = graphviz.Source(dot_data)
graph.render("CART classification")
```

6. To plot the confusion matrix.

```
class_names=[0,1]
fig = pyplot.gcf()
cnf_matrix = metrics.confusion_matrix(y_test, pred_labels)
print(cnf_matrix)
seaborn.heatmap(cnf_matrix.T, square=True, annot=True,
    fmt='d',
cbar=False, xticklabels=class_names,
    yticklabels=class_names,
cmap='summer_r',annot_kws={"size":20})
fig.set_size_inches(2,2)
pyplot.xlabel('true_label', fontsize=20)
pyplot.ylabel('predicted_label', fontsize=20)
```

7. Calculate all the measures to infer more about the classifier's performance.

```
print("Homogeneity: %0.6f" %
    metrics.homogeneity_score(y_test, pred_labels))
print("Completeness: %0.3f" %
    metrics.completeness_score(y_test, pred_labels))
print("V-measure: %0.3f" % metrics.v_measure_score(y_test,
    pred_labels))
print("Jaccard Similarity score : %0.6f"
    %metrics.jaccard_similarity_score
(y_test, pred_labels,normalize=True, sample_weight=None))
print("Cohen's Kappa : %0.6f" %
    metrics.cohen_kappa_score(y_test, pred_labels,
labels=None, weights=None))
print("Hamming matrix : %0.06f"
    %metrics.hamming_loss(y_test, pred_labels,
labels=None, sample_weight=None, classes=None))
print("Accuracy Score : %0.06f"
    %metrics.accuracy_score(y_test,
pred_labels,normalize=True,sample_weight=None))
print("Precision Score : %0.06f"
    %metrics.precision_score(y_test,
pred_labels, labels=None,pos_label=1, average='weighted',
    sample_weight=None))
```

```
print("Mean Absolute Error : %0.06f"
    %metrics.mean_absolute_error
(y_test, pred_labels,
    sample_weight=None,multioutput='raw_values'))
print("F-Score : %0.06f" %metrics.f1_score(y_test,
    pred_labels,
labels=None,
    pos_label=1,average='weighted',sample_weight=None))
print(metrics.classification_report(y_test, pred_labels))
```

The output of the CART classification including various mathematical measures and figures are given below (Table 9.2).

1. Area under the ROC curve is 0.97
2. Homogeneity : 0.831635
3. Accuracy score : 0.973558
4. Precision score : 0.974099
5. Mean absolute error : 0.026442
6. F-score : 0.973552
7. Completeness : 0.832
8. V-measure : 0.832
9. Jaccard similarity score : 0.973558
10. Cohen's Kappa : 0.947123
11. Hamming matrix : 0.026442

Table 9.2 is the classification report. Here, 0 indicates the label is benign and 1 indicates the label is malware. Support is the number of test samples that are taken for the classification task. A decrease in classification error causes an increase in AUC value. As we move off the threshold of the classifier there occurs a trade-off between the true positive rate and false positive rate. Figure 9.5 shows the ROC curve plot for CART classification. The area under the ROC curve is 0.97. The confusion matrix indicating the correlation between actual labels and predicted labels is shown in Table 9.3. The following information can be inferred from the confusion matrix given in Table 9.3.

1. True Positive = 410;
2. True Negative = 400;
3. False Positive = 18;
4. False Negative = 4.

Table 9.2 Classification report

Labels	Precision	Recall	f1 score	Support
0	0.96	0.99	0.97	414
1	0.99	0.96	0.97	418
Avg/total	0.97	0.97	0.97	832

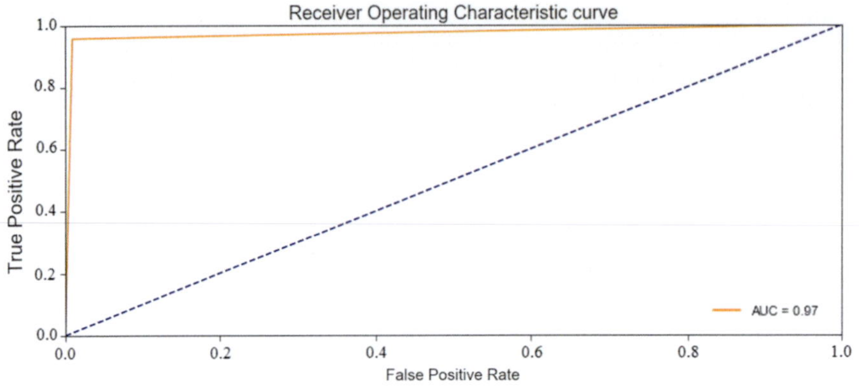

Fig. 9.5 ROC curve

Table 9.3 Confusion matrix

		True label		
		0	1	Total
Predicted label	0	410	18	428
	1	4	400	404
	Total	414	418	832

Confusion matrix is one of the optimal ways of determining the number of labels that were predicted true/false and the number of labels that are actually true/false. The decision tree obtained is shown in Fig. 9.6.

9.11.3 Implementing CART Regression Using Python

```
import pandas as pd
from sklearn import metrics
from matplotlib import pyplot
from sklearn.metrics import roc_curve, auc, roc_auc_score
from sklearn.tree import DecisionTreeRegressor
from sklearn.metrics import classification_report,
    confusion_matrix
from sklearn import tree
import graphviz
import os
import seaborn
pyplot.style.use('ggplot')
seaborn.set(style='ticks')
```

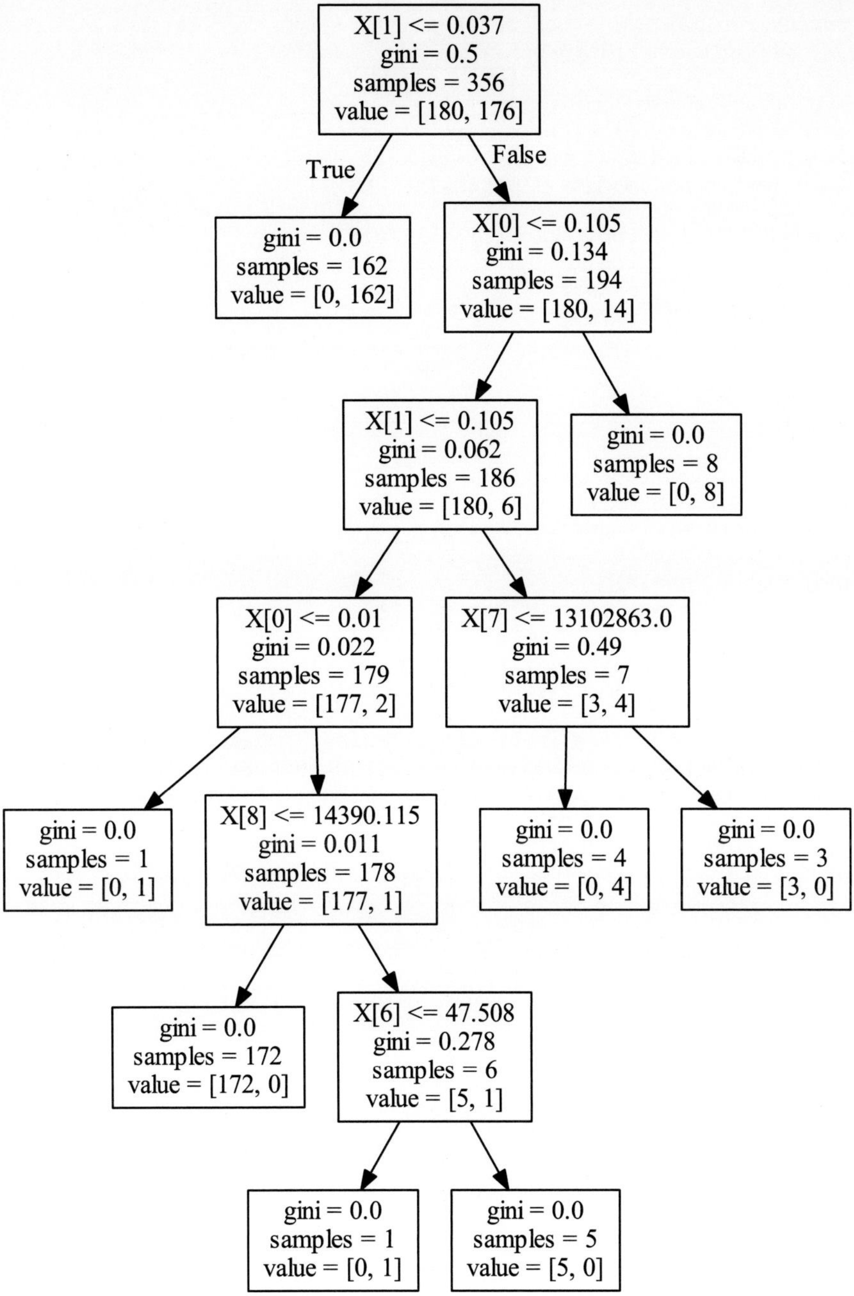

Fig. 9.6 CART classification tree

```
os.environ["PATH"] += os.pathsep + 'C:/Program Files
    (x86)/Graphviz2.38/bin/'

pyplot.style.use('ggplot')
seaborn.set(style='ticks')
data_Train = pd.read_csv('data_1Train.csv')
data_Test = pd.read_csv('data_1Test.csv')

X = data_Train.drop('malware', axis=1)
XX = data_Test.drop('malware', axis=1)
y = data_Train['malware']
yy = data_Test['malware']

X_train = X
X_test = XX
y_train = y
y_test = yy
cls = DecisionTreeRegressor()
cls.fit(X_train, y_train)
pred_labels = cls.predict(X_test)
print("Predicted set of labels are : ")
print(pred_labels)
print("Actual set of labels are : ")
print(y_test)
print(confusion_matrix(y_test, pred_labels))
print(classification_report(y_test, pred_labels))

print("Accuracy Score : %0.06f" %metrics.accuracy_score(y_test,
pred_labels,normalize=True,sample_weight=None))
fpr, recall, thresholds = roc_curve(y_test,pred_labels)
roc_auc = auc(fpr, recall)
pyplot.figure(figsize=(15,6))
pyplot.plot(fpr, recall, 'b', label='AUC = %0.2f' % roc_auc,
    color='darkorange')
pyplot.title('Receiver Operating Characteristic curve',
    fontsize=20)
pyplot.legend(loc='lower right')
pyplot.plot([0, 1], [0, 1], color='navy', linestyle='--')
pyplot.xlim([0.0, 1.0])
pyplot.ylim([0.0, 1.0])
pyplot.ylabel('True Positive Rate', fontsize=20)
pyplot.xlabel('False Positive Rate', fontsize=20)
pyplot.show()
print("Area under the ROC curve is ")
print(roc_auc_score(y_test, pred_labels))

dot_data = tree.export_graphviz(cls, out_file=None)
graph = graphviz.Source(dot_data)
graph.render("dt-regr")
class_names=[0,1]
fig = pyplot.gcf()
cnf_matrix = metrics.confusion_matrix(y_test, pred_labels)
print(cnf_matrix)
```

```
seaborn.heatmap(cnf_matrix.T, square=True, annot=True, fmt='d',
cbar=False, xticklabels=class_names, yticklabels=class_names,
cmap='summer_r',annot_kws={"size":20})
fig.set_size_inches(2,2)
pyplot.xlabel('true_label', fontsize=20)
pyplot.ylabel('predicted_label', fontsize=20)

print("Homogeneity: %0.6f" % metrics.homogeneity_score(y_test,
    pred_labels))
print("Completeness: %0.3f" % metrics.completeness_score(y_test,
    pred_labels))
print("V-measure: %0.3f" % metrics.v_measure_score(y_test,
    pred_labels))
print("Jaccard Similarity score : %0.6f"
    %metrics.jaccard_similarity_score
(y_test, pred_labels,normalize=True, sample_weight=None))
print("Cohen's Kappa : %0.6f" %
    metrics.cohen_kappa_score(y_test, pred_labels,
labels=None, weights=None))
print("Hamming matrix : %0.06f" %metrics.hamming_loss(y_test,
    pred_labels,
labels=None, sample_weight=None, classes=None))
print("Accuracy Score : %0.06f" %metrics.accuracy_score(y_test,
pred_labels,normalize=True,sample_weight=None))
print("Precision Score : %0.06f" %metrics.precision_score(y_test,
pred_labels, labels=None,pos_label=1, average='weighted',
    sample_weight=None))
print("Mean Absolute Error : %0.06f" %metrics.mean_absolute_error
(y_test, pred_labels,
    sample_weight=None,multioutput='raw_values'))
print("F-Score : %0.06f" %metrics.f1_score(y_test, pred_labels,
labels=None, pos_label=1,average='weighted',sample_weight=None))
print(metrics.classification_report(y_test, pred_labels))
```

The output of CART regression including various mathematical measures and figures are given below (Table 9.4).

1. Area under the ROC curve is 0.96
2. Homogeneity : 0.765912
3. Accuracy score : 0.961783
4. Precision score : 0.961791
5. Mean absolute error : 0.038217
6. F-score : 0.961781
7. Completeness : 0.766
8. V-measure : 0.766
9. Jaccard similarity score : 0.961783
10. Cohen's Kappa : 0.923523
11. Hamming matrix : 0.038217

Table 9.4 Classification report

Labels	Precision	Recall	f1 score	Support
0	0.96	0.97	0.96	401
1	0.96	0.96	0.96	384
Avg/total	0.96	0.96	0.96	785

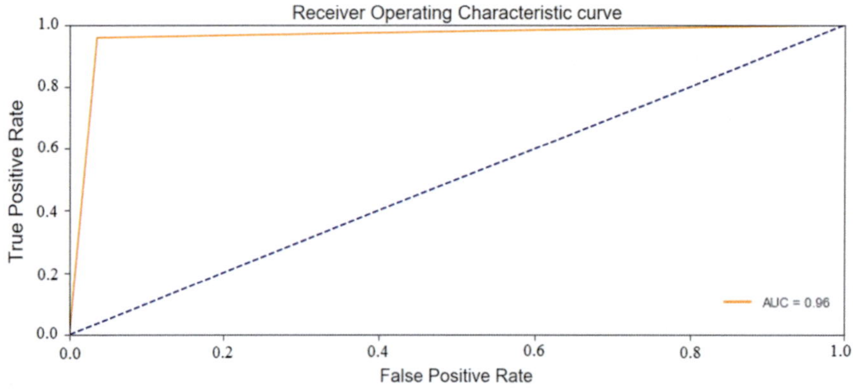

Fig. 9.7 ROC curve

Table 9.5 Confusion matrix

		True label		
		0	1	Total
Predicted label	0	387	16	403
	1	14	368	382
	Total	401	384	785

Table 9.4 gives the classification report; 0 indicates the label is benign and 1 indicates the label is malware. Support is the number of test samples that are taken for the classification task.

A decrease in classification error causes an increase in AUC value. As we move off the threshold of the classifier there occurs a trade-off between the true positive rate and false positive rate. Figure 9.7 shows the ROC curve plot for CART regression. The area under the ROC curve is 0.96. The confusion matrix indicating the correlation between actual labels and predicted labels is shown in Table 9.5. The following information can be inferred from the confusion matrix.

Confusion matrix is one of the optimal ways of determining the number of labels that were predicted true/false and the number of labels that are actually true/false. The decision tree obtained is shown in Fig. 9.8.

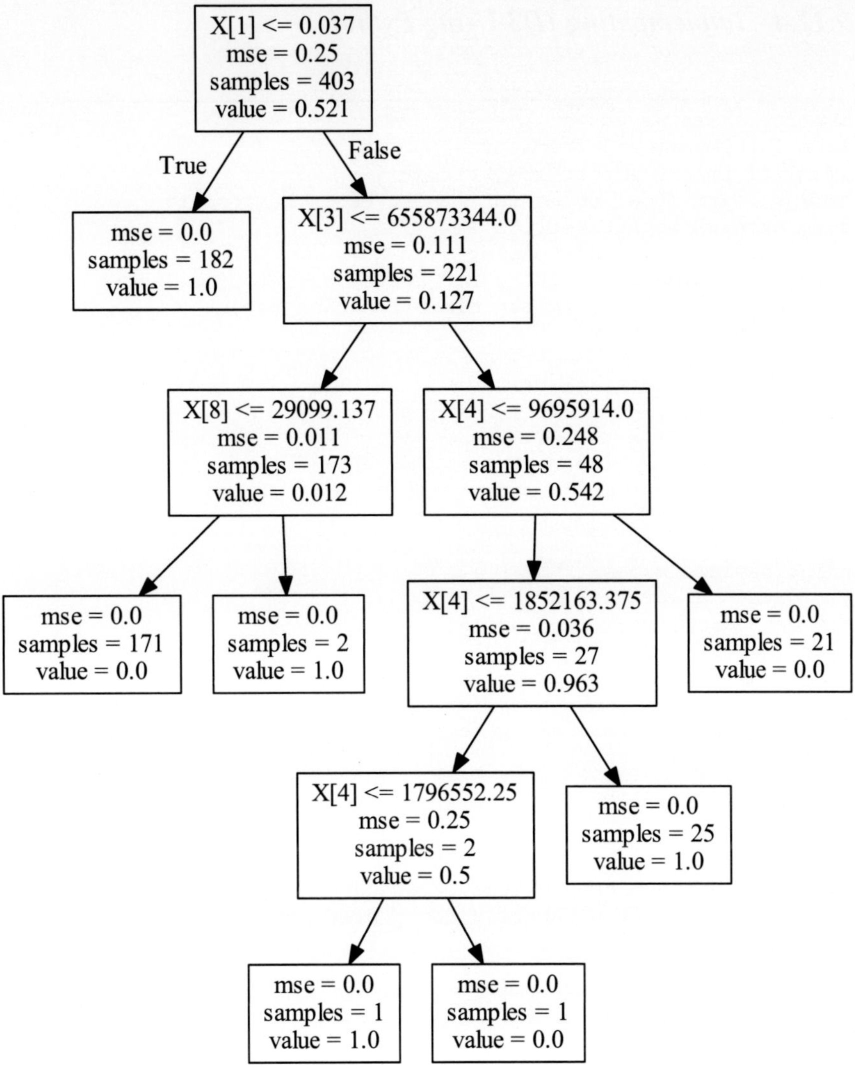

Fig. 9.8 Normalized tree

- True Positive = 368,
- True Negative = 387,
- False Positive = 14, and
- False Negative = 16.

9.11.4 Implementing ID3 Using Python

```
import pandas as pd
from id3 import Id3Estimator
from id3 import export_graphviz
from sklearn.model_selection import train_test_split
from sklearn import metrics
from matplotlib import pyplot
from sklearn.metrics import roc_curve, auc, roc_auc_score
from sklearn.metrics import classification_report,
    confusion_matrix
import seaborn
pyplot.style.use('ggplot')
seaborn.set(style='ticks')

data = pd.read_csv('data_1Normalised-final.csv')
feature_names = ['cpu_sys', 'cpu_user', 'max_pid', 'memory',
    'rx_bytes',
'rx_packets', 'total_pro', 'tx_bytes', 'tx_packets', 'swap']
print(feature_names)
y = data['malware']
X = data.drop('malware', axis=1)
class_names=[1,0]

X_train, X_test, y_train, y_test = train_test_split(X, y,
    test_size=.66,random_state=None)
estimator = Id3Estimator()
est = estimator.fit(X_train, y_train, check_input=True)
pred_labels = est.predict(X_test)
export_graphviz(estimator.tree_, 'id3-3.dot', feature_names)

print(confusion_matrix(y_test, pred_labels))
print(classification_report(y_test, pred_labels))

print("Accuracy Score : %0.06f" %metrics.accuracy_score(y_test,
pred_labels,normalize=True,sample_weight=None))
fpr, recall, thresholds = roc_curve(y_test,pred_labels)
roc_auc = auc(fpr, recall)
pyplot.figure(figsize=(15,6))
pyplot.plot(fpr, recall, 'b', label='AUC = %0.2f' % roc_auc,
    color='darkorange')
pyplot.title('Receiver Operating Characteristic curve',
    fontsize=20)
pyplot.legend(loc='lower right')
pyplot.plot([0, 1], [0, 1], color='navy', linestyle='--')
pyplot.xlim([0.0, 1.0])
pyplot.ylim([0.0, 1.0])
pyplot.ylabel('True Positive Rate', fontsize=20)
pyplot.xlabel('False Positive Rate', fontsize=20)
pyplot.show()
print("Area under the ROC curve is ")
print(roc_auc_score(y_test, pred_labels))
```

```
fig = pyplot.gcf()
cnf_matrix = metrics.confusion_matrix(y_test, pred_labels)
print(cnf_matrix)
seaborn.heatmap(cnf_matrix.T, square=True, annot=True, fmt='d',
cbar=False, xticklabels=class_names, yticklabels=class_names,
cmap='summer_r',annot_kws={"size":20})
fig.set_size_inches(2,2)
pyplot.xlabel('true_label', fontsize=20)
pyplot.ylabel('predicted_label', fontsize=20)

print("Homogeneity: %0.6f" % metrics.homogeneity_score(y_test,
    pred_labels))
print("Completeness: %0.3f" % metrics.completeness_score(y_test,
    pred_labels))
print("V-measure: %0.3f" % metrics.v_measure_score(y_test,
    pred_labels))
print("Jaccard Similarity score : %0.6f"
    %metrics.jaccard_similarity_score
(y_test, pred_labels,normalize=True, sample_weight=None))
print("Cohen's Kappa : %0.6f" %
    metrics.cohen_kappa_score(y_test, pred_labels,
labels=None, weights=None))
print("Hamming matrix : %0.06f" %metrics.hamming_loss(y_test,
    pred_labels,
labels=None, sample_weight=None, classes=None))
print("Accuracy Score : %0.06f" %metrics.accuracy_score(y_test,
pred_labels,normalize=True,sample_weight=None))
print("Precision Score : %0.06f" %metrics.precision_score(y_test,
pred_labels, labels=None,pos_label=1, average='weighted',
    sample_weight=None))
print("Mean Absolute Error : %0.06f" %metrics.mean_absolute_error
(y_test, pred_labels,
    sample_weight=None,multioutput='raw_values'))
print("F-Score : %0.06f" %metrics.f1_score(y_test, pred_labels,
labels=None, pos_label=1,average='weighted',sample_weight=None))
print(metrics.classification_report(y_test, pred_labels))
```

The module used to implement ID3 decision tree algorithm is *decision–tree–id*3. The package comes with an estimator which is called *Id*3*Estimator*. It is imported in sci-kit using the command from id3 import Id3Estimator.

The output of ID3 algorithm is given below:

1. Area under the ROC curve is 0.97
2. Homogeneity : 0.805368
3. Accuracy score : 0.969427
4. Precision score : 0.969643
5. Mean absolute error : 0.030573
6. F-score : 0.969434
7. Completeness : 0.805
8. V-measure : 0.805

Table 9.6 Classification report

Labels	Precision	Recall	f1 score	Support
0	0.96	0.98	0.97	379
1	0.98	0.96	0.97	406
Avg/total	0.97	0.97	0.97	785

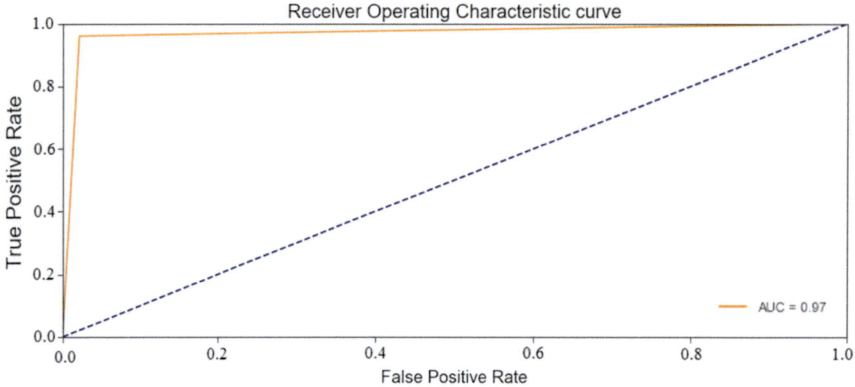

Fig. 9.9 ROC curve

9. Jaccard similarity score : 0.969427
10. Cohen's Kappa : 0.938824
11. Hamming matrix : 0.030573

Table 9.6 shows the classification report; 0 indicates the label is benign and 1 indicates the label is malware. Support is the number of test samples that are taken for the classification task. A decrease in classification error causes an increase in AUC value. As we move off the threshold of the classifier there occurs a trade-off between the true positive rate and false positive rate. Figure 9.9 shows the ROC curve plot for CART classification. The area under the ROC curve is 0.97. The confusion matrix indicating the correlation between actual labels and predicted labels is shown in Table 9.7. The following information can be inferred from the confusion matrix in Table 9.7.

1. True Positive = 390,
2. True Negative = 371,
3. False Positive = 8, and
4. False Negative = 16.

Confusion matrix is one of the optimal ways of determining the number of labels that were predicted true/ false and the number of labels that are actually true/ false. The decision tree obtained is shown in Fig. 9.10.

Fig. 9.10 ID3 decision tree

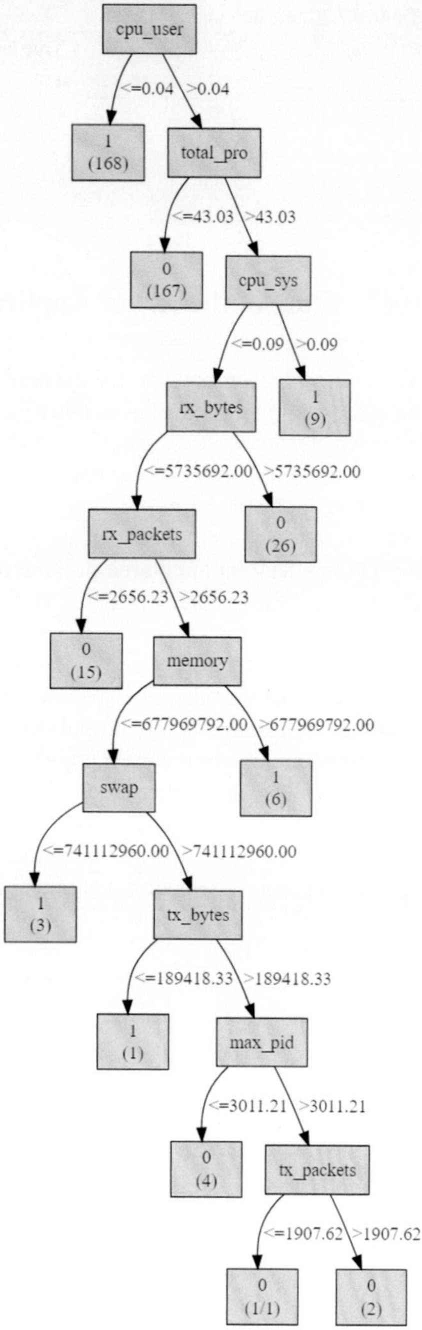

Table 9.7 Confusion matrix

		True label		
		0	1	Total
Predicted label	0	371	16	387
	1	8	390	398
	Total	379	406	785

9.12 State of the Art of Applications of Decision Trees

There is a high probability for cyberattacks in the aviation industry, and this can be addressed by using different machine learning algorithms including the decision trees. Capturing the network traffic and checking the signatures of files transferred are among a few that can be made use of to detect various cyberthreats. Decision trees find applications in detecting virus attacks as well as in mining the security log patterns to identify potential threats.

IDS is a less explored area in the cloud infrastructure, though it can be used in the fog computing over big data. The KDD Cup'99 dataset can be used for this experiment. Do necessary preprocessing on the dataset, for instance, string values in the dataset should be replaced by its corresponding column number. The next step is to normalize the data, after which the decision tree can be constructed using the training set. The tree finally outputs the labels for the test data.

Botnets are one of the most popular methods adopted these days to spread malicious codes via the Internet. They are considered much harmful than malware application as they easily propagate over the network attacking multiple systems within a short span of time. The classification and regression tree (CART) algorithm can be used for feature selection. Features can be extracted by passively monitoring the network traffic to extract information related to TCP connections based on TCP control packets. Further, decision trees can be used to reduce the number of features by eliminating those which have a little influence on the classification problem.

Chapter 10
Adversarial Machine Learning in Cybersecurity

10.1 Introduction

Adversarial machine learning algorithms deal with adversarial sample generation which is creating false input data that are capable enough to fool any machine learning model. For instance, attributes of a goodware can be added to a malware executable to make the classifier identify a malicious sample as benign. As the name suggests, "adversary" means opponent or enemy. If you are thinking what an enemy has got to do in machine learning, this chapter will take you through how vulnerable machine learning models are and how easily they can misunderstand during the learning process. If any set of input data when given to a machine learning model gets misclassified, we call them as adversarial samples. Let us see how adversarial sample generation is adapted in different areas of cybersecurity. With the increase in dominance of machine learning algorithms in defending and early detecting malicious activities in the cyberworld, researchers have started investing time and resource in finding the flaws of machine learning too. The intelligence of a computing machine always depends on how it is taught using what. May it be malware detection or pattern recognition or facial recognition or object identification or self- driving cars or spam email detection, machine learning comes into play.

Research done earlier has also proven that the misclassification rate obtained is pretty high for adversarial samples of malicious executables. Let us consider a binary classification problem, where $X = \{X_1, X_2, \ldots, X_n\}$ are the feature vectors of n malware samples and $Y = \{Y_1, Y_2, \ldots, Y_n\}$ are the set of labels corresponding to each malware sample. The aim of the attacker would be to influence the decision-making capability of the classifier such that the label Y_i moves far from its actual value (flips in the case of binary classifiers). This basically is not applicable to binary classifiers alone but can also be applied for ML models with multiple labels. Let $f : X \rightarrow Y$ be the classification function. The adversarial sample X_i^* corresponding to $X_i \in X$ is given by

$$X_i^* = X_i + \delta_i \tag{10.1}$$

T. Thomas et al., *Machine Learning Approaches in Cyber Security Analytics*, https://doi.org/10.1007/978-981-15-1706-8_10

such that $f(X_i + \delta_i) \neq f(X_i)$ and δ_i is any small perturbation of the feature vector that leads the ML model to misclassify. It is important to test the robustness of any machine learning algorithm against adversarial attacks before the model is deployed for any job. Though the security of ML classifiers continues to be under debate, the effectiveness of ML models make researchers work on how to defend attacks caused due to adversarial samples.

Neural networks are always known to be vulnerable to adversarial samples. Adversarial samples also known as crafted samples are much closer to the actual input data, which finally end up getting classified in a wrong way. It is well known that the adversarial samples are generally difficult to be detected. The following sections would help the reader to find answers to the following questions in specific.

1. How is it possible to produce adversarial samples with high confidence that can effectively fool the machine learning model?
2. What are the different methods available at present to generate adversarial samples?
3. What insights we can get from implementations of practically crafted adversarial samples?

10.2 Adversarial Attacks in Cybersecurity

To craft adversarial samples, slight perturbations are made on legitimate data. The perturbations are made in such a way that they almost go undetected for human sensory organs. But it is not be forgotten that such slight changes are more than enough for a machine learning model to get deceived. Adversaries aim to mislead the prediction done by the machine learning model. Here, in this section, we shall take a quick look at how an adversarial attack leads to security issues in the cyberworld.

Designing adversarial malware executables involve different procedures, one among which is modifying the API call sequences. The generator outputs a modified malware which will be misclassified as benign by changing the API call sequences. C++ programming language supports wrapper functions that are capable of wrapping malware binaries based on its modified API call sequences during runtime. Care should be taken to add API calls without affecting the malicious behavior of the binary. The functionality of the adversarial sample generated can be validated later on by monitoring each sample in a Cuckoo sandbox. There are a number of codes available to generate such functionality-preserving malicious samples that may be used to fool malware detection systems. One among them is the "no-op attack" which is capable of adding API calls without affecting the workflow of an executable.

One of the areas where machine learning finds use is in automated spam email filtering. As we know, there are a number of spammer applications responsible for generating bulk spam emails. Machine learning algorithms have successfully proven their strength in content-based spam email filtering to reduce the spread of unsolicited emails. Though adaptability is one of the major advantages of any machine learning algorithm, it becomes a threat when adversarial samples manipulate the learning phase. In practical situations, it is very easy for attackers to generate crafted samples and thereby make the machine learning models to infer results from ineffective classification rules. In the spam email detection domain, the adversarial samples can craft spam messages such that the underlying machine learning algorithm will get adversely affected while classifying future incoming messages. One of the simplest attacks that can be launched by any attacker is the "dictionary attack" using which a spam filter can be disabled. Attacks like "focused attack" focus on how a victim can be prevented from viewing emails of a particular sort and "pseudospam attacks" are capable of altering the filter in such a way that spam emails enter the user's inbox. In a "causative attack", attackers may be capable enough to influence the training data used by the classifier. In other cases, the attacker might also create an "exploratory attack" by observing how the classifier reacts to new set of emails. A causative adversarial attack involves choosing a desired victim and altering the training set by sending attack messages. Now the spam filter may get infected as it re-trains with the attack messages. This will result in misclassification of new incoming messages.

Speech recognition models are also susceptible to adversarial attacks. Today where research in artificial intelligence is progressing at a rapid rate, automatic speech recognition systems such as Cortana by Microsoft, Siri from Apple, Alexa by Amazon, etc. are found to be susceptible to adversarial attacks. Today, smartphones offer face lock system where a user can unlock the phone by simply focusing the camera to the user's face. This face identification system has also turned out to be vulnerable. Fake images can be generated by adversarial attack algorithms in such a way that humans might identify the image to be real but machine learning algorithms might not. More are the chances for a facial recognition system to be susceptible to poisoning attacks. This is because facial key points can easily be fooled during the training phase. An attacker can wear sunglasses or face masks to fool a face detection system. We will be looking at poisoning attacks in the next section.

One of the areas today where research in artificial intelligence is progressing at a high rate is self-driving cars. An attacker can introduce small manipulations into the image captured by the object recognition system and other sensors attached to the car, thereby introducing an error in the angle to which the car steering should be moved. Sign recognition is one of the most integral parts of autonomous cars. Misclassification that might occur in traffic signs might potentially lead to a disaster.

Polymorphic malware have always been an issue in signature-based malware detection systems while constructing intrusion detection systems (IDS). Here, it is very easy for an attacker to unpack a malware and obfuscate it, thereby resulting in a significant change in its hash value as the detection mechanism would only look for an exact match for signatures. This might allow the malicious sample to bypass the detection mechanism undetected.

10.3 Types of Adversarial Attacks

Adversarial attacks are of two types: poisoning attacks and evasion attacks. We will now discuss the details of these attacks.

Poisoning attacks are a class of adversarial attacks on machine learning models where a small fraction of training data is altered to fool the classifier. As discussed earlier, machine learning has become a vital part of many applications today such as filtering spam messages, computer vision, intrusion detection system, malware detection, etc. Training and testing are the critical components that make a machine learning model more optimal in extracting features and making predictions. Poisoning attack is achieved by injecting malicious data which is capable enough to trick the machine learning model into the training dataset. With increase in the number of malware samples generated each day, lot of research is going on in the early detection and prevention of malware attacks. We iterate each technique in the book for malware detection because malicious intrusion is gaining more attention these days due to the damages it causes. Samples are crafted for poisoning attacks such that features are only added or removed. The features are specific in number, and syntax-based features are used to create crafted samples. An attacker can inject as many as feature variants such that perturbations are applied to each feature within a range to confuse the classifier and make it to take wrong decisions during certain instances. The perturbations are nothing but the variations of features of goodware with the intention of misclassifying a malware as a goodware.

As said in the earlier section, facial recognition systems are more prone to poisoning attacks. The system can be easily manipulated by carefully placing poisoned instances in the training data. Images are less likely to look suspicious as slight changes in image pixels are difficult to be noticed by a human eye.

Evasion attacks are those kind of attacks where an intruder craft samples in the test dataset. The intuition here is that the attacker maximizes the loss on the adversarial sample with the original class to cause misclassification such that the sample gets classified into some other class. Evasion attacks generally occur during decision-making, as the attack primarily aims in launching an attack while the model is tested with some random piece of data.

Though adversarial attacks of different types are capable enough to bring down the performance of a machine learning model, many defensive techniques are also in the process of development.

10.4 Algorithms for Crafting Adversarial Samples

There are a lot many ways for attacking a fully functioning machine learning model. This would make the model perform malicious actions exactly opposite to what the algorithm is intended to do. Not always would attackers have white-box access to the exact machine learning model implemented; in such cases, black-box attacks are chosen to create adversarial samples. This is because black-box models supports transferability. In most of the scenarios, the samples crafted for a particular machine learning model succeed in affecting other ML models as well, provided that all the models do the same task. Thus, with very less amount of information about the ML model responsible for solving problems in the victim's side, an attacker can train a proxy model with crafted samples and transfer it to the victim. This also requires the training feature set to be acquired by the attacker to generate adversarial samples. There are a few research publications that explain techniques capable of conducting black-box attacks without making use of transferability to generate adversarial samples. This section would deal with algorithms that are capable of fooling machine learning models in specific. There are a lot of algorithms available for creating adversarial samples, in which we shall only cover two algorithms in detail along with their implementations. The other algorithms are only briefed here. The different algorithms are as follows:

1. Generative adversarial network (GAN),
2. Fast gradient sign method,
3. L-BFGS,
4. Carlini–Wagner attack,
5. Elastic net method,
6. Basic iterative method, and
7. Momentum iterative method.

10.4.1 Generative Adversarial Network (GAN)

GAN which stands for generative adversarial network is a technique for generating adversarial samples by learning and approximating the distribution of original feature set. Deep neural networks (DNN) have proven themselves to be one of the most efficient machine learning algorithms that are found to work well with some of the large-scale practical applications such as facial recognition, object identification for driverless cars, speech processing, robotics, medical imaging, etc. But experiments conducted in the recent times have found DNN to be vulnerable to adversarial attacks which are capable of introducing small perturbations to the input data, thereby bringing a deviation from the actual prediction made by the DNN. There are a lot of research ongoing in generating adversarial samples for DNNs. Samples are created for experiments done on image processing as well as on malware detection. GAN even has the ability to generate images from noise, thereby posing a huge threat to the current image recognition systems.

GAN consists of a generator G and a discriminator D as said above. Primarily, we have the dataset whose crafted samples are to be created. G captures the distribution of that dataset. D calculates the probability that the sample belongs to the original dataset and not created by G. G aims to craft the sample in such a way that the probability of D misclassifying the incoming sample is maximized. The job of D is to determine the legitimacy of an incoming sample. GANs are DNN architectures. When samples are fed to the GAN, the output of G will be evaluated by D to determine where the sample has come from. Neural network makes use of backpropagation to update the generators weights to produce outputs with less loss. Here, the discriminator is only used as a classifier.

For easy understanding, we may interpret GAN as a game between two players, where one of the players G creates crafted samples and the other player D tries to find out the authenticity of the incoming sample. The generator G by default tries to fool the discriminator D, and the attempt is considered to be a success when D misclassifies the sample generated by G. Training a GAN is a step-by-step procedure. We consider the problem of binary malware classification to explain GAN. The details are given below.

1. Feed some random noise to the generator G. Let (x, y) be an input-label pair which gets transformed into (x', y'). x' being the crafted input and y' being the fake label.
2. Feed the discriminator D with the actual sample x and the crafted input x' alternatively.
3. D returns a probability, which is any number between 0 and 1.
4. Both G and D are feedback loops. G is a feedback loop with D, while D is a feedback loop with the actual set of training feature set.
5. As we had said in the beginning, we consider here a binary classifier which classifies an input sample either as a malware or as a goodware.
6. The loss of D is calculated as the sum of the loss of the neural network when both the actual and crafted samples are fed as input. G calculate its noise separately as each network has a different objective function.
7. An optimization algorithm is applied, and above steps are repeated for a certain number of epochs.

Maximum likelihood estimation is a procedure applied on GAN to choose the parameters for the ML model so as to maximize the likelihood of the training data. This is done by creating a distribution of data by selecting samples from the training set and finding the probability of the ML model over those crafted samples.

Considering both $G(z; \theta_G)$ and $D(x; \theta_D)$ to be multilayer perceptrons, an input noise vector z is defined to study the distribution p_G of the generator G over the input data x. Then, $D(x)$ is the probability that x is a legitimate sample and not crafted by the attacker. D is trained such that its probability of labeling samples created by G is maximized, and G is trained to minimize $\log(1 - D(G(z)))$. Then, the value function $V(G, D)$ can be defined as

$$\min_G \max_D V(D, G) = \mathbb{E}_{x \sim p_{data}(x)}[\log D(x)] + \mathbb{E}_{z \sim p_z(z)}[\log(1 - D(G(z)))]. \quad (10.2)$$

During practical implementation, there are possibilities for the above equation to fail in providing sufficient gradient for G for a better learning. This is because in the beginning stage of the training there are chances for D to misclassify incoming samples, as they might be clearly different from the actual training data. This might result in the saturation of $\log(1 - D(G(z)))$. Hence, it is always better to train G so that it maximizes $\log(D(G(z)))$. Simple codes for the generator, discriminator, and GAN are given below.

```
generator = Sequential([
Dense(128, input_shape=(100,)),
LeakyReLU(alpha=0.01),
Dense(784),
Activation('tanh')
], name='generator')
```

```
discriminator = Sequential([
Dense(128, input_shape=(784,)),
LeakyReLU(alpha=0.01),
Dense(1),
Activation('sigmoid')], name='discriminator')
```

```
gan = Sequential([
generator,
discriminator])
```

10.4.2 Fast Gradient Sign Method (FGSM)

The fast gradient sign method (FGSM) is one of the algorithms to generate adversarial samples proposed by Goodfellow. Gradient descent is nothing but an optimization algorithm so as to find the local minimum of a differentiable function. The gradient sign method makes use of the gradient of the underlying ML model to find the adversarial examples. The actual sample x is crafted by subtracting or adding a slight error value ε to each feature of x if $x \in X$ and X is a malware dataset, or to each pixel value in case an image is crafted. The addition or subtraction is done based on whether the sign of gradient of the pixel (in case of an image) is positive or negative. If the error value is added in the direction of the gradient, then the image will be purposely altered so that the classifier fails.

Let x be any sample data point taken from the actual training dataset X, y be the label of the data point, and θ be the parameters associated with the model. If the cost function to train the neural network is represented as $J(\theta, x, y)$, then it may be linearized to obtain an optimal max-norm constrained perturbation. The perturbation is given by

$$\eta = \varepsilon\ sign(\Delta_x J(\theta, x, y)), \tag{10.3}$$

where $\Delta_x J$ is the gradient of the loss function of the model w.r.t. the original input vector x. Thus, the crafted sample is given by

$$x' = x + \eta \tag{10.4}$$

The sign of the gradient is said to be positive if the noise induced into a sample feature vector increases the loss (increase in pixel intensity in the case of images) and the gradient is said to be negative if there is a decrease in loss (decrease in pixel intensity in the case of images). Recent research works also show that deep neural networks can be deceived by adding perturbations as small as altering a single pixel value of an image.

Max-norm constraint is a form of regularization wherein an absolute upper bound is applied on the magnitude of the weight vector for every neuron in the network and to use project gradient descent to enforce the constraint. This when implemented practically updates the parameters in neural network, thereby clamping the weight vector w of each neuron to satisfy $||w||_2 < c$. It is very crucial to update different parameters during backpropagation while the neural network is trained using gradient descent. A neuron within a neural network is said to be clamped when it is set to a fixed value. While the system is running, the activation levels of the input units are always clamped to desired values.

10.4.3 Limited-Memory Broyden–Fletcher–Goldfarb–Shanno Algorithm (L-BFGS)

Limited-memory Broyden–Fletcher–Goldfarb–Shanno algorithm (L-BFGS), a gradient-based attack, is used to create adversarial samples. It adopts a brute force white-box approach. L-BFGS algorithm can be simply run for a lesser number of iterations to initiate an attack with lower success rate. Let x be a sample taken from the training dataset and x' be its corresponding adversarial sample. The algorithm aims to solve the following optimization problem:

$$\begin{aligned} &\text{minimize} \quad c \cdot ||x - x'||_2^2 + \text{loss}_{F,l}(x') \\ &\text{such that} \quad x' \in [0, 1]^n, \end{aligned}$$

where $\text{loss}_{F,l}$ is a function that maps an input feature set to a positive real number, F is a neural network, and l is the loss function. A suitable constant $c > 0$ is found by line searching which generates adversarial samples of minimum distance. The optimization problem is solved for different values of c.

10.4.4 Carlini–Wagner Attack (CW Attack)

Here, creating crafted samples is formulated as an optimization problem. The aim is to find a small deviation δ that is to be made to an input feature set x so that the ML model assigns it a different label. Experiments conducted have proven that Carlini–Wagner attack produces adversarial examples with very less distortion, even lesser than FGSM attack. In most of the cases, Carlini–Wagner attack is used to generate adversaries where there is zero knowledge about both the detection mechanism and the machine learning model used. The aim of the attack is to minimize the perturbation using gradient descent as

$$\text{minimize}||x' - x||_2^2 + c \cdot l(x'), \tag{10.5}$$

where c is any constant, x is the original data, x' is the crafted data, and $l()$ is the loss function. $l()$ is given by

$$l(x') = \max(\max\{Z(x')_i : i \neq t\} - Z(x')_t, -k), \tag{10.6}$$

where t is the target class and $\max\{Z(x')_i : i \neq t\} - Z(x')_t$ is the difference used to compare the class t with the next most likely class. Z called logits is the final layer of the neural network. The value of k creates an impact over the confidence of these adversarial examples. As the value of k increases, the adversarial samples generated are said to have high confidence and when $k = 0$ the adversarial samples are said to have low confidence. The term *low confidence* indicates that the actual sample and the crafted sample will be assigned the same label after classification.

The Adversarial Robustness Toolbox has the Carlini–Wagner L_2 attack implemented, which can be evoked to carry out the attack while doing experiments.

10.4.5 Elastic Net Method (EAD)

The elastic net method or EAD is one among the attacks inspired from the CW attack discussed in the previous section. EAD makes use of the loss function same as that of CW attack and performs elastic net regularization instead of L_2 (ridge) and L_1 (Lasso) regularization. Elastic net regularization combines the penalties of both ridge and Lasso regularizations, and aims in minimizing the following loss function:

$$\underset{z \in \mathcal{Z}}{\text{minimize}} f(z) + \lambda_1||z||_1 + \lambda_2||z||_2^2, \tag{10.7}$$

where p optimization variables form a vector z, $\mathcal{Z} = \mathbb{R}^p$ is the set of feasible solutions, $f(z)$ is the loss function, λ_1 and λ_2 are the L_1 and L_2 regularization parameters and $\lambda_1, \lambda_2 \geq 0$. $||z||_q$ is the L_q norm of z, and the term $\lambda_1||z||_1 + \lambda_2||z||_2^2$ is the elastic net regularizer of z. The elastic net regularization becomes the ridge regression formulation when $\lambda_1 = 0$ and becomes the Lasso formulation when $\lambda_2 = 0$. The elastic net regularization is capable of selecting highly correlated features to overcome the flaw caused due to high-dimensional feature selection. $f(z)$ the loss function becomes the mean squared error for standard regression problems and z would represent the weights on the features. Let f be the loss function for creating the crafted samples, and then $f(x)$ is given by

$$f(x, t) = \max\{\max_{j \neq t}[Logit(x')]_j - [Logit(x')]_t, -k\}, \tag{10.8}$$

where t is the target class, $Logit(x') = [[Logit(x')]_1, \ldots, [Logit(x')]_K] \in \mathbb{R}^K$ is the logit layer (the last neuron layer of neural network) representation of x' in the neural network, K is the total number of classes considered in the classification problem, and $k \geq 0$ is the confidence parameter which is responsible for ensuring a constant gap between $\max_{j \neq t}[Logit(x')]_j$ and $[Logit(x')]_t$.

10.4.6 Basic Iterative Method

The basic iterative method also known as projected gradient descent is an extension of basic fast gradient sign method. Let x be the input sample and x' be the crafted sample. Then the adversarial examples are generated using the following iterative process:

$$\begin{aligned} x_0' &= x \\ x_{n+1}' &= Clip_{x,e}\{x_n' + \alpha sign(\nabla_x J(x_n', y_{true})\}, \end{aligned} \tag{10.9}$$

where α is the step size. Gradient descent is an optimization algorithm aimed at finding the optimal weights so as to minimize the loss of a function. The step size helps in determining how the weight should be modified, by deciding how much to move while trying to minimize the loss. The lower the step size, the higher the training time and it will take more time to calculate the best weights. $Clip_{x,e}\{A\}$ indicates the element-wise clipping of x, and ∇_x is the model's gradient.

10.4.7 Momentum Iterative Method

Momentum iterative fast gradient method is a white-box attacking algorithm which aims to stabilize optimization and escape local minima by accumulating the gradients of loss function during each iteration. The optimization problem for generating adversarial samples is

$$\underset{x'}{\text{argmax}} J(x', y), \quad \text{such that } ||x' - x||_\infty \leq \varepsilon, \tag{10.10}$$

where $J(x', y)$ is the loss function used to train the ML model, which is defined as $J(x', y) = -y \cdot \log(p(x'))$; $p(x')$ being the predicted probability of any ML model given input x' and ε is the size of the adversarial perturbation. Many research works demonstrate that the adversarial examples generated by momentum iterative methods show higher success rates for both black-box and white-box attacks.

10.5 Adversarial Attack Models and Attacks

As we have seen different models that are capable of deceiving machine learning algorithms by creating crafted samples, it is equally important to understand defensive mechanisms as well. Defensive techniques against adversarial attacks help to make the ML model more resistant to perturbations that might occur in the input data. *cleverhans* is an implementation which provides functionalities that implement machine learning models. It also has modules that has defensive mechanisms implemented. The same concept of constructing adversarial samples is adopted here as well. What would be the result if we purposely provide crafted samples to a machine learning model during its training phase? This would obviously help the machine learning model to improve its performance through continued learning.

The security of machine learning is a field of study that had gained maximum attention from researchers these days. Threat models are one of the methods used to optimize ML models by attacking them on purpose to find the hidden vulnerabilities of the network. These threat models can be attacked using different attack techniques to understand how robust each model is. The three different types of threat models along with the corresponding attack models are given below.

1. Perfect Knowledge Adversary
   Here, adversary is aware of the parameters used by the model and the detection techniques that the ML model uses to secure itself. The attacker can make use of this available information to evade the actual ML model as well as the detector.
   An *adaptive white-box attack* can be used here as an attack strategy. Assuming that the attacker has access to the detector, the attacker has full knowledge about the ML algorithm used, its parameters, and hyperparameters as well as the underlying architecture. Now the aim of the intruder would be to construct a loss function and create adversarial examples that are capable of bypassing the detector and thereby fooling the ML classifier. Finding an appropriate loss function is a crucial part in this attack.
2. Limited Knowledge Adversary
   Here, although the adversary does not have access neither to the actual detector implemented nor to the training data used, it has knowledge about the detection scheme used to secure the ML model as well as the training algorithm.
   A *black-box attack* is one of the most difficult ways to construct an adversarial sample. This is because as the name suggests the attacker would be totally unaware of the underlying architecture and the parameters of the detector. The black-box

attack purely depends on the property of transferability which we have discussed earlier in this chapter. The intruder can create a separate training dataset with size and quality similar to that of the original training dataset, so as to train a substitute model.

3. Zero-Knowledge Adversary
   Here, the adversarial samples are generated with the lack of knowledge on the ML model and the detector used.
   A *strong attack* is carried out mostly using CW's attack strategy, and it is checked whether the defense is capable of detecting the attack. If the strong attack fails in attacking the model, then for sure the two previous attack models also would fail in attacking the detection mechanism. Here, the threat model is said to be very weak as the attacker is not even aware of the defense that has been employed by the underlying ML model.

10.6 Adversarial Attacks on Image Classification and Malware Detection

Here, we shall take a look at two of the attacking methods discussed in the earlier sections, namely, the GAN and gradient-based methods to generate adversarial samples. Artificial intelligence has totally changed the automobile industry by assisting in developing driverless cars. Though it has been around for the past few years, it is gaining much attention these days due to the advancements in ML techniques. Continuous efforts are made to increase the efficiency of object recognition methodologies, speech recognition, driver monitoring, eye tracking, etc. as this would help in building AI-based autonomous vehicles. Let us assume a scenario where an autonomous car while in motion encounters an animal crossing a road and the ML model implemented within the car detects it as some stationary object. This false recognition can lead to serious accidents. This is what adversarial attacks can do to ML models that are implemented in different technologies that substantially affect our daily lives such as face recognition, malware detection, industrial control systems, and so on. In the following sections, we shall look into adversarial attacks on image classification and malware detection problems.

10.6.1 Gradient-Based Attack on Image Misclassification

In this section, we shall try to understand a simple code that adopts a neural network classifier to classify animals and an adversarial code snippet that misclassifies any kind of animal the network receives as input.

1. The first step in any experiment is to import all the necessary libraries.
   keras.preprocessing import image is the data preprocessing module of the Keras

deep learning library which provides utilities for working with images. *inception_v3* is a deep neural network pretrained on the ImageNet and is publicly available in Keras. There are many more pretrained models available such as VGG16, VGG19, Xception, ResNet50, and MobileNet. It is easy to use the pretrained weights of these neural net architectures, as training neural networks from the scratch is time-consuming. Keras being a model-level library has a *backend* implementation of TensorFlow, Theano and CNTK, and deep learning frameworks. PIL stands for python image library which aids manipulating images of different file formats.

```
import numpy as np
from keras.preprocessing import image
from keras.applications import inception_v3
from keras import backend as K
from PIL import Image
```

2. Now load the pretrained DNN and the image of an animal; here, we take the image of a cat. Scale the image to maintain the pixel intensities between $[-1, 1]$. Define the number of samples that should be propagated through the network by specifying the batch size. Carry out the prediction by running the image through the neural network and print the corresponding prediction made.

```
model = inception_v3.InceptionV3()
img = image.load_img("cat.jpg", target_size=(299, 299))
input_image = image.img_to_array(img)
input_image /= 255.
input_image -= 0.5
input_image *= 2.
input_image = np.expand_dims(input_image, axis=0)
predictions = model.predict(input_image)
predicted_classes =
    inception_v3.decode_predictions(predictions, top=1)
imagenet_id, name, confidence = predicted_classes[0][0]
print("This is a {} with {:.4}% confidence!".format(name,
    confidence * 100))
```

This gives the following output predicting the input image as an Egyptian cat.

```
This is a Egyptian_cat with 72.3% confidence!
```

3. Now we shall take a look at how the network is fooled to give a wrong prediction for the image of a cat. After loading the $Inceptionv3$ model, remember to store the first and last layer of the neural network into two variables. This is to make sure that the image we intend to craft is returned after further processing. There are different numbers corresponding to different images such as class 859 is for toaster. Choose any image from $ImageNet$ to fool the network with, and assign its corresponding id to a variable. Repeat all the process said in the previous step.

Load the image to be crafted, scale the image, and add an extra dimension for the batch size.

```
model = inception_v3.InceptionV3()
model_input_layer = model.layers[0].input
model_output_layer = model.layers[-1].output
object_type_to_fake = 859
img = image.load_img("cat.jpg", target_size=(299, 299))
original_image = image.img_to_array(img)
original_image /= 255.
original_image -= 0.5
original_image *= 2.
original_image = np.expand_dims(original_image, axis=0)
```

4. Next, calculate the distortion (amount of change) that we intend to bring over the image to be crafted. Specify the learning rate for each iteration, for making the network understand how the crafted image is to be updated in each iteration. Define the cost function and gradient function, and create a Keras function that can be used to calculate the current cost and gradient. Make use of a while loop to adjust the crafted image so that it shows higher efficiency in tricking the neural network model. Finally, de-scale the image and save it.

```
max_change_above = original_image + 0.01
max_change_below = original_image - 0.01
hacked_image = np.copy(original_image)
learning_rate = 0.1
cost_function = model_output_layer[0, object_type_to_fake]
gradient_function = K.gradients(cost_function,
    model_input_layer)[0]
grab_cost_and_gradients_from_model =
    K.function([model_input_layer,K.learning_phase()],
    [cost_function, gradient_function])
cost = 0.0

while cost < 0.80:
# Check the closeness of the image is to the target
    class(toaster) and grab the gradients to modify the
    image and alter it in that direction.
cost, gradients =
    grab_cost_and_gradients_from_model([hacked_image, 0])
hacked_image += gradients * learning_rate
hacked_image = np.clip(hacked_image, max_change_below,
    max_change_above)
hacked_image = np.clip(hacked_image, -1.0, 1.0)

print("Model's predicted likelihood that the image is a
    toaster: {:.8}%".format(cost * 100))

img = hacked_image[0]
img /= 2.
img += 0.5
img *= 255.
```

```
im = Image.fromarray(img.astype(np.uint8))
im.save("hacked-cat.jpg")
```

5. The output image is a crafted image of the Egyptian cat which gets classified by the neural network as a toaster.

```
Model's predicted likelihood that the image is a toaster:
    1.5992288%
Model's predicted likelihood that the image is a toaster:
    1.7042456%
Model's predicted likelihood that the image is a toaster:
    1.8456187%
Model's predicted likelihood that the image is a toaster:
    1.9906914%
Model's predicted likelihood that the image is a toaster:
    2.1799866%
Model's predicted likelihood that the image is a toaster:
    2.4168948%
.
.
.
.
.
.

Model's predicted likelihood that the image is a toaster:
    41.074491%
Model's predicted likelihood that the image is a toaster:
    73.922229%
Model's predicted likelihood that the image is a toaster:
    88.298416%
```

10.6.2 Creation of Adversarial Malware Samples Using GAN

We know that most of the malware detection systems today adopt machine learning algorithms for effective detection of malicious applications. This is because ML systems help in predicting malicious nature of applications using static and dynamic features more effectively. In this section, we shall take a look at how adversarial malware samples can be created using GAN.

First, acquire the necessary malware samples from AMD dataset or from VirusShare. Use any malware analysis platform such as Cuckoo sandbox to extract the API features. The first step is to build a black-box detector and train it; similarly, build and compile a substitute detector and build a generator. Input the malware and noise into the generator to generate adversarial malware samples. The code used here is publicly available in https://github.com/yanminglai/Malware-GAN. In malware Detection, the true positive rate (TPR) is an indication of the detection rate

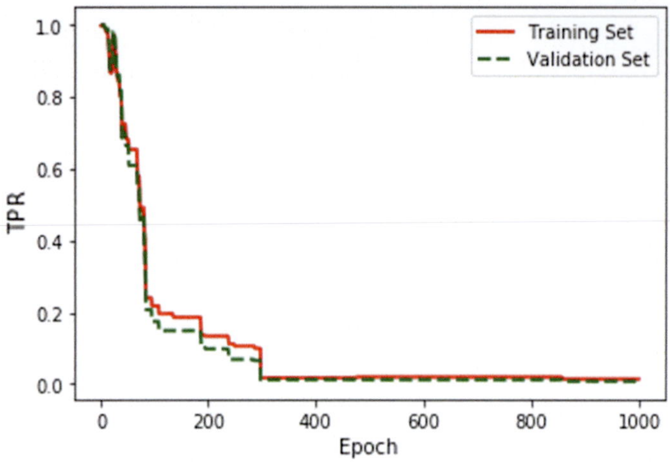

Fig. 10.1 Change of TPR over time

of malware. Once the adversarial attack is carried out, the reduction in TPR would indicate the success rate of malware samples remaining undetected by the detection algorithm.

Figure 10.1 shows the variation of TPR on the training set and the validation set over different values of epochs. The x-axis shows the epoch, while the y-axis represents the TPR. We see that the TPR almost becomes zero when the epoch is 400. Also, the TPR of original and crafted samples indicated that crafted malware were less identified as malware samples by the detector.

```
Original_Train_TPR: 0.979890310786106, Adver_Train_TPR:
    0.013711151736745886
Original_Train_TPR: 0.9854014598540146, Adver_Train_TPR:
    0.0072992700729927005
```

Bibliography

1. Alpaydin, Ethem. 2014. *Introduction to machine learning*.
2. Ayodele, Taiwo Oladipupo. 2010. Types of machine learning algorithms. *In New advances in machine learning*. InTech.
3. Brownlee, Jason. 2016. Supervised and unsupervised machine learning algorithms.
4. Hierons, Rob. 1999. Machine learning. Tom M. Mitchell. Published by McGraw-Hill, Maidenhead, UK, international student edition, 1997. ISBN: 0-07-115467-1, 414 pages. Price: UK£ 22.99, soft cover. *Software Testing, Verification and Reliability* 9 (3): 191–193.
5. Knuth, Donald Ervin, Tracy Larrabee, and Paul M. Roberts. *Mathematical writing*, vol. 14.
6. Masnadi-Shirazi, Hamed, and Nuno Vasconcelos. 2009. On the design of loss functions for classification: theory, robustness to outliers, and savageboost. In *Advances in neural information processing systems*, 1049–1056.
7. Ng, Andrew. Linear regression.
8. Ng, Andrew Y., and Michael I. Jordan. 2002. On discriminative versus generative classifiers: A comparison of logistic regression and naive bayes. In *Advances in neural information processing systems*, 841–848.
9. Quinlan, J. R. 1986. Induction of decision trees. *Machine Learning* 1(1): 81–106.
10. Rokach, Lior, and Oded Maimon. 2005. Decision trees. In *Data mining and knowledge discovery handbook*, 165–192. Springer.
11. Shalev-Shwartz, Shai, and Shai Ben-David. 2014. *Understanding machine learning: From theory to algorithms*. Cambridge University Press.
12. Wasserman, Larry. 2013. *All of statistics: a concise course in statistical inference*. Springer Science & Business Media.
13. Das, Kajaree, and Rabi Narayan Behera. A survey on machine learning: Concept, algorithms and applications.
14. Dey, Ayon. Machine learning algorithms: A review.
15. Harrington, Peter. 2012. *Machine learning in action*. Shelter Island, NY: Manning Publications Co.
16. Langley, Pat. Crafting papers on machine learning.
17. Mohammad, Rami M., Lee McCluskey, and Fadi Thabtah. Phishingwebsites.
18. Marsland, Stephen. 2011. *Machine learning: an algorithmic perspective*, pp 1–25. Chapman and Hall/CRC.
19. Mitchell, Tom Michael. 2006. *The discipline of machine learning*, vol 9.
20. Nilsson, Nils J. (1996). Introduction to machine learning: An early draft of a proposed textbook.
21. Pedregosa, Fabian, Gaël Varoquaux, Alexandre Gramfort, Vincent Michel, Bertrand Thirion, Olivier Grisel, Mathieu Blondel, Peter Prettenhofer, Ron Weiss, Vincent Dubourg, et al. 2011.

T. Thomas et al., *Machine Learning Approaches in Cyber Security Analytics*, https://doi.org/10.1007/978-981-15-1706-8

Scikit-learn: Machine learning in python. *Journal of Machine Learning Research* 12(Oct): 2825–2830.
22. Gunnar, Rätsch. A brief introduction into machine learning.
23. Richert, Willi. 2013. *Building machine learning systems with Python*. Packt Publishing Ltd.
24. Robert, Christian. 2014. Machine learning, a probabilistic perspective.
25. Simeone, Osvaldo et al. 2018. A brief introduction to machine learning for engineers. *Foundations and Trends® in Signal Processing* 12 (3–4): 200–431.
26. Welling, Max. A first encounter with machine learning.
27. Boutaba, Raouf, Mohammad A. Salahuddin, Noura Limam, Sara Ayoubi, Nashid Shahriar, Felipe Estrada-Solano, and Oscar M. Caicedo. 2018. A comprehensive survey on machine learning for networking: Evolution, applications and research opportunities. *Journal of Internet Services and Applications* 9 (1): 16.
28. Buczak, Anna L., and Erhan Guven. 2016. A survey of data mining and machine learning methods for cyber security intrusion detection. *IEEE Communications Surveys & Tutorials* 18 (2): 1153–1176.
29. Chan, Philip K., and Richard P. Lippmann. 2006. Machine learning for computer security. *Journal of Machine Learning Research* 7 (Dec): 2669–2672.
30. Conti, Mauro, Tooska Dargahi, and Ali Dehghantanha. 2018. Cyber threat intelligence: Challenges and opportunities. *Cyber Threat Intelligence*, 1–6.
31. Ford, Vitaly, and Ambareen Siraj. 2014. Applications of machine learning in cyber security. In *Proceedings of the 27th international conference on computer applications in industry and engineering*.
32. Ji, Tiantian, Yue Wu, Chang Wang, Xi Zhang, Zhongru Wang. 2018. The coming era of alphahacking?: A survey of automatic software vulnerability detection, exploitation and patching techniques. In *2018 IEEE third international conference on data science in cyberspace (DSC)*, 53–60. IEEE.
33. John, Teenu S., and Tony Thomas. 2019. Adversarial attacks and defenses in malware detection classifiers. In *Handbook of research on cloud computing and big data applications in IoT*, page to appear. IGI Global.
34. John, Teenu S., Tony Thomas, and Md. Meraj Uddin. 2017. A multifamily android malware detection using deep autoencoder based feature extraction. In *Proceedings of 9th IEEE International Conference on Advanced Computing, CoAC 2017*.
35. Kang, BooJoong, Suleiman Y. Yerima, Sakir Sezer, and Kieran McLaughlin. 2016. N-gram opcode analysis for android malware detection. arXiv:1612.01445.
36. Krishnan, Arya, Tony Thomas, Gayathri R. Nayar, and Sarath S.M. 2018. Liveness detection in finger vein imaging device using plethysmographic signals. *Advances in Intelligent Systems and Computing Series*, 251–260.
37. Nguyen, Khoi Khac, Dinh Thai Hoang, Dusit Niyato, Ping Wang, Diep Nguyen, and Eryk Dutkiewicz. 2018. Cyberattack detection in mobile cloud computing: A deep learning approach. In *Wireless communications and networking conference (WCNC), 2018 IEEE*, 1–6. IEEE.
38. Nunes, Eric, Casey Buto, Paulo Shakarian, Christian Lebiere, Stefano Bennati, Robert Thomson, and Holger Jaenisch. 2015. Malware task identification: A data driven approach. In *2015 IEEE/ACM international conference on advances in social networks analysis and mining (ASONAM)*, 978–985. IEEE.
39. Nunes, Eric, Ahmad Diab, Andrew Gunn, Ericsson Marin, Vineet Mishra, Vivin Paliath, John Robertson, Jana Shakarian, Amanda Thart, and Paulo Shakarian. 2016. Darknet and deepnet mining for proactive cybersecurity threat intelligence. arXiv:1607.08583.
40. Ragendhu, S.P., and Tony Thomas. 2019. Fast and accurate fingerprint recognition in principal component subspace. *Advances in intelligent systems and computing series*, page to appear.
41. Roopak, S., and Tony Thomas. 2014. A novel phishing page detection mechanism using html source code comparison and cosine similarity. In *2014 fourth international conference on advances in computing and communications (ICACC 2014)*.

42. Roopak, S., Tony Thomas, and Sabu Emmanuel. 2018. Android malware detection mechanism based on bayesian model averaging. *Advances in intelligent systems and computing (AISC)*, 87–96.
43. Roopak, S., Tony Thomas, and Sabu Emmanuel. 2018. Detection of malware applications in android smart phones. In *World scientific reference on innovation, volume 4: Innovation in information security*, 211–234. World Scientific.
44. Roopak, S., Athira P. Vijayaraghavan, and Tony Thomas. 2019. On effectiveness of source code and SSL based features for phishing website detection. In *First International conference on advanced technologies in intelligent control, environment, computing and communication engineering (ICATIECE-2019)*.
45. Shalaginov, Andrii, Sergii Banin, Ali Dehghantanha, and Katrin Franke. 2018. Machine learning aided static malware analysis: A survey and tutorial. *Cyber threat intelligence*, 7–45.
46. Veiga, Alberto Perez. 2018. Applications of artificial intelligence to network security. arXiv:1803.09992.
47. Devi, V.S., Roopak S., Tony Thomas, and Md. Meraj Uddin. 2019. Multi-pattern matching based dynamic malware detection in smart phones. In *Energy efficient computing & electronics: Devices to systems*, 421–441. CRC Press.
48. Xin, Yang, Lingshuang Kong, Zhi Liu, Yuling Chen, Yanmiao Li, Hongliang Zhu, Mingcheng Gao, Haixia Hou, and Chunhua Wang. 2018. Machine learning and deep learning methods for cybersecurity. *IEEE Access*.
49. Zamani, Mahdi, and Mahnush Movahedi. 2013. Machine learning techniques for intrusion detection. arXiv:1312.2177.
50. Zhang, Jason. 2018. Mlpdf: An effective machine learning based approach for pdf malware detection. arXiv:1808.06991.
51. Zhang, Peng, Tony Thomas, and Sabu Emmanuel. 2012. Privacy enabled video surveillance using a two state markov tracking algorithm. *Multimedia Systems* 175–199.
52. Zhang, Peng, Tony Thomas, Sabu Emmanuel, and Mohan S. Kankanhalli. 2010. Privacy preserving video surveillance using a pedestrian tracking mechanism. In *MiFor, ACM multimedia 2010*.
53. Zhang, Peng, Tony Thomas, and Tao Zhuo. 2015. An object-based video authentication mechanism for smart-living surveillance. In *The 2015 international conference on orange technologies (ICOT2015)*.
54. Zhang, Peng, Tony Thomas, Tao Zhuo, Wei Huang, and Hanqiao Huang. 2017. Object coding based video authentication for privacy protection in immersive communication. *Journal of Ambient Intelligence and Humanized Computing* 871–884.
55. Zhang, Peng, Yanning Zhang, Tony Thomas, and Sabu Emmanuel. 2014. Moving people tracking with detection by latent semantic analysis for visual surveillance applications. *Multimedia Tools and Applications* 991–1021.
56. Contagio mobile-mobile malware mini dump.
57. Virusshare malware dataset.
58. Weka 3—data mining with open source machine learning software in java.
59. Arp, Daniel, Michael Spreitzenbarth, Hugo Gascon, and Konrad Rieck. 2014. Drebin: Effective and explainable detection of android malware in your pocket.
60. Aung, Zarni, and Win Zaw. 2013. Permission-based android malware detection. *International Journal of Scientific & Technology Research* 2 (3): 228–234.
61. Bose, Abhijit, Xin Hu, Kang G. Shin, and Taejoon Park. 2008. Behavioral detection of malware on mobile handsets. In *Proceedings of the 6th international conference on Mobile systems, applications, and services*, 225–238. ACM.
62. Carrizosa, Emilio, Belen Martin-Barragan, and Dolores Romero Morales. 2010. Binarized support vector machines. *INFORMS Journal on Computing* 22 (1): 154–167.
63. Cortes, Corinna, and Vladimir Vapnik. 1995. Support-vector networks. *Machine Learning* 20 (3): 273–297.
64. Dai, Guqian, Jigang Ge, Minghang Cai, Daoqian Xu, and Wenjia Li. 2015. Svm-based malware detection for android applications. In *Proceedings of the 8th ACM conference on security & privacy in wireless and mobile networks*, 33. ACM.

65. Damodaran, Anusha, Fabio Di Troia, Corrado Aaron Visaggio, Thomas H. Austin, and Mark Stamp. 2017. A comparison of static, dynamic, and hybrid analysis for malware detection. *Journal of Computer Virology and Hacking Techniques* 13 (1): 1–12.
66. Egele, Manuel, Theodoor Scholte, Engin Kirda, and Christopher Kruegel. 2012. A survey on automated dynamic malware-analysis techniques and tools. *ACM Computing Surveys (CSUR)* 44 (2): 6.
67. Ghanem, Kinan, Francisco J. Aparicio-Navarro, Konstantinos G. Kyriakopoulos, Sangarapillai Lambotharan, and Jonathon A. Chambers. 2017. Support vector machine for network intrusion and cyber-attack detection. In *2017 sensor signal processing for defence conference (SSPD)*, 1–5. IEEE.
68. Hearst, Marti A., Susan T. Dumais, Edgar Osuna, John Platt, and Bernhard Scholkopf. 1998. Support vector machines. *IEEE Intelligent Systems and their Applications* 13 (4): 18–28.
69. Kim, Donghoon, and Ki Young Lee. 2017. Detection of ddos attack on the client side using support vector machine. *International Journal of Applied Engineering Research* 12 (20): 9909–9913.
70. Kruczkowski, Michal, and Ewa Niewiadomska Szynkiewicz. 2014. Support vector machine for malware analysis and classification. In *Proceedings of the 2014 IEEE/WIC/ACM international joint conferences on web intelligence (WI) and intelligent agent technologies (IAT)*, vol. 02, 415–420. IEEE Computer Society.
71. Kumar, Ayush, and Teng Joon Lim. 2019. Edima: Early detection of IoT malware network activity using machine learning techniques. arXiv:1906.09715.
72. Lin, Chih-Ta, Nai-Jian Wang, Han Xiao, and Claudia Eckert. 2015. Feature selection and extraction for malware classification. *Journal of Information Science and Engineering* 31 (3): 965–992.
73. Nguyen, Minh Hoai, and Fernando De la Torre. 2010. Optimal feature selection for support vector machines. *Pattern Recognition* 43 (3): 584–591.
74. Rossi, Fabrice, and Nathalie Villa. Classification in hilbert spaces with support vector machines.
75. Sahs, Justin, and Latifur Khan. 2012. A machine learning approach to android malware detection. In *Intelligence and security informatics conference (EISIC), 2012 European*, 141–147. IEEE.
76. Shijo, P.V., and A. Salim. 2015. Integrated static and dynamic analysis for malware detection. *Procedia Computer Science* 46: 804–811.
77. Singh, Tanuvir. 2015. Support vector machines and metamorphic malware detection.
78. Sujyothi, Akshatha, and Shreenath Acharya. 2017. Dynamic malware analysis and detection in virtual environment. *International Journal of Modern Education and Computer Science* 9 (3): 48.
79. Tian, Ronghua, Rafiqul Islam, Lynn Batten, and Steve Versteeg. 2010. Differentiating malware from cleanware using behavioural analysis. In *2010 5th international conference on malicious and unwanted software (MALWARE)*, 23–30. IEEE.
80. Trzesiok, Michal. 2010. The importance of predictor variables for individual classes in SVM.
81. Wei, Fengguo, Yuping Li, Sankardas Roy, Xinming Ou, and Wu Zhou. 2017. Deep ground truth analysis of current android malware. In *International conference on detection of intrusions and malware, and vulnerability assessment*, 252–276. Springer.
82. Weston, Jason, Sayan Mukherjee, Olivier Chapelle, Massimiliano Pontil, Tomaso Poggio, and Vladimir Vapnik. 2001. Feature selection for SVMS. In *Advances in neural information processing systems*, 668–674.
83. Agarwal, Jyoti, Renuka Nagpal, and Rajni Sehgal. 2013. Crime analysis using k-means clustering. *International Journal of Computer Applications* 83 (4).
84. Bora, Mr., Dibya Jyoti, Dr. Gupta, and Anil Kumar. 2014. Effect of different distance measures on the performance of k-means algorithm: An experimental study in matlab. arXiv:1405.7471.
85. Burguera, Iker, Urko Zurutuza, and Simin Nadjm-Tehrani. 2011. Crowdroid: Behavior-based malware detection system for android. In *Proceedings of the 1st ACM workshop on security and privacy in smartphones and mobile devices*, 15–26. ACM.

86. Enayet, Omar, and Samhaa R. El-Beltagy. 2017. Niletmrg at semeval-2017 task 8: Determining rumour and veracity support for rumours on twitter. In *Proceedings of the 11th international workshop on semantic evaluation (SemEval-2017)*, 470–474.
87. Feizollah, Ali, Nor Badrul Anuar, and Rosli Salleh. 2018. Evaluation of network traffic analysis using fuzzy c-means clustering algorithm in mobile malware detection. *Advanced Science Letters* 24 (2): 929–932.
88. Feizollah, Ali, Nor Badrul Anuar, Rosli Salleh, and Fairuz Amalina. 2014. Comparative study of k-means and mini batch k-means clustering algorithms in android malware detection using network traffic analysis. In *2014 international symposium on biometrics and security technologies (ISBAST)*, 193–197. IEEE.
89. Finch, Holmes. 2005. Comparison of distance measures in cluster analysis with dichotomous data. *Journal of Data Science* 3 (1): 85–100.
90. Higbee, Kenneth. 1998. Mathematical classification and clustering.
91. Jain, Anil K., M. Narasimha Murty, and Patrick J. Flynn. 1999. Data clustering: A review. *ACM Computing Surveys (CSUR)* 31 (3): 264–323.
92. Kinable, Joris, and Orestis Kostakis. 2011. Malware classification based on call graph clustering. *Journal in Computer Virology* 7 (4): 233–245.
93. Lathiya, Shital, and M.B. Chaudhari. 2018. Cseit183780 | rumour detection from social media: A review. 10.
94. Li, Yuping, Jiyong Jang, Xin Hu, and Xinming Ou. 2017. Android malware clustering through malicious payload mining. In *International symposium on research in attacks, intrusions, and defenses*, 192–214. Springer.
95. Narra, Usha, Fabio Di Troia, Visaggio Aaron Corrado, Thomas H. Austin, and Mark Stamp. 2016. Clustering versus SVM for malware detection. *Journal of Computer Virology and Hacking Techniques* 12 (4): 213–224.
96. Pai, Swathi, Fabio Di Troia, Corrado Aaron Visaggio, Thomas H. Austin, and Mark Stamp. 2017. Clustering for malware classification. *Journal of Computer Virology and Hacking Techniques* 13 (2): 95–107.
97. Perdisci, Roberto, Wenke Lee, and Gunter Ollmann. 2014. Method and system for network-based detecting of malware from behavioral clustering, September 2 2014. US Patent 8,826,438.
98. Roux, Maurice. A comparative study of divisive hierarchical clustering algorithms. 2015. arXiv:1506.08977.
99. Samra, Aiman A. Abu, Kangbin Yim, and Osama A. Ghanem. 2013. Analysis of clustering technique in android malware detection. In *2013 seventh international conference on innovative mobile and internet services in ubiquitous computing (IMIS)*, 729–733. IEEE.
100. Prajakta, Ms., D. Sawle, and A.B. Gadicha. 2014. Analysis of malware detection techniques in android.
101. Singh, Archana, Avantika Yadav, and Ajay Rana. 2013. K-means with three different distance metrics. *International Journal of Computer Applications* 67 (10).
102. Ye, Yanfang, Tao Li, Yong Chen, and Qingshan Jiang. 2010. Automatic malware categorization using cluster ensemble. In *Proceedings of the 16th ACM SIGKDD international conference on Knowledge discovery and data mining*, 95–104. ACM.
103. Zubiaga, Arkaitz, Ahmet Aker, Kalina Bontcheva, Maria Liakata, and Rob Procter. 2018. Detection and resolution of rumours in social media: A survey. *ACM Computing Surveys (CSUR)* 51 (2): 32.
104. Zulfadhilah, Prayudi, Yudi Prayudi, and Imam Riadi. 2016. Cyber profiling using log analysis and k-means clustering. *International Journal of Advanced Computer Science and Applications* 7 (7).
105. Bansal, Roli, Priti Sehgal, and Punam Bedi. 2011. Minutiae extraction from fingerprint images-a review. arXiv:1201.1422.
106. Jon Louis Bentley. 1975. Multidimensional binary search trees used for associative searching. *Communications of the ACM* 18 (9): 509–517.

107. Bentley, Jon Louis. 1990. K-d trees for semidynamic point sets. In *Proceedings of the sixth annual symposium on Computational geometry*, 187–197. ACM.
108. Beygelzimer, Alina, Sham Kakade, and John Langford. 2006. Cover trees for nearest neighbor. In *Proceedings of the 23rd international conference on Machine learning*, 97–104. ACM.
109. Dolatshah, Mohamad, Ali Hadian, and Behrouz Minaei-Bidgoli. 2015. Ball*-tree: Efficient spatial indexing for constrained nearest-neighbor search in metric spaces. arXiv:1511.00628.
110. Hong, Lin, Yifei Wan, and Anil Jain. 1998. Fingerprint image enhancement: Algorithm and performance evaluation. *IEEE Transactions on Pattern Analysis and Machine Intelligence* 20 (8): 777–789.
111. Jadhav, S.D., and A.B. Barbadekar. Euclidean distance based fingerprint matching. Citeseer.
112. Jain, Anil K., Salil Prabhakar, and Lin Hong. 1999. A multichannel approach to fingerprint classification. *IEEE Transactions on Pattern Analysis and Machine Intelligence*, 21 (4): 348–359.
113. Jiang, Liangxiao, Harry Zhang, and Jiang Su. 2005. Learning k-nearest neighbor naive bayes for ranking. In *International conference on advanced data mining and applications*, 175–185. Springer.
114. Karu, K., and Anil K. Jain. 1996. Fingerprint classification. *Pattern Recognition* 29 (3): 389–404.
115. Kibriya, Ashraf Masood. 2007. *Fast algorithms for nearest neighbour search*. Ph.D. thesis, The University of Waikato.
116. Kovesi, P.D. MATLAB and Octave functions for computer vision and image processing. http://www.peterkovesi.com/matlabfns/.
117. Kumar, Neeraj, Li Zhang, and Shree Nayar. 2008. What is a good nearest neighbors algorithm for finding similar patches in images? In *European conference on computer vision*, 364–378. Springer.
118. Li, Wenchao, Ping Yi, Wu Yue, Li Pan, and Jianhua Li. 2014. A new intrusion detection system based on KNN classification algorithm in wireless sensor network. *Journal of Electrical and Computer Engineering*.
119. Liao, Yihua, and V. Rao Vemuri. 2002. Use of k-nearest neighbor classifier for intrusion detection. *Computers & Security*, 21 (5): 439–448.
120. McCann, Sancho, and David G. Lowe. 2012. Local naive bayes nearest neighbor for image classification. In *2012 IEEE conference on computer vision and pattern recognition (CVPR)*, 3650–3656. IEEE.
121. Omohundro, Stephen M. 1989. *Five balltree construction algorithms.*.
122. Pawar, Vaishali, and Mukesh Zaveri. 2014. Graph based k-nearest neighbor minutiae clustering for fingerprint recognition. In *2014 10th International Conference on Natural Computation (ICNC)*, 675–680. IEEE.
123. Prasath, V.B., Haneen Arafat Abu Alfeilat, Omar Lasassmeh, and Ahmad Hassanat. 2017. Distance and similarity measures effect on the performance of k-nearest neighbor classifier-a review. arXiv:1708.04321.
124. Raja, K.B., et al. 2010. Fingerprint recognition using minutia score matching. arXiv:1001.4186.
125. Rajani, Nazneen, Kate McArdle, and Inderjit S. Dhillon. 2015. Parallel k nearest neighbor graph construction using tree-based data structures. In *1st high performance graph mining workshop, Sydney, 10 Aug 2015*.
126. Rajanna, Uday, Ali Erol, and George Bebis. 2010. A comparative study on feature extraction for fingerprint classification and performance improvements using rank-level fusion. *Pattern Analysis and Applications* 13 (3): 263–272.
127. Shah, Shesha, and P. Shanti Sastry. 2004. Fingerprint classification using a feedback-based line detector. *IEEE Transactions on Systems, Man, and Cybernetics, Part B (Cybernetics)* 34 (1): 85–94.
128. Shakhnarovich, Gregory, Trevor Darrell, and Piotr Indyk. 2006. *Nearest-neighbor methods in learning and vision: Theory and practice (neural information processing)*.

129. Shi, Yang, Fangyu Li, WenZhan Song, Xiang-Yang Li, and Jin Ye. 2019. Energy audition based cyber-physical attack detection system in IoT, 05 2019.
130. Sitawarin, Chawin, and David Wagner. 2019. On the robustness of deep k-nearest neighbors. arXiv:1903.08333.
131. Sproull, Robert F. 1991. Refinements to nearest-neighbor searching ink-dimensional trees. *Algorithmica* 6 (1–6): 579–589.
132. Wieclaw, Lukasz. 2013. Gradient based fingerprint orientation field estimation. *Journal of Medical Informatics & Technologies* 22.
133. Bengio, Dr. Yoshua. Face recognition homepage.
134. Chakraborty, Dulal, Sanjit Kumar Saha, and Md. Al-Amin Bhuiyan. 2012. Face recognition using eigenvector and principle component analysis. *International Journal of Computer Applications* 50(10).
135. Goldstein, A. Jay, Leon D. Harmon, and Ann B. Lesk. 1971. Identification of human faces. *Proceedings of the IEEE* 59 (5): 748–760.
136. Lata, Y. Vijaya, Chandra Kiran Bharadwaj Tungathurthi, H. Ram Mohan Rao, A. Govardhan, and L.P. Reddy. 2009. Facial recognition using eigenfaces by PCA. *International Journal of Recent Trends in Engineering* 1 (1): 587.
137. Paul, Liton Chandra, and Abdulla Al Sumam. 2012. Face recognition using principal component analysis method. *International Journal of Advanced Research in Computer Engineering & Technology (IJARCET)* 1 (9): 135.
138. Samaria, Ferdinando S., and Andy C. Harter. 1994. Parameterisation of a stochastic model for human face identification. In *Proceedings of the second IEEE workshop on applications of computer vision, 1994*, 138–142. IEEE.
139. Sandhu, Parvinder S., Iqbaldeep Kaur, Amit Verma, Samriti Jindal, Inderpreet Kaur, and Shilpi Kumari. Face recognition using eigen face coefficients and principal component analysis.
140. Shemi, P.M., and M.A. Ali. A principal component analysis method for recognition of human faces: Eigenfaces approach.
141. Turk, Matthew, and Alex Pentland. 1991. Eigenfaces for recognition. *Journal of Cognitive Neuroscience* 3 (1): 71–86.
142. Turk, Matthew A., and Alex P. Pentland. 1991. Face recognition using eigenfaces. In *Proceedings CVPR'91, IEEE Computer Society Conference on Computer Vision and Pattern Recognition, 1991*, 586–591. IEEE.
143. Bengio, Dr. Yoshua. Facial keypoints detection kaggle.
144. Bourdais, Florian. A convolutional neural network for face keypoint detection.
145. Deshpande, Adit. A beginner's guide to understanding convolutional neural networks.
146. Alauthaman, Mohammad, Nauman Aslam, Li Zhang, Rafe Alasem, and M. Alamgir Hossain. 2018. A p2p botnet detection scheme based on decision tree and adaptive multilayer neural networks. *Neural Computing and Applications* 29 (11): 991–1004.
147. Burnap, Peter, and Matilda Rhode. 2018. Behavioural machine activity for benign and malicious win7 64-bit executables.
148. Advisors Enplus. 2017. Decision trees.
149. Gupta, Bhumika, Aditya Rawat, Akshay Jain, Arpit Arora, and Naresh Dhami. 2017. Analysis of various decision tree algorithms for classification in data mining. *International Journal of Computer Applications* 163 (8).
150. Han, Jiawei, Jian Pei, and Micheline Kamber. 2011. *Data mining: Concepts and techniques*. Elsevier.
151. Peng, Kai, Victor Leung, Lixin Zheng, Shangguang Wang, Chao Huang, and Tao Lin. 2018. Intrusion detection system based on decision tree over big data in fog environment. *Wireless Communications and Mobile Computing*
152. Quinlan, J. Ross. *C4. 5: Programs for machine learning*. Elsevier.
153. Rhode, Matilda, Pete Burnap, and Kevin Jones. 2018. Early-stage malware prediction using recurrent neural networks. *Computers & Security* 77: 578–594.
154. Taleqani, Ali Rahim, Kendall E. Nygard, Raj Bridgelall, and Jill Hough. 2018. Machine learning approach to cyber security in aviation. In *2018 IEEE international conference on electro/information technology (EIT)*, 0147–0152. IEEE.

155. Bailey, Michael, Thorsten Holz, Manolis Stamatogiannakis, and Sotiris Ioannidis. 2018. *Research in attacks, intrusions, and defenses: 21st international symposium, RAID 2018, Heraklion, Crete, Greece, 10–12 Sept 2018, Proceedings*, vol. 11050. Springer.
156. Bhowmick, Alexy, and Shyamanta M. Hazarika. 2016. Machine learning for e-mail spam filtering: Review, techniques and trends. arXiv:1606.01042.
157. Carlini, Nicholas, Guy Katz, Clark Barrett, and David L. Dill. 2018. Ground-truth adversarial examples.
158. Carlini, Nicholas, and David Wagner. 2017. Adversarial examples are not easily detected: Bypassing ten detection methods. In *Proceedings of the 10th ACM workshop on artificial intelligence and security*, 3–14. ACM.
159. Nicholas Carlini and David Wagner. Towards evaluating the robustness of neural networks. In *2017 IEEE Symposium on Security and Privacy (SP)*, pages 39–57. IEEE, 2017.
160. Chen, Pin-Yu, Yash Sharma, Huan Zhang, Jinfeng Yi, and Cho-Jui Hsieh. 2018. Ead: Elastic-net attacks to deep neural networks via adversarial examples. In *Thirty-Second AAAI conference on artificial intelligence*.
161. Dong, Yinpeng, Fangzhou Liao, Tianyu Pang, Xiaolin Hu, and Jun Zhu. 2017. Discovering adversarial examples with momentum. *CoRR*. arXiv:1710.06081.
162. Dong, Yinpeng, Fangzhou Liao, Tianyu Pang, Hang Su, Jun Zhu, Xiaolin Hu, and Jianguo Li. 2018. Boosting adversarial attacks with momentum. In *Proceedings of the IEEE conference on computer vision and pattern recognition*, 9185–9193.
163. Duddu, Vasisht. 2018. A survey of adversarial machine learning in cyber warfare. *Defence Science Journal* 68 (4): 356–366.
164. Goodfellow, Ian. 2016. Nips 2016 tutorial: Generative adversarial networks. arXiv:1701.00160.
165. Goodfellow, Ian, Jean Pouget-Abadie, Mehdi Mirza, Bing Xu, David Warde-Farley, Sherjil Ozair, Aaron Courville, and Yoshua Bengio. 2014. Generative adversarial nets. In *Advances in neural information processing systems*, 2672–2680.
166. Goodfellow, Ian J., Jonathon Shlens, and Christian Szegedy. 2014. Explaining and harnessing adversarial examples. arXiv:1412.6572.
167. Hu, Weiwei, and Ying Tan. 2017. Generating adversarial malware examples for black-box attacks based on gan. arXiv:1702.05983.
168. Kurakin, A., Ian Goodfellow, and Samy Bengio. Adversarial machine learning at scale. 2016. arXiv:1611.01236.
169. Madry, Aleksander, Aleksandar Makelov, Ludwig Schmidt, Dimitris Tsipras, and Adrian Vladu. 2017. Towards deep learning models resistant to adversarial attacks. arXiv:1706.06083.
170. Nataraj, Lakshmanan, Sreejith Karthikeyan, Gregoire Jacob, and B.S. Manjunath. 2011. Malware images: Visualization and automatic classification. In *Proceedings of the 8th international symposium on visualization for cyber security*, 4. ACM.
171. Nelson, Blaine, Marco Barreno, Fuching Jack Chi, Anthony D. Joseph, Benjamin I.P. Rubinstein, Udam Saini, Charles Sutton, J.D. Tygar, and Kai Xia. 2009. Misleading learners: Co-opting your spam filter. In *Machine learning in cyber trust*, 17–51. Springer.
172. Norton, Andrew P., and Yanjun Qi. 2017. Adversarial-playground: A visualization suite showing how adversarial examples fool deep learning. In *2017 IEEE symposium on visualization for cyber security (VizSec)*, 1–4. IEEE.
173. Papernot, Nicolas, Fartash Faghri, Nicholas Carlini, Ian Goodfellow, Reuben Feinman, Alexey Kurakin, Cihang Xie, Yash Sharma, Tom Brown, Aurko Roy, et al. 2016. Technical report on the cleverhans v2. 1.0 adversarial examples library. arXiv:1610.00768.
174. Sanjeevi, Madhu. Generative adversarial networks (gan's) with math.
175. Szegedy, Christian, Wojciech Zaremba, Ilya Sutskever, Joan Bruna, Dumitru Erhan, Ian Goodfellow, and Rob Fergus. 2013. Intriguing properties of neural networks. arXiv:1312.6199.
176. Vorobeychik, Y., M. Kantarcioglu, and R. Brachman. 2018. *Adversarial machine learning*. Synthesis Lectures on Artificial Morgan & Claypool Publishers.
177. Wang, Beilun, Ji Gao, and Yanjun Qi. 2016. A theoretical framework for robustness of (deep) classifiers against adversarial examples. arXiv:1612.00334.

178. Xiao, Chaowei, Bo Li, Jun-Yan Zhu, Warren He, Mingyan Liu, and Dawn Song. 2018. Generating adversarial examples with adversarial networks. arXiv:1801.02610.
179. Yuan, Xiaoyong, Pan He, Qile Zhu, and Xiaolin Li. 2019. Adversarial examples: Attacks and defenses for deep learning. *IEEE transactions on neural networks and learning systems*.
180. Zuo, Chandler. 2018. Regularization effect of fast gradient sign method and its generalization. arXiv:1810.11711.

MIX
Papier aus verantwortungsvollen Quellen
Paper from responsible sources
FSC® C105338

If you have any concerns about our products,
you can contact us on
ProductSafety@springernature.com

In case Publisher is established outside the EU,
the EU authorized representative is:
Springer Nature Customer Service Center GmbH
Europaplatz 3, 69115 Heidelberg, Germany

Printed by Libri Plureos GmbH
in Hamburg, Germany